The Crisis
of Our Time

*Reflections on the Course
of Western Civilization,
Past, Present, and Future*

David Burnett King

SELINSGROVE: Susquehanna University Press
LONDON AND TORONTO: Associated University Presses

Associated University Presses
440 Forsgate Drive
Cranbury, NJ 08512

Associated University Presses
25 Sicilian Avenue
London WC1A 2QH, England

Associated University Presses
2133 Royal Windsor Drive
Unit 1
Mississauga, Ontario
Canada L5J 1K5

The paper used in this publication meets the requirements
of the American National Standard for Permanence of Paper
for Printed Library Materials Z39.48-1984.

Library of Congress Cataloging-in-Publication Data

King, David B.
   The crisis of our time.

   Bibliography: p.
   Includes index.
   1. Civilization, Occidental.   I. Title.
CB245.K544   1988   909′.09821   86-63055
ISBN 0–941664–78–3 (alk. paper)

PRINTED IN THE UNITED STATES OF AMERICA

To
Nita, Laura, Bonnie, Thomas, Stephen, and Hannah

Today is always partly tomorrow and can only be understood in movement, futuristically, speculatively.

—Michael Harrington, *The Accidental Century*

We may very well stand at one of those decisive turning points of history which separate whole eras from each other.

—Hannah Arendt, "Home to Roost: A Bicentennial Address"

What is the explanation of this crisis of European civilization, which has long been obvious from many aspects and is today reaching its full manifestation? Modern history, now coming to an end, was conceived at the time of the Renaissance. We are witnessing the end of the Renaissance.

—Nicholas Berdyaev, "The End of the Renaissance"

All the civilizations that we know of, including the Greek, have already broken down and gone to pieces with the single possible exception of our own Western civilization—and no child of this civilization who has been born into our generation can easily imagine that our society is immune from the danger of suffering the common fate.

—Arnold Toynbee, *Civilization on Trial*

Only a major crisis will force the kind of constitutional change advocated by serious students of government today. I believe such a crisis is likely to occur because to avoid it, too many things have to go right, all over the world, for a long period of time.

—Felix Rohatyn, "The Coming Emergency and What Can Be Done about It"

They developed a system of cooperation up here that worked and the population grew and grew and grew, just as we're doing today. And they bumped into the limits of their capabilities to manage what they were doing.

—Richard Loose, "The Chaco Legacy"

. . . the vaunted "progress" of modern civilization is only a thin cloak for global catastrophe.

—Barry Commoner, *The Closing Circle*

If the earth must lose that great portion of its pleasantness which it owes to things that the unlimited increase of wealth and population would extirpate from it, for the mere purpose of enabling it to support a larger but not a better or a happier population, I sincerely hope for the sake of posterity, that they will be content to be stationary, long before necessity compels them to it.

—John Stuart Mill, *Principles of Political Economy*

But we cannot allow, nor need we, the future to be the past writ large.

—Krishan Kumar, *Prophecy and Progress: The Sociology of Industrial and Post-Industrial Society*

The twentieth century is a time when everything cracks, where everything is destroyed, everything isolates itself, it is a more splendid thing than a period when everything follows itself. So the twentieth century is a splendid period, not a reasonable one in a scientific sense, but splendid.

—Gertrude Stein, *Picasso*

How can you say this and that when this and that hasn't happened yet?

—Yogi Berra

Please note that I do not say *predict* the future. We cannot predict the future, but we can anticipate it—we can look forward to it and in some sense prepare for it.

—Carl Becker, *Modern History*

You need to seek the underneath world. That's the one that's going to come up in the next century!—except for houses; they don't grow underground.

—Hannah King, age 7

Contents

Preface

I should begin by emphasizing that much of what follows is opinion. I have not attempted to write a narrative history, but rather to provide an essay, a work of analysis and projection. Should it from time to time take on too dogmatic an appearance, then that is a fault, yet one that can be partly explained away by the requirements of style: it is very hard to follow an argument while having to wade through a host of qualifications. Therefore, reservations have been neglected in order to favor the development of the themes. I am aware, however, of the risks involved in generalizing at the level of civilizational history. We know both too much and too little: too much about the parts, making difficult any attempt to pass through the domains of the specialists without getting it all wrong; and too little about how the parts relate to the whole. That is equally true whether we choose to look backward or forward.

And here the intention is to do some of both: to look backward at the past, the past of Western civilization, and forward through the present, where the West and the world would seem to have become one and the same, to the future. There is nothing mysterious in the procedure; what has happened will be used to speculate about what is going to happen. In the course of using what has happened, we shall impose an order on the facts—an order, but not to be sure the only conceivable order—and in the course of speculating about what is going to happen, the implications of this reconstruction will be brought to bear upon the future. The intention is to provide, then, a view of history designed to assist in reflecting on both where this civilization has been and where it may be heading.

To summarize here at the very beginning, my conclusions can be reduced to the following points:

1. The present finds itself in the midst of a general crisis, one that has put its mark upon the entire century. Its effects have been and are being felt throughout our culture and society; the crisis is not restricted to aspects within our civilization but is, rather, a crisis of the civilization itself.

2. It is not at all unusual for civilizations to pass through periods of crisis. Their histories are filled with alternating eras of stability and flux. And usually the latter, the times of crisis, do nothing but interrupt for a while the previous directions of development. Occasionally, however,

they have much more profound effects, wheeling everything around and setting the civilization moving along a different path. This contemporary crisis is of the latter sort. It marks a turning point, or, if point is too fine, then a time of fundamental transition and redirection.

3. As such, it is the fourth great transition in the long history of the West: the first occurred in obscurity, in the privacy of the illiterate centuries at the very beginning of the first millennium before Christ, as the Greeks emerged from their Dark Age; the second when the Romans, now presiding over the mainstream of Western development, faltered in their attempts to continue to expand and began instead to collapse, this from about the second century A.D. on; and the third around the end of the first millennium A.D. when the West, now the medieval West, finally in its descent reached bedrock and found the firm footing from which it could launch another period of growth. Now, with the fourth, the crisis of the twentieth century, it would seem that we are leaving growth once again and reorganizing our civilization along other lines. That puts the matter too simply, especially since growth is not the only thing that we are leaving. For we are making our departure also from the Modern Age that it built, with all that that means with regard to the structure of culture and society.

4. A final point: if we indeed are leaving the Modern Age, it is also true that we have not seen the last of it just yet. Those who have announced its end are undoubtedly correct, but premature. They have mistaken a turning point for a conclusion. It takes about as long, however, to build down an age as it does to build one up. Or at least it has in the past.

Building down an age: that has necessarily a melancholy ring. I should hasten to add that my own reaction is not altogether pessimistic. There is much to criticize in the West's recent history. The Modern Age has been spectacular during its centuries of ascent, but also ruthless and even cruel. And it has created predicaments of unique danger. If during these last modern centuries we should shed some of the bad features while keeping some of the good, we might be able to create for ourselves if not a golden then at least a silver age. We shall explore the possibilities towards the end of this essay.

But what is to be made of those dangers just referred to? Is it not entirely possible that the future will be ruled not by transition but by chaos, brought upon us by a true catastrophe, be it the result of economic disintegration, mass famines, nuclear destruction, or some combination of these? It will be argued here that, being a civilization, we as such wish to persevere and shall therefore seek effective remedies; and that these indeed are implicit in the very process of devolution, that which is occasioning the departure from the Modern Age that we are already experiencing.

A word about the sources that have influenced my opinions: I have benefited especially from the texts and monographs of Crane Brinton,

Robert Palmer, Richard Pipes, Franklin LeVan Baumer, H. Stuart Hughes, Geoffrey Barraclough, Warren Johnson, Krishan Kumar, Leopold Kohr, Warren Wagar, Roland Stromberg, Shepard B. Clough, Robert Heilbroner, Hugh Trevor-Roper, and Theodore Rabb. As for the theoreticians of civilization, I came to their systems relatively late, with ideas of my own already formed or forming, and therefore profited all the more, but without being tempted to accept anything whole—an approach that I recommend as well to the reader with regard to my own presentation. I began with Marx, one of the few nineteenth-century social theorists who still seems to have much to say to us. I have also found Toynbee very much worth reading. It is true that his pedantry forced him into unreasonable conclusions, but he has not deserved the abuse that he has received. The same is true of Spengler. Of the two great historical anthropologists, Sorokin and Kroeber, I have learned more from the latter. I have also been impressed by the ideas of Romano Guardini, Nicholas Berdyaev, T. E. Hulme, Ortega y Gasset, and John Lukacs. I am especially indebted to Professor Lukacs, who as a reader for Susquehanna Press has made several valuable suggestions. Finally, I should mention my students, whose questions and comments over the years have both informed me and forced me to rethink my positions.

I wish to thank the Oregon Committee for the Humanities for a fellowship that permitted me to write without interruption for one summer; Oregon State University, from which I received a three-month released-time grant; and the O.S.U. LaSells Stewart Foundation for a very helpful award during the final stages of the work. I also owe a debt of gratitude to my colleagues Don McIlvenna and Darold Wax, who have provided me with many insightful criticisms; to David N. Wiley, Beth Gianfagna, Ron Roth, and Thomas Yoseloff, my editors at Susquehanna and Associated University Presses; and to my family, which has tolerated my neglecting other chores. In addition, I wish to express my sincere appreciation for both the diligence and patience shown by Julia Bruce, Karen Force, and Treena Martin, whose skills with the word processor have made the preparation of the manuscript so much easier; and to Kim Smith for her excellent work with the index.

The artisans of the Navaho culture left an intentional flaw, I am told, in each piece of work. This was done lest the gods assume that, the tasks of these artisans on earth completed, they were ready to move on. Although the temptation to write a flawless book has been considerable, I have successfully resisted it and managed to retain a few errors. For these, I of course claim full responsibility and benefit.

The Crisis
of Our Time

1
The Crisis in Review: The Present

Throughout the West today there exists a profound feeling of unease. Without knowing quite why, we assume that we are passing through some sort of crisis, riding out a sea change that will somehow make the future very different from the past. But every epoch tends to see itself in a state of crisis, and, to a certain extent, every epoch is correct. History is change, and the process of transition never stops, with each turn producing its discomforts. Yet, of course, every epoch is not equally correct. Some periods are finally distinguished by their stability, others by the lack of it. If the course of human affairs forms a seamless web, then certainly the structure of that web is uneven. Long stretches of relative continuity alternate with shorter periods of relative discontinuity. Historical development is clearly spasmodic.

Even so, most of the discontinuities are but temporary. The force of the previous momentum eventually has its way, and the original inclinations are confirmed. So many crises, perceived at the time as momentous, turn out to be only trivial interruptions. Sooner or later, however, there occurs something like a real break, marked by pronounced and simultaneous disintegration and rejuvenation, at which time the inevitable and always-present movement begins to bend in a new direction. These last are the times of true crisis. For the West, and now also the world that it has made over in its own image, the twentieth century is one such time. We have, it is becoming increasingly clear, arrived at some sort of fundamental turning point.

It is not a turning point, not a crisis, with regard to only politics or only economics or only culture. It is, on the contrary, very much a turning point and a crisis of all of these together. And that means that what is happening is civilizational in scope: the individual dislocations being experienced can best be explained as a crisis of the civilization itself. More specifically, it is a crisis generated by the transition of the West from one age to another. The Modern Age has held sway since the fifteenth century. But now it is beginning to take leave of us. Just as the West several times before has had to adjust to its passage from one age to another, with all that that implies, now we are once more witnessing the trauma of conversion—this time as we make our way painfully and warily from the Modern Age to whatever lies beyond it. That is not to say that the Modern Age is at its very end. That too will come, but, if the past is still an adequate guide—and let us hope that it is not entirely wrong—then not immediately, and perhaps not for a century or even two.

What is at an end is the period of modern vitality. For the last five hundred years, Western civilization has been infused with the spirit of creation. It has been obsessed with discovering, knowing, ordering, building, and dominating, and has indeed realized many of its dreams—while at the same time producing, inadvertently if predictably, the stuff of nightmares. At last it has come, and entirely naturally, by a more or less normal progression, to a new turning point. Thus the West finds itself in the midst of a period of sweeping change. The old energies have been dissipated, and it is beginning to move not only in a different direction, but also at a different pace. And it is also beginning, surely, to search for solutions to the problems generated by some of the later products of modern creativity, those that have contributed to that odd predicament we find ourselves in lately, where the grand achievements of recent progress threaten us with extinction.

We view other great historical transitions long after the fact and from the outside, and they manage to appear reasonably precise. This one we see from the inside, and it gives the impression necessarily of being a very ragged matter. Crises abound, but the connections that bind them together are seldom obvious. Thus we are not encouraged to see the big picture. But all of history's great movements have seemed to lack coherence when observed from within by contemporaries. Ours in this regard is certainly no exception. We can focus on individual dislocations. We find it difficult, however, to think in terms of ages and civilizational change. For we have little experience with these.

And today the perception of the civilizational condition is further confused by the much-noted disparity between twentieth-century culture and society. Our culture—that part of the civilizational whole that describes our aesthetic dimensions and accounts both for the formal explanations by which we justify ourselves as well as the less than fully conscious but nonetheless very real mood, or *Zeitgeist,* that envelopes every coherent historical unit—would seem to be saying one thing, while our society, whether we look at its economic or political constitution, would appear to be giving out a different message. Contemporary culture has already become what we might call antimodern, that is to say, it has already rejected the traditional modern canons, those of the Modern Age. In the great cultural revolution of the early part of this century, every facet of Western culture rather suddenly experienced the overthrow of its modern past. We shall turn to the specifics in a moment. Yet society continues, or at least struggles to continue, in its modern ways: its political system, its economy, and many of its social constructions are extensions of work the foundations of which were laid during the early modern centuries. That is puzzling. Our society is modern. But our culture is not. Western civilization has been apparently split down the middle. The division is superficial, however, and perhaps in the long run not very significant. Western culture and Western society will soon enough be moving in the same direction. The break with the modern past already made by culture is even now being followed by a similar societal break. Ultimately coming together, Western culture and society will again present a unified whole, as they move in what passes for harmony in such matters toward a new age. Given the necessarily reciprocal and mutually dependent nature of their relationship, there is no other option.

This essay, then, will explore the West's twentieth-century crisis as a single phenomenon and consider its implications for what lies ahead. The discussion is divided into three parts, the first, contained in chapter 1, centering on the present, meaning here the twentieth century taken as a whole; the second, presented in chapters 2, 3, and 4, on the past, without some knowledge of which can we hardly hope to gain true perspective; and the third, in chapter 5, on the future, our final destination. That said, it should be at once acknowledged that the divisions with regard to present, past, and future are not and could not be adamantly maintained, especially so since the selection of a scheme whereby a commentary on the present is put first has occasioned some inevitable overlapping and repetition. I have begun with the present, however, for a reason, and that is to focus at the start on the crisis that the Modern Age is going through, assembling its various parts in such a way that the single over-crisis of which they are but instances becomes discernible. I am assuming that this departure from a strictly chronological approach will lend more by way of insight than it detracts; and that where certain things are dealt with more than once the different contexts will justify going over the same ground a second time.

While we are previewing matters of design and organization, allow me to add a few more words about the purpose of each of the five chapters. Chapter 1 will attempt, as said, to offer a summary sketch of the present, yet one not made in isolation, but set, rather, against the backdrop of the Modern Age, that great segment of our civilizational history that began with the Renaissance and extends to the present. The presentation will follow an outline that will then become the pattern for the subsequent commentaries on the past and future: we shall initially look at the West's culture, dividing the discussion into two parts, the first treating style, the artistic component of culture, with its implicit statement on the contemporary state of things; and the second thought, the reflective, analytical component, that which is committed to making an explicit statement. Together, these two constitute an ongoing record of our perception of our nature and significance.

Then we shall go on to an overview of society, again dividing the subject into two parts, the first to consider politics, the governmental component, where one finds the struggle to resolve the major societal problems and to set directions; and the second to consider economics, the productive component, the function of which is to provide material well-being. We might say that the sum of style and thought is culture, while the sum of politics and economics is society. And, if that is so, then the sum of culture and society is civilization. Thus in following the distinct but related histories of the components of culture and society we shall be plotting the course of the civilization itself. Here, with regard to the present, it will be argued that our culture has already made a distinct break with its modern forms, as true for style as for thought; and that our society is now in a condition that can only result in its also breaking with those forms, likewise as true for politics as for economics.

Chapter 2 will begin the treatment of the West's long-range past, the whole of this survey being intended to make available in shorthand form an account of our experience with ages—to observe, that is, how the West has moved from its prehistorical condition to its first age, the Greco-Roman, or Classical; then from the Classical Age to the Middle Ages; and finally from the Middle Ages to the Modern Age. The purpose here is obvious enough: if we are changing ages, if, that is, the West is again undergoing the sort of fundamental transformation that will eventually force us to recognize that the world about us is no longer the old, modern one to which we had grown accustomed, but rather a new one, then it is good to know something of what changing ages has meant in the past. But in order to do this, the focus cannot be restricted to the points—here, centuries—of change alone; rather, to get a sense of the rhythms involved, it is necessary to rethink the West's entire course.

While chapter 2 confines itself to the first great transition, from the prehistoric to the classical, that long period of growth that was the work of Greece and Rome, chapter 3 goes on to deal with the second, in which the West moved away from its classical peak toward the medieval nadir around the end of the first millennium A.D. Chapter 4, the last of the historical chapters, then traces the outlines of another long growth period, one that saw the West expand from its medieval resting point to a new peak in the nineteenth and twentieth centuries, only then to falter and, it would seem, once again reverse directions.

The last chapter of this essay, chapter 5, is, then, the receptacle for our commentary on the future. Again, the underlying assumption that serves as the ordering principle for these remarks is that we are indeed in the process of beginning another lengthy civilizational journey, one that will take us toward a new age—an age in which quite likely our present problems will tend to disappear. But also an age, of course, in which new ones will replace them. If the West does indeed move away from its modern predicaments, it will undoubtedly find others. Still, perhaps it is now time for that.

In any case, we shall speculate on what is in store for the West. Yet can we, it can be legitimately asked, say anything to describe a future that will bear a reasonable resemblance to the one that will actually happen? Yes, I think we can. The civilizational future is just as dependable—and just as erratic—as our personal futures. As the individual operates within his or her milieu, struggling to sustain a certain course, so does the civilization act within its own network of circumstance. Even the results would appear to be rather similar.

As for our personal lives, we make assumptions about the future all the time, and usually these prove correct: the sun does come up tomorrow, the appointments are met, as foreseen. Also most of our long-range expectations are realized, if not always in just the form anticipated. When our assumptions with regard to either the immediate or distant future are badly off, then the result is traumatic. The sudden death of a loved one, the unexpected end of a relationship, the unforeseen loss of a job—these are tragic. And they are that for the very good reason that we have been conditioned by the great success of our homely and continual efforts at predicting the future not to expect tragedy. We are in fact so good at predicting that the interjection of a failure into the series has a shattering effect. For those unfortunate enough to have the experience repeated frequently, the result is often the onset of neurosis, or worse. We as individuals rely on our ability to look ahead. It is such a commonplace activity that we are usually conscious of it only when we are proved wrong. Then we are apt to shrug and find some solace in the momentary belief that the future—necessarily with regard to human affairs, because humans are essentially unpredictable—cannot in any case be accounted for. And then, of course, we rightly go right back to work accounting for it. If we did not, we would perish.

On the grand historical level, where we see civilizations rather than individuals moving upon the stage, things are really not that much different. Civilizations can be civilizations only if they are coherent and relatively stable. And because of that coherency and stability, they are necessarily predictable: we can depend on them to go on doing what they have been doing in the past. That does not mean that there is an absence of change. Not at all. As with individual lives, there is with regard to civilizations indeed an abundance of change. But the fact is that in both cases the change is not essentially random. It flows along, more or less holding to a pattern. Just as we can say, "I would expect that person to act that way in that sort of situation," we can also say, "Yes, given that historical record, we can expect this particular civilization to do the following": to behave, that is, as it has in the past.

Should that be true for the West at this particular time, however, if, as is being asserted here, we are at a point in our history where discontinuity prevails over continuity? Can we still manage a reasonable view of our future at a moment when we would seem to be on the threshold of a very different set of experiences? Again, the answer is that, yes, we can—that is to say, we have the potential to do that; in theory, we can do it. That does not mean necessarily that the view presented here or indeed any view will prove accurate. Yet insofar as the West continues to be also *discontinuous* as it has in the past—and our discontinuities have a lengthy history, too—then we have at least some basis upon which to form an image of the future.

Nevertheless, there is one way in which the future must and will differ from every attempt to describe it: views of the future are necessarily schematic. If they are to have any worth at all, then they must follow some sort of scheme, whether derived from the past, as in this case, or from whatever sources. And they have to be limited by that scheme. Yet quite obviously the future will have its accidents. Even if we hit on precisely the right scheme, then the unfolding of the actual events will still turn out differently because of chance—the predictable recurrence of the unpredictable. For all of the deterministic weight that the past and present bring to bear on the future, there will still occur happenstance events of great significance.

We realize this. We do not need a philosophy of history to tell us. It is all too evident. Still, for all that, the schematic approach to the future is the only possible approach. We must take the organized path or none at all. It will give us at best an imperfect impression. But, nevertheless, one worth having. The accidents that will interfere with what we might think of as the normal course of events will probably not be influential enough to alter the major directions set by the past. If that proves incorrect—if, for example, we should become the victims of a full-scale nuclear war—then that sort of accident would indeed make for a future cut off from our previous experience. And, consequently, once we have done what we can to prevent it—and in commenting on the future we shall take up the matter of just what that might be—then there is little point in worrying about life after such a cataclysm. Civilization and possibly human life itself would come to an end.

So the task undertaken here is not to portray a future that is more the result of accident than history, but rather the opposite, to portray one that is more the result of history than accident. Each of our past futures has been a more or less logical extension of its own past, even when that has meant taking a new course. We shall expect that this future will oblige us by continuing to observe the custom. If our efforts at dealing with the problems that the Modern Age has bequeathed to us are so unsuccessful that we manage finally to poison the world or even to blow much of it up, then there will not be many of us left to reflect on how useless a view of the future based on the past alas turned out to be.

But if we were indeed convinced that tragedy is our most likely future, then we would want all the more to increase our concern with what is to come. And that is the purpose of this essay: to contribute to an awareness of the future and of our relationship to it. Our present neglect of the future is remarkable. No doubt that is a habit acquired during the long pre-historical era when the future came on so slowly that it was all but irrelevant. The present, that is to say, the circumstances of the moment, could be expected to prevail and prevail and prevail. Population, methods of production, social customs, religious beliefs, habitat—everything re-mained quite stable, the underlying movement primarily determined for a long time by the advance and recession of the glaciers. Things moved very literally at a glacial pace.

Even with the coming of civilization, the rate of historical change remained slow, especially for the vast bulk of the population, committed as it was to an agrarian life that was altered but little over the millennia. With the advent of Western civilization, a new dynamic element was intro-duced, yet still the future approached at a moderate speed. Then came the Modern Age, the very essence of which has been rapid movement and constant renovation, especially, of course, since the waves of new tech-nology hit the West beginning in the eighteenth century. Our most recent history has been in this respect entirely unique. For it has been charac-terized by a refusal to stand still. And we are now experiencing the most restless period of a restless age, itself the product of a restless civilization. We are making it our unending work to destroy the past in order to hasten through each present to ever-new futures.

Given the fact of our extremely dynamic nature, of this commitment to a frenetic plunge forward, our disinterest in the future is not only inappropri-ate, but also dangerous. Yes, there are signs that we are awakening to the predicament. The last several decades have seen the growth of a variety of future-oriented studies. Still, our concern for the future remains pe-ripheral. That would seem to be indicated by the ease with which our governments are able to preserve present prosperity by measures that are clearly prejudicing the future's chances for survival. Yet this particular future, our present future, is no longer out there somewhere over a distant horizon. On the contrary, it lies directly before us. We are going to be soon experiencing the effects of our choices, as they settle in upon us—certainly that will be true for our children and every subsequent generation, but also even for ourselves, the present generations of adults. The future these days is too close to the present to permit us to ignore it. Regardless of how inadequate our means for considering it may be, we are compelled to do so. We can no longer simply ignore the future. For, given our technological power, we necessarily act on the future as we act on the present. But detrimentally. We are using up the future. If only for that reason, we should be forced to incorporate in our consciousness a very real concern for what is to come.

We shall now turn to the present crisis. Our attempt to think about the West's future will begin, then, with an attempt to think about the West's present, starting, as indicated, with a look at the cultural upheaval of the twentieth century. The intention, again, will be to place that upheaval within the context of the history of the last several centuries, treating in turn the changes in style and thought, each both basic and fascinating.

STYLE

The interrelationship of culture to society is obscure. Theories abound with regard to the reciprocal influence, but all that can be said with certainty is that in the final analysis they tend to hang together. When one experiences a long era of stability, so does the other. And it is the same at the time of major transformations. To repeat: these cannot occur in society without soon being imitated by cultural change, not in culture without soon being paralleled by societal change. Whatever their internal ties, culture and society are obviously parts of a larger whole, the civilization itself. Thus when we witness a fundamental set of changes in either culture or society, we are made aware of the implications for even greater change. We have, it is now clear, just experienced such an upheaval, the cultural revolution that in the course of the last century has challenged the old modern world view, abolished its corresponding style, and begun the introduction of a new world view and a new style.

But before going on to look at this great discontinuity in recent cultural history, beginning with style, it will be helpful to acknowledge two problems. The first concerns a semantic difficulty that continues to make a complex matter needlessly even more complex: the existence of two usages for the word *modern*. Perhaps modern, since it retains the meaning "most recent," should never have been used to designate an age, but it was, and we are stuck with it. We cannot forbid either the reference to the forms that originated after the Middle Ages as modern; or to those that are now supplanting them also as modern. In this essay, however, modern will be used in the historical rather than current sense, to refer to the original modern, the modern of that Modern Age that first emerged into the light of day at the time of the Renaissance. That which is now emerging or in some cases has already emerged to replace the modern will be called, for want of a more descriptive term, the postmodern.

In this way we shall here avoid having to label as modern a twentieth-century style in painting and sculpture that has totally rejected modern canons; a twentieth-century architecture that bears no resemblance to modern architecture; a twentieth-century music that has consciously striven to renounce its modern origins; literary conventions that have clearly separated the work of the twentieth century from that of its modern predecessors; and so forth. Most semantic difficulties once revealed go away quickly enough, but not this one. The consistent employment of modern for cultural phenomena that have as their first purpose the destruction of the modern does much to deprive them of their significance and to play down the fact that there has been a revolution. They are made to seem to be the latest in a long line of modern substyles, when they are not that at all.

The second problem arises from the attempt to see a single culture, when in fact there are many. Generalization with regard to any subject produces similar dilemmas, and one accepts the neglect of the parts as the price paid in the effort to make sense. But here there is an additional consideration, the existence side by side and often in contradiction of a high and a low culture, the culture of a certain sort of elite and that of the masses. The line separating the two is partly indifferent to traditional divisions, such as class, and rather blurred; nevertheless, the distinctions in production are clear enough. Indeed, they are now clearer than ever, despite or perhaps because of the tendency of the democratic assumption to deny their separate existence. Can, then, one depict the culture of a period? Or must the effort stop short, with only the portrayal of high and low cultures? The answer lies in the nature of the relationship between the two. The fact is that they are not entirely separate, but move sooner or later along the same paths, with high culture in the vanguard, low culture working the interior dimensions. One might say that high culture probes and produces, while low culture consoles and consumes. And it is the eventual meeting of the two that gives an age its cultural definition. The high culture produces the initial forms. The society as a whole then gradually makes a selection. It puts its stamp on the high forms that will survive.

Thus we shall look to the high culture, but not to the extremities, where experimentation is intense. Rather, our interest is directed to the central, essential styles and ideas that are already beginning to achieve societal acceptance: to high culture, as it were, in the process of confirming its connection to society. Were we concerned with culture for the sake of culture, then we would be more ready to explore the various dead ends—to view, that is, experimental efforts as things in themselves. But here our use of culture as an index to civilizational directions makes us wary of the unique.

It is now appropriate to proceed to a commentary on style in the twentieth century. In seeking to delineate its outlines, we turn first to painting—for if style is the index of civilization, then painting is the index of style. So often it is in painting that the first hints of epochal change are to be found. No doubt this circumstance is the result of the fact that the painted work is a purely aesthetic achievement, done relatively easily and cheaply, and by a single individual. The other arts, with more obligations—architecture, for example, must produce buildings that do not fall down—are consistently somewhat more conservative. Painting is on the cutting edge of cultural change. Accordingly, the history of painting offers a shorthand version of the history of civilization itself. We come to expect from it a clear and early announcement of new directions.

What, then, is the essential message of twentieth-century painting? It is that modern style is finished. Twentieth-century painting has flatly rejected the style of the Modern Age. And the break has been as precipitate as one can imagine with regard to such matters. To put this in its proper perspective—and, again, we shall not be able to avoid the past in our discussion of the present—let us review very briefly the high points in the course of modern painting.

The modern style came into its own in the fifteenth century, after, to be sure, a lengthy medieval preparation, dating from the eleventh. It was a new art, distinct not only in its use of perspective and attention to naturalistic detail, but also in its general mood. Even though the subjects were often, indeed usually, religious, it was not an art of piety. Rather it was one of ebullient humanism. Renaissance painting brilliantly expressed with its naturalism the sweeping cultural revolution of which it was the centerpiece. A new age had found a new art.

It is not true, of course, that once the modern style was established change came to an end. The Modern Age in painting has had its distinct divisions. The sixteenth century Mannerists distorted somewhat the more naturalistic renditions of the High Renaissance, and the painters of the baroque carried this experiment to the point where it began to look as if a thoroughly new art was just around the corner. But the slide away from Renaissance canons came to a halt short of the brink, and a neoclassical revival during the eighteenth century restored the old forms, if perhaps without the old quality. The neoclassical was a revival of a revival, the Enlightenment imitating the Renaissance imitating the Greeks and Romans. And that was probably one imitation too many. But whatever the difficulties, the modern style was restored. The painting of the eighteenth century had nothing of the revolutionary about it, even when depicting revolution. It offered a calm classicism for a securely modern time.

Then at this point dawned the Romantic era. From roughly 1780 until 1830—the dates are somewhat different depending on the specific national tradition[1]—a new emotionalism and a sense of mystery were making themselves felt in Western culture, and these were, of course, reflected in painting. Yet Romantic art did not reject the basic modern conventions. There was a new vitality that strained to break out of the old forms, but break out it did not. When it was superseded by the mid-nineteenth-century realist movement, the modern tradition was still intact—now some four hundred years old and apparently in good health.

Realism, however, was in several ways subversive. As with all truly modern art, it was an attempt at naturalism. But it departed from modernism in three ways. First, it looked to the byways of the civilizational path. It was humanist, but it sought out the commoner rather than the hero. Second, its comment was critical rather than adulatory. And third, in its quest for a sharper view of reality, it began to postulate a truer reality beyond the natural, thereby launching the art of the Modern Age on a course that could only lead to its demise and replacement.

The very next movement, impressionism, which emerged in the 1860s, began that replacement; although it was also clear that the process would be rather circuitous and take some time. If with the realist Manet (1832–1883) it had seemed as if the leap from an interest in abstract patterns within nature to a fully abstract art might have been made directly, with Monet (1840–1926) and the impressionists another tack was taken. In the long run, the result would be the same. For the next several decades, however, Western art seemed to test the limits to which naturalism could be put without actually leaving it. The impressionist way was to blur the focus, yet never so much that the natural form was lost. The expressionists then added some distortion to the blurred effect. Next the cubists divided the scene into blocks. And finally, just before World War I, the avant-garde took the last step, that which brought it to the predominantly abstract art of the twentieth century. From that point on there was not much left to do to complete the revolution, except to apply the new canons in new ways and pursue a mop-up action against the lingering pockets of resistance. In fact, the efforts to eliminate the Renaissance style have not been relentless, for one of the principles of the new art is that there should be no single style. Eclecticism has been tolerated and even encouraged, and thus satiric and also straight imitations of a variety of Renaissance schools are permitted to coexist along with the abstract. One can imagine, too, a series of significant realist revivals, the first of which has already made its appearance. If the past is any model, however, the revolution will not be undone. The chasm has been crossed and modern art left behind. The West may cherish the memory, but a return is impossible.

We have been close enough to this change of styles to be unawed by it and are thus apt to underrate its importance. To give it its proper due, it should be kept in mind that upheavals of this magnitude in the world of art are just as rare as are those general ones that mark the decline of ages, with which they of course exactly coincide. The suggestion is hard to ignore: whatever the causal relationship, when the West's style of painting changes, the age also begins to change.

The West's sculpture during the last century has experienced much the same history as has painting, and of course the implications are also the same. From the Renaissance through the middle of the nineteenth century, the modern style prevailed: naturalistic, fully three-dimensional, and concentrated on the human figure—thus also a humanistic sculpture for a humanistic age. Here too there have been periods of deviation, first baroque and then Romantic. But again, by the eighteenth century the neoclassical forms were reestablished. Then, a little later than with painting, those neoclassical, modern forms underwent a fundamental change, clearly perceptible by 1900. The result was a new, postmodern sculpture, no longer representational and humanistic, but rather either distorted or abstract, or both together. Sculpture, like painting, had by the early twentieth century entirely overthrown the modern style. Again, the new sculpture is known, confusingly, as "modern," but whatever one calls it, it is in its inspiration, style, and execution entirely different from the sculpture of the Modern Age.

The history of architecture repeats the same story. Here, too, there was a modern style, established during the Renaissance. That style then lasted, with similar deviations, for about four centuries. It has now been rejected. Beginning in the last decades of the nineteenth century, the Renaissance forms, that is, the Greek and Roman shapes and trappings that the Renaissance had revived, began to disappear. Thereupon a postmodern set of conventions established itself.

It is interesting to note that when this new style began to emerge, it did not proceed from either the baroque or Romantic dissenting traditions, but rather came increasingly to resemble the move in art toward abstraction. Hence the break with the neoclassical past was fairly precise. Bauhaus functionalism was cubist in appearance, with all of the old devices swept away. Not columns, pediments, and friezes, but boxes—boxes without topses, if you will—had become the West's new architectural essences. As with painting, the basic features of this severe style had already been created by the eve of World War I, although the use of the old models continued until about mid-century. From then on, however, the new style has been employed almost exclusively. The West's cities are today spectacular monuments to this great architectural revolution.

If we ask for the causes of the crisis in architecture and the resultant new style, the answers often given point to the new materials and technologies that made the changes possible; also to the theory of functionalism that proposed to bring the efficiency and precision of the machine age to architectural design; and finally to the machines themselves, which were so useful in providing the imagery. Yet the change is bigger than the sum of the explanations. New means of building cannot force the appearance of a new style, only permit it. As for functionalism, there are several objections to the arguments that insist on its influence in creating a postmodern architecture. For one, the buildings themselves were only dubiously functional. For another, the theory has passed, and the essential style remains. Postfunctional architecture has made adjustments, not another revolution. In addition, the new style, as already remarked, nicely resembles the parallel development of the abstract in painting and sculpture, where the application of a functionalist motive has no meaning. As for the style of architecture imitating that of machinery, one should also note that the new style of machinery has imitated that of the new architecture, both eager in their design to move beyond the old classicism. Perhaps it is best to say that the architecture of the West's Modern Age has come to an end because the cultural vigor of the age itself has come to an end.

Turning to music, we come upon yet another aspect of the twentieth century's stylistic crisis. Here, too, the course of development has again followed that now-familiar pattern. Out of the medieval tradition a new music evolved during the early modern centuries. It was melodic, tonal, and took a rather simple and direct approach to rhythm. It was logical, introducing recognizable themes, repeating them, and then returning to the point of origin. And it gave a sense of being enframed, with each piece complete within itself, not unlike in this regard the modern piece of art or modern building. There was change, of course, with music also experiencing baroque, neoclassical, Romantic, and realist phases. But in all of these the modern essentials were preserved. Then, again in the late nineteenth century, they quickly succumbed. Beginning with an impressionist phase, the old music proceeded to drift away, and soon it had disappeared. What is referred to as serious music has ceased to be classical. Nor is it now always serious. As in art, novelty is in, tradition out. If there is a new convention, it is, as one critic has suggested, the eclectic search for novelty itself.[2] In any case, the crisis in music has put an end to the modern style.

As for unserious or popular music, the revolution has been muted and uneven. On the one hand, it is true that jazz has been in touch with the emerging new style since the thirties. Also, while rock has been more conservative in choosing its forms, it has nevertheless achieved an animal primitivism, even vulgarity, that is a clear departure from the popular music of the past. And of course its sensuality and hyper-volume are hardly reminiscent of Mozart. On the other hand, much of adult popular music adheres to the traditions—melody, harmony, stable rhythm, and enframement—that have been abandoned elsewhere. One wonders why classical music, where traditions are revered, should have made such a complete break; while popular music, where traditions are often despised, should have held back. We come again here to the matter of the relationship of high to low culture and the notion of a time lag. It would seem that there is fairly consistently a chronological gap between the point at which intellectuals, in this case the composers of society's "sacred" music, begin to feel the need for fundamental change and the point at which it is perceived by those composing for popular tastes. There is nothing remarkable in the fact. The two sets of artists have very different purposes: the popular composers to entertain people busy living in the present, their classical counterparts to venture insights into what the present is in the process of becoming. The lag can be seen in many areas and was especially acute in the early part of this century, as the intellectuals began to grope for a postmodern culture to replace the dying modern. The resultant much-talked-about alienation would seem in retrospect to have been the result not of intellectuals and the bulk of society moving in different directions, but of the two moving, as already noted, in the same direction at different times, at an interval. If that suggests that intellectuals are an avant-garde that leads society along, then that is mostly wrong. Rather they would seem to serve as a true avant-garde. Although they consistently view the new terrain first and are able occasionally to send back dramatic reports, still they take their marching orders from the large army to the rear, which continues to make the final decisions regarding the movement of the whole. When a Miles Davis, then, decided that jazz would improvise on the work of Igor Stravinsky, it was not an act of imitation so much as one of acceptance: the commander had received the suggestion of his scout and approved it.

What of the crisis in twentieth-century literature? Literary content is an aspect of thought. If history, to paraphrase Bolingbroke, is philosophy searching for truth by attempting a factual reconstruction of reality, then literature is philosophy searching for truth via an intuitive reconstruction. As an aspect of thought, we can best deal with it in our commentary on thought in general. Literature has another aspect, however, that is unique, and that is style. Other forms of thought cannot escape style, but they do not emphasize it. With literature it is given, as it were, equal billing. Thus literature has two histories, each worth noting. And with regard to style, it is more of the same. The modern forms that were used since their emergence in the later Middle Ages and Renaissance have now been discarded. While they had undergone considerable evolution and been occasionally challenged, particularly by the Romantics, they had survived intact through the middle of the nineteenth century. The beginning of the end can be traced once more to the next several decades, from ca. 1880, with a new style yet again already present by the outbreak of World War I, but still not predominant; and then fanning out to put its mark on the whole of the West by mid-century. It was subjective, symbolic, with neither rhyme nor reason, and often unintelligible, although in the hands of a few masters strangely awesome. In short, the new literary style was almost the very opposite of that of the Modern Age. If it too has been labeled "modern" and "modernist,"[3] then this confusing nomenclature should not obscure the obvious: the new modern, better, postmodern style, is not a refinement of the old modern style, but rather its rejection.

And that is the point that can be made here to sum up this quick review of the stylistic aspect of this century's crisis: during the last hundred years, the old modern style, the style of the Modern Age, has been cast aside and replaced by a startlingly different style. The modern style was naturalistic and neoclassical. But this new postmodern style has shunned naturalism for abstraction and has dropped all of the traditional neoclassical hallmarks. The changes began to take place in the last decades of the nineteenth century and were more or less complete by the 1920s, in some cases even somewhat earlier. There then followed a period, extending into the 1950s, during which the new forms struggled to be accepted. Finally, the second half of our century has seen the new style's assimilation and extension. It has arrived.

If this treatment seems rather abrupt, then it should be said that the purpose here is only to point to the discontinuity and to identify it as one of those few times when the West has, as it were, put on a new face. We shall have more to say about its characteristics in chapter 4. But now we shall move on to an equally brief review of the crisis in the thought of the twentieth century.

THOUGHT

The thought of the Modern Age, like everything modern, began to assume its characteristic shapes at the time of the Renaissance. It was founded upon four essential assumptions. The first of these was the belief in human dignity, with its concomitant assertion of the individual's efficacy, especially with regard to the ability to achieve goals without divine interference. The second was the belief in the priority of life in this world, whatever one's expectations concerning an afterlife. The third was the belief in mankind's capacity for obtaining knowledge about the things of this world, given both an orderly nature, subject neither to the caprice of the gods nor an irregular fate, and a mind capable of the rational methods necessary to permit perception. And the fourth was the expectation of an ameliorative condition, that is, of the fundamental improvability of the secular life, this in the earlier period only implicit but later emerging as a formal theory of progress. Thus these four: commitment to the individual, affirmation of the primacy of the secular, assertion of the accessibility of knowledge, and faith in progress. These were the components of the modern mind.

They were not, to be sure, fully developed during the Renaissance. And, like all things modern, they met with severe challenges during the periods of reaction, particularly in the seventeenth century and again during the Romantic era of the late eighteenth and early nineteenth centuries; but for a long time nothing could permanently halt their advance, as they came to put their stamp on modern thought. By the middle of the eighteenth century, they had permeated the upper segments of society; by the middle of the nineteenth, the middle segments; and by the middle of the twentieth, the remainder. Yet, even as they were making their final conquests, a new revolution had begun.

For by the last decades of the nineteenth century, modern thought was beginning to undergo basic change. Each of its essential assumptions was being brought under attack, with much of the work of annihilation accomplished, as in the other compartments of the West's culture, even before 1914. Yet while it is scarcely no more difficult to recognize the demise of modern thought than of modern art, architecture, music, or literary style, one cannot, as with these, speak of the creation of a new entity that has replaced the old. But, if the old assumptions have not yet been replaced, they have nonetheless been discarded.

For example, human dignity and free will, the essentials of individualism, have been victimized by an assault that has come not from one side but two: from Freudianism, with its insistence on the persistent effects of infantile depravity, and also from behaviorism, which has attempted to demonstrate the absence of a human personal core that could be considered either dignified or free; or, for that matter, even depraved. If the modern opinion of man's nature was set in the fifteenth century by Pico's *Oration on the Dignity of Man*,[4] it was just as clearly reversed in the twentieth by B. F. Skinner's *Beyond Freedom and Dignity*.[5] Thus this crucial premise of modern thought has been flatly rejected. The Western mind has changed: it simply no longer believes in the individual as conceived of by humanism.

With regard to secularism, the concentration on life in this world, there have been two very different reactions, both dissenting. One is to be found in existentialism, which has renewed and even exaggerated the modern preoccupation with the secular, but at the cost of renouncing every other modern tenet and reconciling itself to the sense of futility that has accompanied the failure of the modern world view. Existentialism has not pretended to offer new hope. Rather, in recommending commitment in the face of absurdity, it has merely pointed to a practical cure for too much despair. Secularism has been here preserved, but stripped of all those appurtenances that had made it originally attractive. If the behaviorists have denied man dignity while leaving a meaningful world, the existentialists have left him dignity but in turn denied the meaning.

The other negative response to secularism has taken the form of a renewed interest in religion, in which the antisecular, fundamentalist, and transcendental elements have been given emphasis, thus bringing to an end the long history of the secularization of religion. To describe the West in the twentieth century as a society beyond secularism is not, however, correct. Our present point is perhaps best characterized by Heidegger's remark, which joins the existential and religious positions: that God is indeed dead, but that we are awaiting His return.[6] Secularism has gone sour, but as yet the West as a whole has found no adequate substitute.

As for knowledge of the world, the twentieth century has again departed from the modern beliefs. By the nineteenth century, the modern credo had evolved into an optimistic positivism that expected, having cast aside superstition and speculation and restricted itself to the methods of science, to obtain at last the final answers to the problems put by both society and nature. Yet it was by way of the positivistic tradition that the West arrived at some very unpositivist conclusions, more damaging in the long run to modern epistemology than Hume's skepticism, Kant's reinsertion of the subjective element, or Hegel's revival of Divine Providence. For the new positivism that developed step by step out of the old confessed finally that its methods could be applied only narrowly, and not at all to those crucial matters—such, for instance, as the meaning of life—that were usually taken to be the main concern of philosophy. On these subjects, philosophy, said Wittgenstein, could only remain silent.[7] And with that frank evaluation, modern epistemology expired. The same conclusion, to be sure, could have been and indeed was reached through other channels. T. S. Eliot's context was different, but the point was very similar when he complained that the proliferation of knowing was moving mankind further away from real knowledge.[8] When the twentieth century was offered systems that might serve as a restored epistemology, they have proceeded not from science, but either from religion or a sort of secular intuition, as with Bergson's vitalism.[9] But nothing as generally persuasive as positivism once was has taken its place, and where the positivist effort has chosen despite its problems to continue, it has bypassed the question of how one knows to concentrate, as with pragmatism and behaviorism, on results.

Regarding the modern assumption of progress, the twentieth century has been equally critical. Faith in progress had reached a peak around the middle of the nineteenth century. When Schopenhauer (d. 1860) condemned the doctrine, most Western intellectuals, Marx included, were still believers. But when Nietzsche (d. 1900) attacked it some decades later, a significant number had begun to join in the dissent. And from that point on the balance swung steadily, until the vast majority of those who give articulation to the current state of the mind of the West had abandoned progress. And it was obviously not only those, either, for by the latter third of the twentieth century a general pessimism has come to be shared at all levels, as Robert Nisbet has noted in his *History of the Idea of Progress.*[10]

Thus the modern era in thought has come to an end. Some have taken the aberrations of the last century to be the result of a temporary lapse. Others have seen them as the result of a betrayal by the intellectuals. Given the absence of a new thought ready to provide for the West a clear postmodern *Weltbild,* the changes lend themselves to all sorts of explanations that have little connection to the disintegration of modern things in general, to the loss of the modern direction. But whatever validity these specific arguments may have, it is difficult not to believe that what has happened to thought has something to do with what is happening to the entire culture: the end of modern thought has come about as the culture of which it was a part has also come to an end.

There has been a revolution in twentieth century science, too, of course. Stable space has been replaced by curved space; fixed time by relative time; hard matter by hints of abstraction; specific predictability by aggregate predictability; and, perhaps most significant, the optimism that foresaw endless progress through discovery and invention by a new pessimism. And that new pessimism is fed by doubts both with regard to the possibility of extending the present limits of fundamental knowledge and the wisdom of doing so, of continuing, that is, to follow where theory leads, oblivious to the dangers.[11]

But should the innovations in science be taken to be part of the larger cultural transition? Or does its methodology and commitment to a suprahistorical position exempt it from the sorts of influence that would join it to the other cultural movements of an age? That is a difficult question, and the answers are rightly debated. Certainly science is not as free to follow fluctuating intellectual predilections as is, say, painting. Yet every major epoch has produced a science that, whatever its procedures, has managed to match its views of nature to those of the prevailing culture. Not that science produces lies for the occasion. Ortega y Gasset was undoubtedly right, however, when he suggested that from the many possible correct descriptions science can be relied upon to elaborate those to which it is already predisposed. An age inclined to think of the universe as a machine will find a Newton; an age inclined to see it as an abstraction, a distortion of the old nature, will find an Einstein.[12] Thus we are right to place this century's scientific upheavals alongside the other cultural changes. The Modern Age, beginning with the generation of Copernicus, produced a modern science. After the usual challenges—among them, Luther's disdain, the Catholic resistance to heliocentrism, and Pascal's sophisticated warnings—it became the dominant Western position with regard to the physical world. It then remained that throughout the Modern Age. But with the passing of modern culture, it too has given way.

These changes in science theory, for all the casual talk about the cultural significance of relativity and the quantum theory, have been kept in the background by the enormous attention given to technology, science's pragmatic offspring. In applied physics and biology, the move to a new position has been much slower. In fact, it can be said that if the original ambitions of the Modern Age are harbored anywhere in the West in relatively unchallenged fashion, it is here, among the engineers and applied scientists, who continue to insist that nature can be mastered for the benefit of mankind. They make use of the new physics to the extent that it is applicable, but are hostile to its philosophical implications. The one concession, and it is not an insignificant one, is the offer to apply technology to the problems created by technology. But their hearts remain with the era of growth and the old dedication to progress, to the achievement of the secular utopia. Indifferent to theory, it will take a more practical demonstration, one that would seem to be in preparation, to convince the technologists of the futility of their ambitions.

We conclude this review of the crisis in twentieth-century culture with a look at education. Here the changes are less obvious. In some respects, educational procedures and goals are now more in keeping with those of the modern model than ever before. Modern education from its inception during the Renaissance has been secular, coeducational, devoted to the development of the individual, and humanistic, that is, committed to the assumption that at the core of any program of study should be the humanities. In the twentieth century, Western education has remained secular. It has become more completely coeducational than ever before. It continues to be oriented to individual development. And the condition of the humanities is with regard to certain indices still very healthy. In the schools entire populations are supposedly offered the rudiments of a humanistic education, and at the higher level the humanities departments do what they can to carry on the old traditions. Yet gradually a new system has replaced the old. Its essential ingredient is professionalism. The Modern Age had rejected the medieval notion that education should be primarily professional. We have now rejected the modern notion, returning to professionalism. For despite the prominence of liberal studies, large numbers of those educated in Western universities have in fact shifted to the professional colleges, where the classical portion of the curriculum has been reduced to an insignificant minimum. Even if this were not the case, the failure of the preparatory levels to develop the basic skills necessary to pursue humanistic studies at the university level has created an almost insurmountable problem. Of reading, writing, and arithmetic, the last is the only one to survive, and then with the help of a calculator.

Thus education in this century, and especially since the end of World War II, has witnessed some profound changes. Perhaps it is because these have occurred during a period of tremendous growth, particularly in higher education, that they have not received much attention. The traditional areas have been able to preserve themselves, but still, only as islands, surrounded by the flood. And it is the flood itself, not those islands, that determines the essentials of contemporary education. Through the nineteenth century, the Renaissance idea in education prevailed. It does no longer. Certainly of all the discontinuities experienced by the West's culture during this century of crisis, this in education is of the greatest significance. An age's education is its propaganda. Modern culture might yet survive without some of its trappings, but not without a population educated to believe in its ideals.

In art, architecture, sculpture, music, literary style, thought, science, and education, then, we have witnessed the same process unfolding: in the course of the last century those cultural structures that were created during the Renaissance and then endured throughout the vital modern centuries either have collapsed or reveal themselves to be in an advanced state of decay. The individual changes have been summarized only with regard to their essentials, thereby to emphasize their relationships as parts within a whole. And it is that whole, the Western cultural experience in this period of fundamental transition, to which we return here at the end of this short survey in order to stress a single point, and that is that there has been one experience, not many. Western civilization has a culture. That culture between roughly 1500 an 1900 was in its ascendant modern phase. Since roughly 1900 it has been in the process of becoming something else.

POLITICS

Proceeding now to the great crisis in twentieth-century society, the first observation that should be made is that treating it as we shall do here, separately from the cultural crisis, is somewhat artificial. They are thoroughly intertwined, of course, and the division is made only to give us the opportunity to concentrate on each in turn before rejoining them. The same applies to the parts into which the societal crisis is here divided, the political and economic. We can also note again that the societal crisis differs at this point from that which has been experienced by the West's culture, in that the cultural transition is much further along. Modern society continues in some respects to be quite successful. Things run along smoothly enough, so smoothly that talk of a crisis sometimes seems at best premature. Yet beneath the surface the situation is ominous. The institutions and systems of modern society continue to function, but they would seem to be seriously flawed. Caught in a rapidly changing world, their ability to change with it appears to have been lost.

Certainly with regard to the political structure of the West it is hard to be optimistic about the future. Any sort of general commentary quickly focuses on the nation-state and its prospects. For clearly it is that nation-state that has been the fundamental unit of politics for the past half millennium, thus for the entire history of the Modern Age. Modern politics has been both centered on and contained by the nation-state. And now, while in some respects at the peak of its power, it would appear to be headed toward almost certain destruction.

Let us consider the nation-state for a moment within its larger historical context. Its origins—as with modern style and thought—lie in the Renaissance. Precisely why it emerged just when it did is not altogether clear. In each of the major unifications, a different set of circumstances seems to have accounted for the success: marriage and *Reconquista* in Spain, victory over the English and Burgundians in France, the success of the Tudors in England, and the work of the princes of Moscow in Russia. But it was not just a coincidence of unique circumstances that produced so many new nations in such a short time. Rather it is more likely that the nation-state was created to fulfill certain needs that were at this time present, if not everywhere to the same degree, nevertheless throughout the West. One can identify three of these. The first was economic. By the beginning of the Modern Age, the localized economy of the early Middle Ages had been replaced by one consisting of broader commercial networks. These were clearly facilitated by the establishment of the national political units, which were capable of maintaining order, setting standards, giving protection, and removing internal tariffs. Perhaps the national solution was not the only one possible, but certainly it was an appropriate response to the economic facts of the time. A larger political unit was needed to support the new economy, and the nation-state provided it.

The second need that the nation-state fulfilled concerned the search for military security. A political structure to be effective must not only provide economic order within its boundaries, but also give protection against competing foreign units, whatever the system. The Roman Empire had managed by absorbing the competing units and continuing to dominate them with the most effective military organization of its day, the legion. In a much different way, the fief of the Middle Ages had rendered a comparable military service. But by the eve of the modern period the West's military system was no longer providing adequate defense. A new weapon and a new attitude were operating together to make the feudal host rapidly obsolete.

The new weapon was the infantryman, employed in large numbers by the new national army. And the new attitude was that which permitted that infantryman, a commoner, to be used in battle, to be introduced with devastating effect into a military operation that had for several centuries been restricted to the aristocracy. From that point on, the national army, gradually elaborated by the addition of artillery, a national navy, and much later, a national air force, became the ultimate arbiter. It could be seriously hurt neither from below nor above. Smaller territorial divisions did not have sufficient resources, and armed alliances of several national states proved effective only temporarily, lasting no longer than it took to keep any one of them from establishing a thorough hegemony.[13] It is true that during the confusion of the seventeenth century it seemed that the national army might be destroyed, as the various strands from which it drew its strength began to unravel. But the damage was soon repaired, and that army continued to insure that the nation-state was the supreme source of military power throughout the remaining modern centuries.

The third need that came to be well provided for by the nation-state was for leadership. Successful societies do not merely exist; rather, they are directed by select segments of the citizenry, a party, class, or priesthood representing something of a consensus and capable of setting directions. Rome's imperial elite had done that. So had the medieval aristocracy. In the Modern Age, it has been the men of business, the entrepreneurs—put in terms of class, the bourgeoisie, and especially the high bourgeoisie—who have either made the political decisions directly or provided the impetus that has carried others along with them. This was true even in those early modern centuries during which the kings and aristocrats occupied almost all of the offices of authority. The business of the Modern Age has been business, and businessmen have set the fundamental directions from the Renaissance on. The quality of this leadership has been often criticized, but it is difficult to argue that it did not exist. Without it, the Modern Age would have been something entirely different.[14]

These, then, were the needs that gave rise to the national state: for a new political framework to support the new economy, for a new armed force that could provide security, and for a new leadership, capable of replacing an increasingly purposeless aristocracy. It has been this state's ability to continue to fulfill these needs that has accounted for its remarkable durability. And its future will, in all likelihood, be determined by its success in continuing to do so. Yet with regard to each, there would now seem to be insurmountable obstacles.

Taking first the matter of the nation-state's relationship to the economy, it can be said that while there are still services being rendered, by and large economic development has taken the situation beyond the point at which the nation-state can offer the most efficient conditions for operation. The original national economy was, to use the terminology offered by Emanuel Wallerstein, a world economy, but not a global economy.[15] That is to say that, while nation-states dabbled here and there at the world level, there existed no true economy encompassing the globe. But now there is one. A new network has emerged that is not at all contained by the old politics. Both the opportunities offered to this new economy and the factors restraining it range far beyond the limits of the national economy and its nation-state. Markets are increasingly overseas, and—ironically, precisely because of the fact that the world web of nation-states is now complete—well beyond the sorts of controls available in the era of colonialism. The ability of major nation-states to influence minor ones is still great, but not an acceptable substitute for the dominion once held over colonies.

This loss of control is even more true with regard to raw materials. Access to resources has become increasingly a problem as the development of new industries has made the national economies dependent on minerals found at home either in insufficient quantities or not at all. The United States, for example, depends on imports for 90 percent of its columbium, manganese, chromium, cobalt, bauxite, and platinum; 75 to 90 percent of its tin and nickel; and 50 to 75 percent of its zinc, antimony, tungsten, and cadmium.[16]

Nor has the nation-state been able to solve what may be the ultimate economic problem—the pollution of the oceans and atmosphere. National jurisdictions stop short precisely where the difficulties begin. And international agreements in this area have proved as undependable as in every other. The nation-state was not designed with such problems in mind and can cope with them but poorly.

Thus the nation-state that functioned so nicely during a long and crucial part of the evolution from the local to the world economy has, it would seem, been rendered relatively useless by the completion of the process. With the emergence of a true global economy, the old national boundaries are proving more cumbersome than helpful. And now even the collapse of the world economy—which, I shall later argue, is in the long run quite likely—could hardly restore the purpose of the national unit, for the bases of national autarky have already been destroyed. The economic life of the nation-state has become too involved with that of the world system to survive a major breakdown of that system. Hence the national economy would seem not only to have lost its place of primacy, but also to have failed to retain a self-sufficient inner economy as a possible refuge.

As for the nation-state's ability to continue to offer security, the prospects are no better. For the national army and navy are no longer the supreme source of power. The very technology that formerly enhanced their position has now made them obsolescent. If before the advent of the nuclear bomb the national armed force was the ultimate power, that distinction now belongs to that bomb itself. And while it can be employed by the nation-state, it can more easily be employed against it. Nor does the nuclear bomb require, as did the national army and navy, the economy and population of a nation-state for its production. The potential for wielding the greatest force, then, has passed from the traditional nation-state to small states formerly on the peripheries and to various infranational and supranational groupings. Never has a civilizational structure surrendered the means of its maintenance quite so suddenly.

Still, the national army and navy are not going to disappear overnight. If they are obsolescent, they are not quite yet obsolete. The tenacious survival of cavalry into the Modern Age serves as a reminder of how enduring military forms can be. The national armed force will stay on for a while; but its ability to provide either security or the means of aggrandizement has been all but eliminated. At home it can offer no defense against terrorism, and abroad its every effort is restrained by the danger that any conflict can bring the escalation to nuclear warfare in which, even in victory, army and nation-state together would be destroyed. Hence the sphere of national war making has been tremendously restricted, limited now to only those areas where the chief adversaries have agreed to tolerate its activity. There have been so far considerable benefits from this odd circumstance: the world since Hiroshima has witnessed many small wars, border skirmishes, as it were, between the major powers; but no big wars. There were only two decades between the end of World War I and the beginning of World War II. There have now been more than four decades since the end of World War II. But lest we congratulate ourselves too readily, we need to remember that World War III will be the end of everything—the real war to end all wars. In any case, the relevant point here is that the national military has been deprived of its *raison*. It can no longer serve as the final decision-maker in the game of international rivalry, except, to be sure, when the decision is to be "death to all." Linger on as this force may, it is an anachronism and, unlike the latter-day feudal host, not merely an anachronism but a terrible danger.

What are we to make of the problem of leadership and the national state? The upper echelons of the bourgeoisie can still be found in the key positions of influence. Yet the old leadership has faltered, it would seem.

The sense of aimless drift that has become more acute as the century has grown older is not merely another manifestation of our growing anxiety, it is rather a reflection of the political realities. Even the idea of leadership has given way, and that to the false promise of conflict-resolution. Governing constellations come and go and nothing happens, while the fundamental predicaments of our times go unaddressed.

Perhaps the dearth of leadership in part derives from the fact that power within the modern state has been widely dispersed in the course of the last century. Just at about the time Marx was predicting that the bourgeoisie was soon to be overthrown by the proletariat, that proletariat instead began to become absorbed into the bourgeoisie. The result was much more destructive to the latter than the outcome of any revolution could have been. For a single class was finally created, and a single class is no class at all. The aristocracy had already been reduced and incorporated. Now the proletariat was elevated and incorporated. The result was that the coherence of the old middle class was destroyed. Rather than a political society directed from a particular vantage point, the state as a result has become an arena in which all interests contend with more or less equal advantage.

And if there is a consensus, it is negative, based not on a willingness to contribute to the making of crucial decisions, but rather on an implicit agreement not even to put the crucial questions. Bourgeois leadership has been replaced by an unpolarized, amorphous condition in which leadership has become impossible. Thus the national state has been also rendered incompetent with regard to this function. The bourgeoisie created the consumer society as a receptacle for its goods. Then, following rather helplessly the logic of democratic theory that had been invented by it to use against its monarchical and aristocrat opponents, it turned the control of politics over to that consumer society, a giant without a brain, a floundering mass awaiting, it would seem, a new organizing principle.

The nation-state, then, continues to survive in the midst of this civilizational transition, but its prospects are not good. It no longer is able to do the things that it was designed to do. It can offer neither a suitable economic framework, nor security, nor essential leadership; and it is therefore highly vulnerable. The world for which the nation-state was made is passing. And the nation-state, in all likelihood, will eventually pass with it.

ECONOMICS

How much different is the picture if one turns to an overview of the West's present economic situation? Certainly here there are a number of very large problems. At the root of most of these is a circumstance that would seem to predetermine the destruction of the modern economy as surely as the inadequacies of the modern political structure foretell the latter's collapse. It is the disturbingly harmful and ultimately unresolvable tension created by the modern economy's need to expand in a world that has reached the limits of its ability to tolerate such expansion. This conclusion rests upon a number of more or less separate assumptions, each of which needs to be examined with regard to its merits. To begin with, has there indeed been a modern economy, a single economic entity corresponding to the Modern Age? If so, is this modern economy in fact irrevocably committed to growth? And, if that should also prove to be the case, then is it correct to assume that growth can no longer continue?

Taking each of these in turn, we can begin with the matter of the existence of a modern economy. If there is no modern economy, then it is not very helpful to assert that it is coming to an end. But there is one, of course, and it is capitalism. Yet the issue is not quite that simple. If capitalism is a system with private ownership and open markets, then its history is somewhat checkered. While it has clearly served as a sort of ideal economic type for the Modern Age, nevertheless it cannot be said to have characterized the actual operation of affairs all that consistently. By capitalism, however, we have come to mean more than a manner of ownership and marketing. We have sensed, rightly, that the Modern Age as a unit is distinct economically from the medieval period that preceded it, and distinct, too, from all other periods. Thus we use *capitalism* as a catch-all phrase to describe this distinction, even when mercantilism and other varieties of state capitalism have pushed private ownership and open markets temporarily into the background.

We have been able, then, to find consistency despite capitalism's tendency to defy on occasion its theoretical descriptions. That this is so is due to the presence of another, more fundamental factor, and that is growth, that condition of more or less permanent expansion that is sometimes taken as a result but is in fact an integral part of the system itself. The medieval economy, it should be remembered, was static—not stagnant, but stable, designed to continue on and on without structural change. The modern economy grew out of it, and one can notice the stirrings as early as the eleventh century; but it was not until the fifteenth and sixteenth centuries that this new economy became the dominant mode. When it did, the pattern of stability was thrust aside. And from the Renaissance to the present, dynamic expansion has continued to be a basic characteristic of the West's economic activity, interrupted only, as with all aspects of the West's modern development, by the general crisis of the seventeenth century. Growth is, then, the feature that has finally given the modern economy its identity and essential quality.

This brings us to the question of whether or not growth and the modern economy are separable. The answer must be no, for the modern economy is growth. When it ceases to grow, it will also cease to function. The modern economy has become so thoroughly molded to the growth over which it has presided that it will not be able to continue without it. That need not have been the case. It would have been possible, at least theoretically, for the medieval economy to have been supplanted by an economic system that could have been many of the things that the modern system has been without being wedded to the growth phenomenon. An urban-directed, commercial, even private-ownership economy dedicated to maintaining but not expanding the new society was a possibility if we view, that is, the issue with exclusive regard to the mechanics of economics. There is nothing inherent to any of these mechanisms that would have forced a modern economy to set itself upon the path of continuous growth had it not chosen to for other reasons.

Chosen is perhaps not the right word, for certainly societies cannot be said truly to choose their directions. Nor can we describe adequately the processes that substitute for choice. All that can be said is that the West's civilization toward the end of the medieval era was developing a remarkable dynamic quality that would put its mark not only on the economy, but also on every other aspect of Western life. Somehow Europe had emerged from the devastations of the fourteenth and early fifteenth centuries with a tremendous energy that it felt compelled to dissipate through every imaginable form of conquest. The West suddenly exploded. Thus the new economy, although it might have been put to other purposes, was constructed in such a way that it would facilitate expansion. Capitalism, therefore, while not of necessity dynamic, became that as a result of the use to which it was put. And because the period of that use lasted for five hundred years, capitalism and growth were finally one and the same. The modern economy was forced at an early age into an addiction to growth. Now in its old age, it is much too late to consider kicking the habit. Put another way, the modern economy can be compared to a creature that, having only moved forward for its entire life, can hardly be expected to move backward or even to shuffle a bit to the side. This fact is just as true for the state capitalisms of Marxist allegiance. The modern world's economies know only growth.

And one finds it at every level. Modern economic theory almost unanimously endorses growth, even in the face of increasing difficulties and obvious ecological dangers. The nation-state assumes that it must continue to grow, and faster than its competitors, or perish. Also it relies upon growth to avoid a forced redistribution of goods and services that would be foreign to the modern tradition. Even the short-term halts to growth, which had been tolerated when the modern economy was younger and still contained within it large segments not yet fully modernized, can no longer be permitted. For they are now far too destructive.

Thus the nation-state exerts a constant pressure in favor of growth. But in addition, each enterprise seeks to expand, convinced of the dogma that insists that growth is good for it and for society, too. In addition, the individual presses for his or her own economic growth. And finally, as if the force of modern ideology were not already sufficient to keep us at our task, we have the persuasions of professional advertisement. Without wishing to belabor the point, one can suggest that these various attitudes and aspirations are interconnected in such a complex way that the removal of growth from the modern economic system is unthinkable. Unless it can continue to grow, it will come to an end and be replaced. There will always be an economy. Possibly we can even invent a better one. But without growth it will not be much like its modern predecessor.

Next, then, we must estimate our ability to go on growing. Prior to the last several decades, almost no one doubted that it would be possible to sustain expansion indefinitely. It had come to be taken for granted—the material manifestation of the progress that would continue forever. A few, to be sure, did not see it quite that way, and wondered whether growth and progress were synonymous. Yet hardly anyone doubted that growth was technically possible. Then rather suddenly the West was submerged under a wave of pessimism. Characteristic of the new attitude and instrumental as well in shaping it was the Club of Rome's *Limits to Growth,* which appeared in 1972.[17] But rebuttals followed, and the consensus seems to have stabilized around a middle position. Here the threats to future growth have been acknowledged—the energy shortages of 1973–74 had made them all too palpable—but it has come to be assumed that science will find a way out. Present energy sources can be recycled, new ones found, people taught to do with less, the heating of the atmosphere and pollution controlled, agricultural production coaxed to continue to increase in order to feed the new billions, and, at the same time, the demographic explosion curbed short of disaster. Trying times are to be expected, but not catastrophe. The modern economy will continue. A few have adhered to their pessimism, notably Robert L. Heilbroner, whose alarming estimate, "The Human Prospect," first appeared in January 1974 in the *New York Review of Books.* Nor has Barry Commoner changed his views. The government task-force report *Global 2000* has also restated the vast problems, as have the essays edited by Daniel Yergin and Martin Hillenbrand under the title *Global Insecurity: A Strategy for Energy and Economic Renewal.* And Aurelio Peccei has continued to press the Club of Rome position in various publications.[18] But the mood seems to have shifted away from long-term fears to immediate difficulties; and because the only envisaged solution to the latter is continued growth, it has been assumed that it must be possible.

Who is right? There is much evidence to suggest that it is the optimists, for despite the doomsayers and also despite occasional inflation and recession, the economy does roll on. Growth continues. And in 1980, China, the largest nation in the world, paid the West the highest compliment when it decided to join the quest for rapid growth. Yet the fact is that the underlying reality with regard to the West's economic life remains extremely precarious and the outlook bleak. In trying to find the way to a future that can be built upon the hopes and methods of the modern economy, it is essential not to ignore three basic points.

The first is that we are beginning to experience serious shortages. In the past, growth came cheap. It will no longer. The industrial revolution was facilitated tremendously by its ability to take what it needed from pools of resources close at hand. Those pools are no longer available, and the costs and dangers of finding substitutes are becoming increasingly more clear.

The second point has to do with the impact of the industrial economy on the global environment. For half a millennium modern man assaulted nature and managed to come away with rewards while leaving his victim more or less intact. Perhaps the aesthetic quality of the world was even enhanced, although that is a matter for personal judgement. But aesthetically and functionally as well, in the course of the twentieth century the natural world has begun to suffer—and, most important, to lose its capacity to sustain man in the future. Pollution is more than an annoyance. Its accumulating impact ultimately threatens all life on this planet. Long before it reaches such proportions, however, it will begin to rearrange the structure of civilization.

We can of course do something about it. Already there have been remarkable demonstrations of our skills of reclamation, as lakes and rivers and sometimes even neighborhoods have been restored. Yet the big picture remains unchanged: because pollution cannot be dealt with alone, given its dependence on the dilemmas created by shortages, it will not go away until growth and capitalism as we know it—we should also add, socialism as we know it—come to an end. Consider the predicament that arises from the search for a source of energy to replace oil, which, whatever the pattern of fluctuation between momentary glut and scarcity in the short run, will no longer be available in the necessary quantities to sustain present rates of usage by sometime early in the next century. If we switch to nuclear energy, then we are dependent on soaring costs of construction, so far unsolved waste-disposal problems, unacceptable threats from accident, and, perhaps worst, the dilemma inherent in not being able to separate peaceful from potential military and criminal use.

Coal seems to be the other alternative. But here we run the risk, or, better put, accept as the almost inevitable by-product, an increase in world temperatures by several degrees over the next half century, thereby significantly changing weather, crop seasons, tide levels—indeed everything dependent on the ecology of the seasons, as locally established over the years. Thus a resource problem becomes quickly a pollution problem, which threatens to go on to create a greater resource problem. Passing from the one to the other and back again in the search to continue the conditions of the frontier, when in the midst of virgin growth and deposits all was to be had for the asking, the West is letting itself down deeper and deeper into a dark hole.

The third point concerns the number of people being served by the West's modern economy. Throughout most of the modern past, intensive use of the system has been highly restricted even within those nation-states at the center of things. But it has reached the majority in the older areas and is now spreading out to encompass the entire population of the world. Further, this is happening in the very century in which that world population has undergone a tremendous acceleration. The Modern Age has of course seen from its inception remarkable demographic growth. Yet from 1500 to 1900 the number of people on earth merely tripled, raising the total from 0.5 to 1.6 billion. This was a significant increase, of course, but unimpressive compared to what was to come. For at present we have reached 5 billion,[19] and by the year 2000 there will be approximately 6 billion, 3.75 times as many as in 1900 and 12 times as many as in 1500. By 2025, according to the World Bank Development Report for 1984, we shall have added yet another billion, upping the total to 7. And the modern economy, having won out in its competition with the more stable but less powerful traditional economies of the pre-Western world, will be asked to support each of those people in the consumptive style of middle America.

Or can that be avoided? That is to say, would it be possible to restrict the Western pattern of usage to part of the globe—our part, of course. No. As long as the modern economy provides for some, there will be great pressure put upon it to provide for all. In part because of the nature of terrorism and the lack of proper defenses, but also due to the fact that many of the resources necessary to the modern economy are in the less developed areas, that pressure cannot help but be effective. Therefore the West if it is to continue to grow is necessarily committed to trying to finish the task that it undertook five hundred years ago, that of remaking the world in its image.

If we project the course of that effort into the near future, what are the foreseeable obstacles? Let us make an assumption or two and then a few simple calculations. We shall assume that there will be no harmful unforeseeable obstacles—no major wars, weather changes, or other disasters; also that the world at the moment is in reasonably good shape, even though with millions starving (estimates differ, but it would seem that the figure approaches half a billion) that is clearly not the case. Thus we can begin with, in a sense, a clean slate. As for the calculations, they derive from recent use figures for the world's production: the United States, where the modern economy has found its most intensive application, has been consuming about one-third of that production. Yet it amounts to only one-twentieth of the world's population. If we assume that level of consumption as a constant, although in fact it is rising, and project it onto the remaining nineteen-twentieths, then we would need for the world twenty thirds rather than three thirds, a world production almost seven times as large as today's. By some time in the next century, when the global population has doubled (again, estimates differ widely with regard to the decade), we would then need another twenty thirds, about thirteen times present output. If we are already beset by the problems of shortages and pollution, at what point along the way to the thirteen-fold expansion will the system collapse? That we cannot know. But we can be fairly confident that there is such a point. The modern growth economy with its program of production will remain workable only if it is restricted to a part of the world's increasing population. And because that will prove impossible, it is destined to fail.

Continuing the modern growth economy on a global scale is, then, a task that is beyond the resources of the best of worlds, to say nothing of the one we live in. We can expect that there will be helpful new inventions, that birth control will have its successes, that the affluent sectors will use relatively less, and that the poor sectors will never come close to achieving their goal of equivalent consumption. But not all of these together will permit the modern economic model to continue now that it has been taken over by the rest of the world. Either a new sort of economy will replace the modern gradually, or the modern will continue full steam ahead until it destroys itself.

Before closing these remarks on the modern economy, we should pause to take special note of the relevance of China's shifting relationship to the West, mentioned above. Under Mao, China resisted the temptation to call upon the West for economic assistance, preferring ideological purity to technological progress. After Mao, the priorities were slowly reversed, and at the Fifth National People's Congress in the summer of 1980 the commitment to a partial economic Westernization was endorsed. This turn-about has been welcomed in the West, and of course it will continue to bring new markets and improve relations. But the most important result will be to hurry the already harassed modern economy along toward its point of dissolution. If the Chinese fulfill their announced ambition of reaching by the end of the century America's present level of economic sophistication, it would mean for them an eighteen-fold increase in production—and that for one-sixth of the world's population. Surely such progress is not likely to be made that quickly, but an advance to the present Russian level is not inconceivable, and that would mean almost a seven-fold increase. A seven-fold increase for one-sixth of the world's population would double the production of the world as a whole, assuming that the rest of the world remained perfectly stable, which of course it will not.

Thus if we are indeed nearing the world's limits to sustain an increase in production, then it is clear that China has become a much greater threat to the West's own future growth since the decision to open up to the West than during those decades when she remained hostile and self-reliant. And because of China's ability to organize one must take the threat very seriously. Something of China's ancient culture survives—it faltered under the impact of the first Western contacts but, ironically, was rescued by Marxism—and is capable of generating, just as was Japan's a century earlier, a dynamic industrialization. If the danger inherent in much of the Third World's modernization lies in the possibility of early failure, the danger with regard to China is that she will succeed much too well. The prospect of one billion Chinese sipping one billion cokes may seem quite appealing to Western business. Yet one billion fully industrialized Chinese competing for ever scarcer raw materials while contributing massive doses of pollution to the atmosphere and oceans can hardly be welcome to a Western economy dedicated to continuing its own present patterns.

So far in this essay we have reviewed the crisis of the twentieth century, both in its cultural aspects, where in most areas a clear transition has already been made, and in its societal, where the imminence of a comparable transition is apparent. Taken together these are assumed to signify a turning point for the civilization as a whole. Henceforth, the West, I am suggesting, not only will cease to develop its modern themes, but also will continue, and it has already begun, to fashion the components of an age that will eventually succeed the modern. Next we shall move backward, into the West's history, in order to provide a perspective on the present. But first, two matters for speculation, the first having to do with the seeming remoteness of these changes from everyday life; and the second with a question already referred to, that which inquires into the relationship between the several parts of the crisis, in particular between those two major categories, culture and society.

As for the seeming remoteness, it is no doubt partly attributable to the fact that we are not accustomed to thinking much about the implications of long-range developments. We remain remarkably presentist. For a long time, the modern scheme of progress taught us to look to the future as a place of almost inevitable triumph. And now that that mood has passed, it would seem that we are not interested in what is to come. To look can only force us to consider changes that we are not eager to make, and in any case do not know how to make. As long as we are able to live out our lives within a modern society in which the threats have yet to become a reality, we are not going to be particularly concerned about such theoretical stuff as the implications of this all-too-quiet crisis.

Possibly even more important, we still find ourselves preoccupied with the working out of a large number of essentially modern propositions. We are in some respects still building the Modern Age. The search for material abundance, despite accumulating disappointments, has not been called off. We continue in it, tenaciously insistent on keeping alive the modern dream. And it takes a great deal of our attention. Especially so since the path has become more difficult.

We are also still much involved in the great modern search for emancipation for the individual. The Modern Age, true to its humanist conceptions, promised freedom to all, and in every practical respect: the right not only to civic participation and property, but also to the pursuit of happiness, to the fulfillment of the unique potential for expression supposedly harbored in each of us. The demands of emancipation are so strong that it is even now difficult to view them in any context that would seem to detract from their status as fixed imperatives. Freedom as an ideal continues to be cherished in the West. It is a legitimate modern heritage, and the consciousness of it still surrounds us, making a different perception of the world all but impossible. That the thrust of modern emancipation will eventually go the way of all modern phenomena is most probable. At the moment, however, its energies continue unabated.

Even in those areas where we are more immediately in touch with the larger changes, we tend not to notice. That is not to say that we are oblivious, only that when we do perceive what might be interpreted as pieces in a fundamental process our inclination is, quite naturally, to concentrate on the local and urgent elements. One example comes from education, where in connection with the cultural revolution we have already noted the demise of the modern system, especially with regard to the substitution of professional for humanistic goals. Rather than this significant innovation being taken as an indication of a reversal of directions, however, it has been instead received as just the opposite, a renewal of the dedication to growth and material progress—which, of course, it also is.

Another example comes from the transformation that is taking place in and around the West's cities. Over the course of the decades since World War II, our cities have experienced remarkable changes. The core areas have decayed; problems of social management have become more acute as a combination of factors has created massive urban unemployment; and crime, following in the wake of poverty and drugs, has added a dimension of fear for rich and poor alike. But while these are serious problems, they are not in a true sense epochal in nature. We have witnessed them before. We should not forget the past difficulties of the city in the Modern Age. Yet there is now a new threat. And it well may alter the city beyond recognition. It is the threat of urban sprawl. The old city is simply disappearing before our eyes as it grows outward, reducing the inner city to a condition of near irrelevance and merging the fringes with the suburbs of the next sprawling city.

Here again we are experiencing a process that has great significance, but our very involvement in its immediate development tends to obscure the larger outlines. Observed from within, one gets the impression of more of the same: the city was big, now it is spreading and becoming bigger still. The picture from the outside, however, from the vantage point of a longer history, is quite different. The city for the past five centuries, for the entire period of the Modern Age, has been at the center of the West's civilization. That was not the way it was in the early Middle Ages, and even in the later Middle Ages the city was still somewhat incidental. It was not until the Renaissance in Italy that it became the focal point of both culture and society. Then throughout the Modern Age it has continued to grow, both in size and significance. There was, to be sure, a period of hesitation in the seventeenth century, but the trend continued thereafter. And of course it was very much reinforced by the effects, felt from the late eighteenth century on, of the urban-based industrialization. Certainly by the middle of the nineteenth century the city and the Modern Age were all but synonymous.

It is for this reason that one views today the obliteration of the city's boundaries, the blurring of the distinction between countryside and city (the point is not original and has been noted by John Lukacs and others[20]), with more than casual interest. If the city is indeed undergoing a transmutation to something else, then, however mundane and familiar these alterations may seem, they can be counted among the rapidly accumulating indices that alert us to the profundity of what is happening. Here is something that is already taking place, something very untheoretical and concrete (as it happens, literally concrete). As we participate in the dissolution of the city, we necessarily participate in the dissolution of the Modern Age as well. Just what lies ahead, at the end of the transition, we can only guess at. What we can see is that the city is being transformed into something else. As that happens we are experiencing firsthand the crumbling of one of the foundation blocks upon which the Modern Age was constructed.

There is yet another point at which we would already seem to be in direct contact with the larger historical context, and that with regard to the oft-noted gap between the generations. The twentieth century, and in particular, it would appear, our part of the twentieth century, is witnessing a sharp conflict between young and old—more exactly, between, on the one hand, those who are in their teens and twenties and, on the other, those from about thirty on.

But certainly generational tensions are not wholly new. They are present always, as any look at the literature of the past will readily attest. Yet they are stronger now than they have been in a long time. The sides are more clearly drawn, and there is less of a sense of commonality, less of an agreement on goals, on the nature of life and the purpose of social organization. And where once adolescents hastened to live through the period of restriction in order to achieve adult status as soon as possible, at present the young—"youth," as we say, somewhat reverentially—are content to postpone the leaving of childhood as long as possible. They have turned inward to enjoy a culture of their own, one that includes all the things formerly forbidden. As Andrew Hacker once put it, they have taken out citizenship in a separate country.[21]

How did this happen? Again, the answers are probably to be found in the circumstances of the epochal transition. The young of our society have not invented their life styles, at least not alone, nor are they chiefly responsible for the sharpness of the line of demarcation between their world and that of their parents. Rather it is the latter, the parents themselves, who have created the new polarity; for it is they who have removed the old barriers. Why have they done this? There are other possibilities, but it is likely that it is because the adult West no longer believes in the venerable maxims that served to control the upbringing of the young during the better part of the Modern Age. The old rules were designed to prepare boys and girls for the tasks of family and business, for life in a bourgeois world in whose future the middle and older generations still had great faith. Now the young are no longer directed toward such roles in a consistent, disciplined way. They receive a very minimum of guidance. Neither the home nor the school wishes to provide the firm models taken from the traditional order that were given to earlier generations. And in the absence of models of a new sort forthcoming from any source, the young have evolved their own, elaborating upon the more latitudinarian tenets of the modern code and rejecting those more disciplinarian and rigorous. The adult world has looked on, sometimes amused, sometimes repelled, but more often indifferent. Without faith in the old values and without new ones to replace them, it has had little choice.

Yet the young eventually even today grow older, and most of them succeed in rejoining the society from which they took leave. The alienation of youth so far leads to nothing. It is an episode, a sort of ritual. However, it is worth noting that it is a ritual not of initiation but of refusal, both an

effect and appropriate symbol of the predicament of successive generations caught in the transition between world views. With neither confidence in its present societal structures nor a plan for the future, the older
generation has permitted the younger to act out a rejection that it is not
quite ready to make its own.

Finally, let us briefly consider within this particular context our contemporary experience with regard to the family. The family as we in the
Western world have come to understand it is as much a part of the Modern
Age as any of the other institutions we have associated with it. It appeared
during the later Middle Ages and Renaissance. It acquired its characteristic features through its long association with the town and city middle
classes, coming to serve not only social and educational purposes, but
also economic ones as well. And it reached its apex in that most bourgeois
of the bourgeois centuries, the nineteenth. Now it would appear to be
undergoing a great change.

It is not that the family is disappearing, but consider what has happened
to it in the course of the twentieth century: its economic significance (only
with a minority of families did it have such, but it was an important
minority) has been remarkably reduced by both tax laws and the evolution
of the corporate structure away from family ownership; its educational
mission has been all but rescinded by the spread of full-day, kindergarten-
to-college public schooling; its children, who returned to the inner circle
of the family in the early modern period, have left it again, for even when
they are not in school they live, as noted, within the social world of the
peer group; and, finally, its authority, its moral credibility, as it were, has
been badly undermined by divorce—one for every two marriages in the
United States at present, a two-and-one-half-fold increase since the late
fifties. Even alone any of these alterations would have presented the
modern family with a serious challenge. Together their effect is tremendous.

But still, are they enough to occasion a real discontinuity, to move the
family after its five modern centuries into a new era? Or are they more
likely to make for modifications, noteworthy but not essentially destructive? So far, judging on the basis of what has happened to this point, it is
impossible to say. Surely, however, our suspicions are aroused by the
proximity of the other elements of the crisis: the impression of a dying age
that is gained from our familiarity with what is taking place in other areas
necessarily strengthens the conviction that here too, with regard to the
family, we are approaching a turning point. Yet it is entirely possible—the
argument will be left to the speculations about the future in chapter 5—
that the initial effects of the West's withdrawal from its modern ways might
in fact strengthen the family in certain regards, as some of the detrimental
tendencies are themselves reversed. But the point here is that the changing

nature of the family can be viewed as another of those areas in which we are in direct and personal contact with the civilizational transformation that we are passing through.

There are, then, clearly more manifestations of the general crisis impinging upon everyday life than one might expect to find. These alterations that we have touched on—with regard to education, to the city, to the gap between generations, and to the family—all have their disparate immediate origins; yet they fit together to make a pattern, and it is not difficult to see therein another indication, common and familiar though the consequences may be, of the world of civilizational change. The societal crisis is obviously far from complete; and, as has been suggested, it is in many ways still merely a potential, if one with an aura of inevitability. In quiet ways, however, it is making its presence felt. It is probably not necessary to add that it is easy to be wrong when indulging in such analyses. One forms a hypothesis and then in merciless procrustean fashion proceeds to reshape any and every available phenomenon to fit the mold. To be sure, when we talk of the future we are guessing. Still, there is good guessing and bad guessing, informed and uninformed. And the factors informing the guessing here are two: first, the anticipated inability of our society to find within its modern constructions solutions to the giant problems confronting it; and, second, the all-but-completed cultural revolution that has so clearly rejected the modern essentials. These provide the context within which our speculations take place and, accordingly, suggest the association of developments that might otherwise appear to have little to do with one another.

This brings us back once again to the problem of the relationship to each other of the various parts of civilizational history, especially with regard to culture and society. As I shall try to show in the next chapters, the major outlines of the West's cultural and societal histories are remarkably similar. Culture and society have experienced their ups and downs not separately, at widely different times, but together, roughly—although seldom exactly—contemporaneously. What causes this simultaneity? Some of our attempts at answering this question assume the existence of a single causative ingredient—for example, an idea and its history or an evolving economic system—which is identified as the responsible agent, thereby explaining the similarities. If the decline of Rome, for example, can be attributed to a failed ideal, then all of the changes are logical, even inevitable derivatives, traceable to the one cause. The loss of the ideal is seen to lie behind the devolving economy, the disintegrating art style, the political collapse, and so on. Or, if a change in the economic system is assumed to be the cause, then everything is taken to derive from the economic factor. In the first case, the cultural ingredient has caused the societal; in the second, the societal the cultural.

But there is another approach to the problem that does not opt for a single cause. Rather, a coincidence of lesser reasons is built into a causative force large enough to affect the course of both culture and society, as when natural catastrophes can be seen to have been accompanied by otherwise unconnected upheavals, such as the movement of peoples, perhaps joined by still other fortuitous circumstances. If single causes are preferred in theoretical works, it is the texts that champion, if unobtrusively, multiple causation. Eschewing the adventuresome and intending to reflect a consensus, the texts necessarily reinforce a growing tendency among historians to reject single causation.

Both of these approaches to what remains an intriguing and yet extremely difficult question leave much unanswered. Multiple causation because it relies on a chance coming together of random events necessarily slights the element of predetermination, which cannot be removed entirely since it represents the accumulated force of all previous events. If the past does not have some sort of influence then there would be no history at all, that is to say, no meaningful story to tell. And there is one.

Yet determinism can easily be overworked, to the detriment of the random. Also, the selection of the determining factor forces us frequently into chronological fudging. Changes in style are explained by, say, a particular political cataclysm, when in fact the aesthetic alterations began considerably before that cataclysm. And of course if an event does not necessarily cause everything that happened after it, it can never cause anything that happened before it. If in dealing with civilizational movements we are to find specific causes, then we need a sound chronology. But is it very difficult to achieve one. Just when did in fact Rome's imperial political institutions begin to become ineffective? Just when was it that the transition to a new economy or to a new set of ideals got under way? Such instances are all but impossible to establish. And without a workable chronology the search for insight into the causative relationships begins to break down. If the explanation that relies on multiple, more-or-less coincidental causation is unsatisfactory because it is too mushy, too indifferent to the obvious weight of the past bearing on each new moment, then the explanation that relies on single causation breaks down in the effort to establish the chronology necessary to the assertion of cause and effect.

Thus when we come to ask whether in a specific case culture causes society or society culture, we find that we cannot even say in which the innovation came first. Possibly our difficulties in establishing a plausible connection between culture and society derive from the fact that we are asking the wrong questions. Rather than worrying about the reciprocal effects, perhaps it would be more reasonable to assume that neither in the final analysis has an independent existence, that they are only parts, and at that hardly distinct parts, within a larger whole, the civilization itself.

There is a great reluctance among many of those who think and write about civilization to credit it with a life of its own. Civilization is taken to be a giant receptacle into which effects are poured. It is assumed to be passive, not a thing that can act. Toynbee and a few others have been exceptions. They have insisted that not only is civilization a vital unit of history, but also that it is the only unit—that almost everything happens as it does because of its place within the civilizational context.[22] That would seem to go too far. Yet Toynbee and the civilizationalists have been undoubtedly right in guiding us toward a view of civilizations as active historical phenomena, certainly as capable of responding to various stimuli as those other units—classes, communities, nations, and the like—to which we attribute something of a life of their own.

Therefore the relevant question may ask not what culture or society is doing to influence the course of the civilization, but rather what the civilization is doing to influence the course—and thus common course—of culture and society. We gain a different perspective if we begin with the civilization itself, attributing to it a certain willful independence, and only then proceed to a consideration of the parts. This different perspective is not the true and only perspective. But it is a useful one if we seek to understand the relationship between culture and society: although they may indeed act upon each other and with considerable results, their consistent coordination, that is, their habit of traveling along together, is best accounted for if we choose not to concentrate on those reciprocal effects, but instead upon the existence of culture and society as subordinate and somewhat artificial (if for purposes of discussion highly convenient) entities within an organic whole.

If we bring this assumption to bear upon the crisis of the West in the twentieth century, the result is to suggest that both the contemporary cultural crisis and the contemporary societal crisis are but aspects of a single civilizational crisis. It is not a matter of the cultural crisis inducing a societal crisis and not either a matter of the societal crisis inducing a cultural crisis. It is, rather, the civilizational crisis itself that is at the root of the matter.

With these reflections, we come to the end of this introductory overview of Western culture and society in the twentieth century. Again to summarize, I have argued, first, that there has occurred a fundamental revolution with regard to culture, with the result that both the style and the thought that we have come to identify with the Modern Age have been in large part rejected; second, that, while society would seem to be attempting to continue in its modern forms, it too has arrived at a turning point, and that the road now before it is one of descent; and, third, that we have little choice but to infer that these dual crises mark not to be sure the end, but rather the beginning of the end of the Modern Age. We would seem to be at one of those grand moments in history when movement in one direction comes lurching to a halt and movement in another, just as erratically, begins.

Some of the ways in which this reorientation of our civilization already touches our lives have been mentioned. But just how much more do we have coming? What would seem to be in store for those of us living out our lives in the late twentieth century? No doubt the best quick answer is that the immediate effects of this great transition will be both more and less profound than we might expect: more, because each step will lead to the definition of a future very different from our past; and less, because these single steps will usually have nothing of the dramatic about them and will proceed in a logical fashion. Even the greatest discontinuities of macrohistory unfold from the individual's standpoint with a certain reassuring slowness—unless, we must now always add, the nuclear option should this time radically and tragically alter the pace.

But more profound or less profound, the best guide to our civilizational future is to be found in our civilizational past—in the threads that when brought together create the history of the civilizational whole, of the civilization itself. It is, then, to a review of that past that we now turn. Certainly our current crisis is partly unique and therefore beyond the reach of historical instruction. Yet just as certainly it is not entirely unique. History will have something to say, even if its auguries, true to the tradition, are apt to be ambiguous and given to a variety of interpretations.

2

Historical Perspectives: From the West's Prehistory to the Classical Age

The West's history does not abound with major turning points. Once directions are set, Western civilization, like all civilizations, tends to adhere to its established tasks. Periods of doubt and confusion do indeed appear with a certain regularity. But the usual end result, as noted earlier, is merely a return to the original pattern or something much like it. Only occasionally is the course fundamentally altered. During the three millennia of Western history prior to this century, it has happened, to say it again, only three times: first, at the very beginning, as the first of the Western peoples, the primitive Greeks, stimulated by contact with the southern cultures with which their invasions had brought them in contact, began to move toward civilization; second, a millennium later, as Rome reached the limits of its long period of expansion and started the trek downward; and, third, still another millennium later, as the medieval West began yet another ascent. Thus the crisis of the twentieth century marks the fourth great turning point in the West's three-thousand-year history. We shall look back at the first three, then, with a certain sense of kinship, but, more to the point, also with the hope of gaining by the inevitable comparison some additional insight into our contemporary experience.

We want, however, more from the past than knowledge of those moments—and moments are in civilizational history rather half centuries and centuries, not instants—where the West's course was reversed. We also wish to look at the eras in between the moments, for only then will the latter appear in the proper perspective. That is not to say that we shall require a long and thorough history. Too much information can sometimes be even more of a handicap to understanding than too little. What we require here is an intelligible outline. And that is what I hope to provide: not the only possible outline, but a clear and valid one.

In this chapter and the next two, we shall be discussing not only turning points and the crises that envelope them, but also ages. An explanation here of the assumed relationship between turning points and ages will make what follows a little clearer. It has already been said that while the twentieth-century crisis represents a turning point, it should not be taken to mark the end of the Modern Age. Now we can make the point at somewhat greater length. After changing directions, a civilization begins to reject its old ways and develop new ones. But between the point at which it turns around and the point at which we can recognize that the new ways have in fact come to prevail there is usually a period of several centuries. A new age is not the immediate result of setting out upon the new direction, but rather the eventual result. The first turning point did not immediately move the Greeks beyond their Dark Age, but it did set them on the path that would then later result in the West's civilization in its classical form, its Classical Age. The second turning point did not immediately put an end to Rome and bring on the Middle Ages. But it did begin to move Rome toward its fall and at the same time Europe toward the early medieval remedies to the problems Rome could not solve. The third turning point, the one that occurred as the medieval West began to ascend from the nadir it had reached at the end of the five "dark" centuries that followed the Roman collapse, did not bring the Middle Ages to an end and begin the Modern Age. Far from it, for, as we shall see, some of the more distinctly medieval phenomena were still to come. But that turning point did witness the beginning of the development of those processes that would finally cause the bulk of medieval institutions and conventions to be blown away rather suddenly, revealing in their place their modern counterparts.

Ages, then, result from the new directions taken at turning points, but they are not coincident with them. A new movement takes considerable time to break the hold of the older civilizational habits, about as long a time as the older movement took to acquire those habits. Perhaps an oversimplified model can best fix the relationship in mind. Let us say that in 1000 B.C. the first turning point occurred. By 500 B.C. (in fact earlier) the Classical Age had dawned. Five hundred years later (in fact, still later) occurred the next turning point, at about the time of Christ. Another five centuries elapsed before the Classical Age came to an end and the Middle Ages began. Then another five hundred years, and the West arrived at the third turning point, around A.D. 1000. Again five centuries passed, and the West around A.D. 1500 entered the Modern Age. Five more centuries, and we stand at the twentieth century turning point, in the general vicinity of A.D. 2000: thus graphically, as in the figure (opposite).

Such a depiction will do more harm than good if it is taken too seriously, especially if we let ourselves be mesmerized by its fearful symmetry. It has the advantage of being lucid. But of course it is wrong in almost every

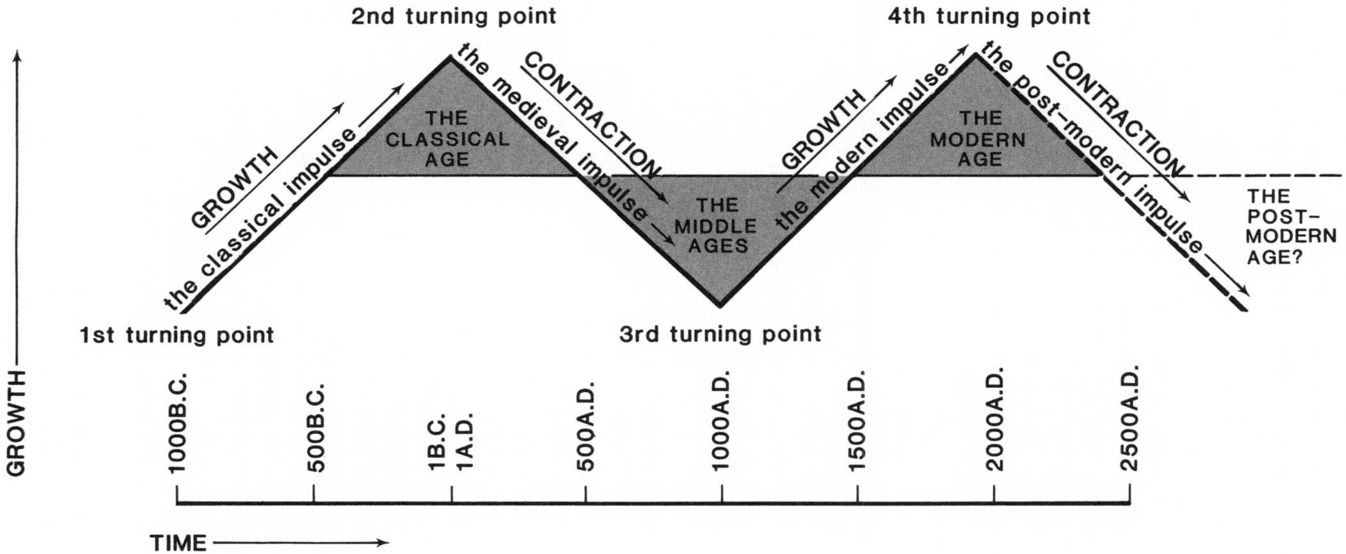

SCHEMATIC OVERVIEW, COURSE OF WESTERN CIVILIZATION

GROWTH

TIME

1st turning point

1000B.C.

GROWTH
the classical impulse

500B.C.

2nd turning point

1B.C.
1A.D.

THE
CLASSICAL
AGE

the medieval impulse

500A.D.

CONTRACTION

3rd turning point

1000A.D.

THE
MIDDLE
AGES

GROWTH
the modern impulse

1500A.D.

4th turning point

2000A.D.

THE
MODERN
AGE

the post-modern impulse

2500A.D.

CONTRACTION

THE
POST-
MODERN
AGE?

particular, and suggests a numerical rigidity that does not in fact exist. Still, it is better, I think, to offer a clear and memorable portrayal and then make the necessary qualifications than to remain throughout correct and obscure.

To sum up, then, we can say that the West has experienced prior to the twentieth century three turning points; that each of these has involved the entire civilization, both culture and society, in a prolonged crisis that has lasted about a century; and that a millennial impulse, emanating from the crisis, has then later resulted in a newly constituted version of the civilization. This newly constituted version we call an age. That age has thereupon persisted until a new impulse, after emanating from a new turning point and enduring several centuries, has in turn caused the age to collapse and be replaced by yet another age—and repeat.

Unfortunately, the process has further complexities. Even between turning points, the West's history has failed to run in a straight line. Not that we should expect it to in its day-by-day or even year-by-year and decade-by-decade operation. But it is also irregular in the very largest sense, although one might add that there is a certain rhythm to the pattern of irregularity: this is to say that the West's major directions, those along which the civilization moves between turning points, are interrupted from time to time by counterimpulses, that is, reactions that interfere with the course of development, yet without in the long run being able to terminate it. These reactions, like the turning points themselves, manifest themselves in profound crises, which also last for about a century. They are not, however, to be confused with the true turning points, for they do not succeed in turning the West around. One of these interrupting, intermediate, within-the-age crises—if permitted a new word, we can call them "intra-eval" crises—has already been mentioned in our discussion in chapter 1 of modern culture and society, that is, the crisis of the seventeenth century. It threatened the modern impulse, harried it and slowed it; but finally the reaction was overcome, and the Modern Age continued. In this history we shall look, if briefly, at several other of these intra-eval crises, some that interrupted growth, others that interrupted decline. Specifically, they are the Hellenistic crisis that for a time obstructed the upward movement of classicism; the Roman century of recovery, the fourth A.D., that sought with some immediate but no lasting success to halt Rome's fall; the Carolingian era, another attempt at recovery that faltered far short of its goals; and the disastrous crisis of the fourteenth century, which, after the preceding several centuries had indeed produced new growth, tore away at it, yet again without ending it for long.[1] Also, we shall look once more at the seventeenth-century crisis; and then finally at the Romantic reaction of the late eighteenth and early nineteenth centuries.

To update our schematized graph to account for these lesser crises, we might impose on it an overlay to make it look something like the presentation in the figure on the following page.

Again, I wish to emphasize that no history, least of all the civilizational variety, happens so neatly. Yet such reductions can help our thinking, if, that is, we accept them for what they are and only for what they are.

The purpose in bringing these intra-eval crises into the story is not only to acknowledge their important effects, but also to recognize them as such and thereby to distinguish them from the true turning points. And they can be distinguished. It would be wrong, I wish to stress, to see the twentieth-century crisis as just another crisis, a crisis among crises. It has its like, to be sure, but not in the more frequent and far less revolutionary crises that challenge without changing; it is, rather, one of those few which challenge *and* change. The twentieth-century crisis is not another crisis like that of the seventeenth, or even that of the fourteenth. It is a major crisis, like the three before it that have been turning points. Also perhaps we can add the obvious, and that is that of these three it is most like the Roman crisis, during which the classical world began to retread the path that had led to the summit.

In speaking of various crises, big and little, and the impulses and counterimpulses that they generate, the language used here sometimes tends to suggest that our history is controlled by mysterious forces. Crises and impulses, even centuries, are given credit for acting, for being in and of themselves independent, generative sources of historical movement. That is wrong, of course. People act. And I think we are also right to speak, as we do here, of those institutions in which people operate in the aggregate—again, communities, states, civilizations, and so forth—as acting. But when we make impulses and the like act, we are using a sort of shorthand. This should be mentioned, for it is all too easy to permit a subtle shift in our assumptions, with the result being that we begin really to believe in the separate existence of our symbols.

Another question, before we set out upon the historical review: if it is indeed people acting, even here upon the broadest of historical stages, why then do they act as they do? Why all the shifting about, with reactions and reversals and so on? Cannot people simply decide where they are going and go there? Apparently not. They drift along together, contained in their several social bodies, not quite sure of what is happening. Yet their collective actions take on inevitably a certain coherence. They begin not just to drift aimlessly, but to drift in a particular direction. And at some point in this drift in a particular direction, who is to say just when, they come to formulate intentions, aspirations with regard to what now begins to loom as a foreseeable future.

But as they push forward, as they strive to create a new order out of the old, dissatisfactions arise. Was not the old order better after all? Have not

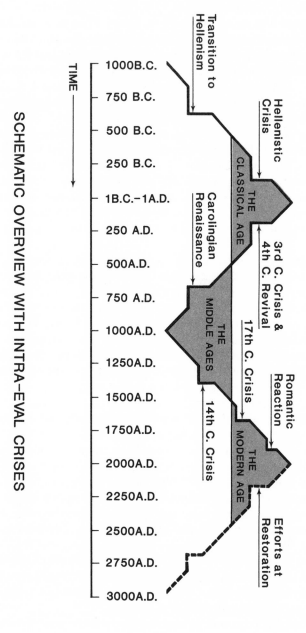

GROWTH ⟶

TIME ⟶

SCHEMATIC OVERVIEW WITH INTRA-EVAL CRISES

Transition to Hellenism

1000B.C.

750 B.C.

Hellenistic Crisis

500 B.C.

250 B.C.

THE CLASSICAL AGE

1B.C.–1A.D.

Carolingian Renaissance

3rd C. Crisis & 4th C. Revival

250 A.D.

500A.D.

17th C. Crisis

750 A.D.

THE MIDDLE AGES

1000A.D.

1250A.D.

Romantic Reaction

1500A.D.

14th C. Crisis

1750A.D.

THE MODERN AGE

2000A.D.

2250A.D.

Efforts at Restoration

2500A.D.

2750A.D.

3000A.D.

the gods, the ancestors, the spirits of nature been offended? And look what is happening to the younger generation! Gradually the objections, originally voiced by isolated minorities, come together to dominate and are now heard throughout the entire civilization, at every level. The civilization thereupon experiences a crisis, with decades, or perhaps a century or even more of turmoil. Styles are altered, the world view is altered, institutions are altered. Everything undergoes fundamental change.

And what is the result? There are essentially two possibilities: if the momentum of the original movement is able to prevail over the reaction—if, that is, people acting in the aggregate determine that they prefer the original directions to those modifications suggested by the reaction—then, barring a catastrophe, the reaction is overcome and the original movement continued. If, however, and this is the other possibility, the reaction prevails, then the civilization sets off in a new direction. The crisis has become a turning point, and the long process of transition to a new age is begun.

We would of course like very much to know why some crises bring only the interruption of a line of development and others its end. Why are some—most—intra-eval and others, but a few, turning points? Here we can only wonder. Perhaps all civilizational crises, those rare ones in which the force for change comes from outside the civilization excepted, are the results of the civilization trying to correct some sort of error. Without trying to argue that survival is the sole purpose of a civilization, it would seem that we can safely assume that it is one purpose. Civilizations are the work of people; and thus civilizations like to survive because people like to survive. When things begin to go poorly for a civilization, its members, although they may well be for the most part unaware of the existence of such a highfalutin thing as a civilization, are able to sense it. For even at the familiar levels, in fact, probably most acutely at the familiar levels, the many little failures are noticed. And therefore a general reaction: people reacting, at this point and that, to this issue and another. If it is something gone wrong that can be put right—possibly the pace of change was too rapid or the benefits too unevenly distributed—then when it is put right, or forgotten, and that can happen too, the journey continues as before. But when the problems are greater than that, when to continue means risking the death of the civilization, then the civilization, the functioning result of all of those millions of individual inclinations, pauses and then pulls back from the danger, finally moving off along a different path. It then begins to exchange its old styles, orders, aspirations, and ideals for a new complement and marches on. The impulse is dead, long live the impulse! The existing system, formerly beneficial but now detrimental, is slowly abandoned. The work of inventing the successor begins immediately. And the transition proceeds.

We shall never know, however, precisely why civilizations behave as they do. Certainly it is not the sort of subject where a few more thousand monographs will bring us closer to the truth. But while we are speculating, we can raise a related question that also cannot be answered, and that is that which asks why turning points are so much more prominent in Western history than in the histories of other civilizations. Other civilizations have changed directions, but their movements have been slower and more deliberate. And the new path has not been so different from the old. Other civilizations have been, in short, more stable. Claude Lévi-Strauss has distinguished between hot and cold societies. The cold ones do not go anywhere. They never change. But the hot ones are constantly changing.[2] While no civilization is cold—only prehistorical societies can be truly stable—most of them have been lukewarm at best. The West alone is a civilization of aggressive movement. Therefore the importance of its turning points. With the West, it is up or down.

This Faustian quality has been often noted. The West is indeed different. Would anyone but a Christian be willing to sell his soul to the Devil? Not that Christianity should be made responsible for the Western will to power. Rather it is the other way around. Christianity is just another of that fierce will's representatives, and hardly the most strident. The West has never been willing to accept the world as it is. It has taken in turn its models of perfection very seriously and, rejecting the Eastern conception of a balance based on a system of complex contradiction and mystery, tried to remake itself in those models' successive images, first as a world state with the Romans, then as a world religion during the Middle Ages, and finally as a world ideology in the modern period, with its faith in the secular utopia based on the conquest of nature.

But if the West's habit of experiencing radical turning points is derived from its inherent dynamism, what produced that dynamism? If we are peculiar in this regard, how did that happen? Again, we are speculating: most of the world's major civilizations have been primary, that is to say, they invented themselves, or at least more so than not. They evolved from primitive beginnings through their own gathering, hunting, and agrarian phases, with little influence from the outside, and that even when thousands of years separate their crossing of the line into the civilized condition from the crossing of that line by others. Mesopotamia, Egypt, India, China, Crete, the American Indian civilizations, and also some of the sub-Saharan centers were pretty much self-starters. A number of civilizations, however, were not. They are secondary civilizations, owing their existence in the greater part to stimuli and models from already established civilizations. Of this sort one counts the Byzantine, the Islamic, the Japanese, and the Western. And of these perhaps only the last, the Western, has been entirely secondary. Byzantium was in too many ways merely a continuation of the West's late Classical Age and proceeded from it without a break. Islam emerged at the meeting place of several older civilizations and soon became absorbed into the mainstream of later Mesopotamian culture. And Japanese civilization was never entirely independent of that of China.

Only the West was the product of a peculiar set of circumstances that made it at the same time a genuinely secondary civilization, clearly profiting from the work of its predecessors, and yet an original, with its immediate origins in the wilderness. We should remember that the Greeks as they entered their eventual homeland had come into contact with Minoan civilization, which they would finally dominate. We know these Greeks as the Mycenaeans, named after their later capital on the Peloponnesus. Had Mycenaean society not broken down under the pressure of new waves of Greek barbarians, then there would have been a direct line of development, stretching from the primary civilizations of Mesopotamia and Egypt through Minoa and Mycenae to the new West. But the line did break down, and between Mycenae and the reemergence of the Greeks there were three dark centuries of barbarism.

The Greeks, therefore, had to begin all over again. Still, they were never far enough removed with regard to either time or place from the older civilizations to escape their influence. Not only were the Greeks surrounded by latter-day forms of the Egyptian and Mesopotamian civilizations, but also the memory of the Minoans and the Greek participation in their civilization lingered on. There was no need, then, to invent basic technology or cultural and societal systems out of nothing. Released from that obligation, the Greeks were free to innovate. Emancipated from the restraining influences of the original civilizations but informed by their heritage, the Greeks moved rapidly beyond the compromises with primitivism that the solutions of the Egyptians, Mesopotamians, and Minoans had represented to more radical positions.

This unique confluence of events, then, may have stimulated the Greeks, and thus the West that they in a sense had invented, to become more innovative than either the primary or the other derivative civilizations. These other civilizations looked inward and sought stability. The Greeks looked outward and sought improvement. With the original tasks of civilizational construction done for them and ready at hand for imitation, but yet free from the older traditions of careful conservatism, they launched an adventuresome experiment. Or, better, they launched a civilizational experiment the essence of which was adventure. The horizon for the West became not a limit but a temptation. And so our civilization emerged: unique, ambitious, creative, and dangerous—dangerous to tradition, to established orders, both human and natural, and finally to itself.

But now we need to go back to the beginning and look at the unfolding of the West's history somewhat more methodically. Again, the purpose is the limited one of offering only a sketch of the directions of the civilizational course. The task will have been successfully accomplished if enough is provided to give an adequate context to our various crises and ages without so much that these become lost from view.

STYLE

The first and inevitably the greatest turning point in the West's history occurred as the West took the leap from its primitive condition to civilization. To be sure, we should acknowledge that there was not a single point at which everything turned, but rather many points, and these stretched out over the centuries of the Greek Dark Age (ca. 1100–800 B.C.). Yet the West did change its directions, here at the beginning of its civilizational course. And it did so in much the same manner that it later would, with parallel innovations occurring throughout culture and society. For fundamental change characterized every aspect of life. Perhaps we should note, too, that these were not changes from nothing to something, from some sort of primitive void to the activity of civilization, but rather from one way of doing things and thinking about things to another way of doing things and thinking about things. Western civilization came into existence by transforming and ultimately replacing an older set of prehistorical traditions.

To see just what took place, to view, that is, the profound transformations that followed upon the turning point, we shall, in keeping with the scheme for this historical summary already presented, look in turn at style and thought, the chief components of culture; and then at politics and economics, the chief components of society. Beginning with style, then, let us introduce the subject with a conclusion: the essential effect of the West's first change of directions was to inaugurate a long movement from the abstract to the natural. Primitive art had been mostly abstract (although one must admit that it could be highly realistic at times, except, very significantly, when dealing with the human figure), while classical art was fundamentally naturalistic.[3] And the story of the transition from the primitive style to the classical is that of the conversion from abstraction to naturalism.

Primitive art had been an art with practical and specific goals. The artist had had no intention of putting before his viewer and, more importantly, his gods an objective and dispassionate rendition of the visual facts.

Rather, he had wished to make a plea, or at least a point. Therefore he had selected the essentials and given them marked emphasis. The primitive mind had simply lacked the desire found in the naturalistic artist to portray the world as an end in itself. It had wished, rather, to act upon it, to produce through the art work an immediate physical effect. Style was never free to go its own way. It had remained subordinate to the purposes of a practical magic. Naturalism per se had no place. Only as we move forward into the world of the early civilizations does that circumstance begin to change.

What, then, was the role of those primary civilizations in this history? The answer would seem to be that they here, as in so many regards, went halfway and then stopped. A compromise with the tendency to naturalism was achieved early on; but there the development came to a halt, and seldom were newer conventions permitted to break through the restraints—the Amarna realism sponsored by Akhenaton during ancient Egypt's New Kingdom was one of the rare exceptions. Yet much had been done. And when the Greeks emerged from their Dark Age, they were of course influenced by the primary stylistic traditions, with which they had a certain familiarity. There was not only the Minoan-Mycenaean heritage, but also direct contact with Egypt and, less so, Mesopotamia. One can therefore conclude that the Greeks came into the world of civilization already aware of the seminaturalistic accomplishments of Egyptian, Mesopotamian, and Minoan art.

For that reason the move to naturalism, when it came, was made relatively rapidly. The very first efforts, to be sure, and both in painting and in sculpture, were directed at creating a Greek version of the old style. Egyptian art was reborn with a Hellenic face. But from about 600 B.C. on, the transition to a full naturalism took place quickly. The archaic forms fell away and were replaced with a new fluidity. Still there were obstacles, not so much with regard to technique but to theory. The same compulsion to symmetry and logic that inspired classical architecture made classical art for a long time a little less than natural. It was not until just before a new tendency to distortion set in during the Hellenistic period that the Greeks finally were ready to accept nature more or less on its own terms, and then only briefly. Yet for all the exceptions, a naturalistic style had been devised that had broken free of both the primitive and the primary-civilizational conventions. By the Athenian Golden Age of the fifth century B.C., it had come to prevail.

But what has naturalism to do with architecture? Can we also speak of naturalism as the essential characteristic in Greek architectural style? Certainly not without qualification, for buildings are not natural. It is easy enough to apply the canons of an abstract style to architecture, but nature provides no models. There can be no such thing as a naturalistic building.

Yet the Greeks did their best, attacking the problem from two different directions: first, they amply decorated their buildings with increasingly naturalistic sculpture. Pediments became battlefields and columns maidens. If the structure itself could not be copied from nature, at least it could be adorned with nature's work, especially with the greatest examples of that work, the gods and mankind—and for purposes of portrayal there were no distinctions, a fact significant in its own right, between the two.

The second means that the Greeks hit upon to reconcile architecture to naturalism—to impose, that is, the naturalistic style upon their temples and public buildings—consisted in rooting them firmly in nature. Nature, at least as the Greeks conceived of it, was logical, here-and-now, and organically complete. Architecture should be that too, and it was. The Greeks built buildings that were tightly rational, earth-bound, and confidently unified, following Aristotle's advice that works of art should have a proper beginning, middle, and end, so that they might thereby resemble a "living creature."[4] Thus architecture did its best to conform to the new style.

The Greeks, then, were able to achieve a degree of naturalism that far surpassed anything that had preceded it. It has been suggested that that had something to do with the West's being a secondary civilization. But whatever the explanation, the artistic revolution was clearly not an isolated splinter, and its history is only disentangled from the general flow of development with some difficulty. The same is of course true not only with respect to the other changes that took place at this particular turning point, but also regarding those that occurred at the later turning ponts that will be surveyed. The point is made here, where it is obvious enough—perhaps so much so that calling attention to it would seem superfluous—with a view of the conclusions drawn from the present crisis. If the West has behaved consistently as a civilization over so many centuries, with its various components fluctuating in keeping with the larger civilizational course, is it not reasonable to suggest that that is happening now as well?

Once launched upon its course, classical naturalism, to return to its history, had a long and fairly smooth evolution. But eventually, and perhaps unavoidably, it was subjected to a dissenting reaction. The challenge came in the fourth century B.C., shortly after the collapse of Athenian hegemony in the late fifth, and its effects were felt through the Alexandrian period and even beyond. In retrospect, what was happening is reasonably clear: if it is true that civilizations move from turning point to turning point, they do not, as said, do that directly, as the crow flies. Occasionally they would seem to undergo a period of hesitation. The lines of evolution falter and begin to reverse themselves—not all of them, surely, at just the same time, but singly, in a seemingly random and superficially unconnected fashion that only gives the look of coherence if we back off

sufficiently. And then usually, after a century or two, the original directions are restored. The style, world view, and institutions withstand the
challenge and prevail. We have used the adjective "intra-eval" to describe
these crises within an age, thus distinguishing them from those that begin
the work of building a new age. It was an intra-eval crisis that was
emerging at this point within the Greek world. We shall see its effects with
regard not only to style, but also—just as we should expect, if we are
indeed dealing with the history of a civilization—to each of our major
categories. The Greeks had moved too far too fast and now were entering a
time of reappraisal. That would seem to be the larger significance of that
period we refer to as the Hellenistic.

The Hellenistic era extended from the fourth century until the Romans
imposed their new order on the Mediterranean.[5] With regard to style, there
were some dramatic alterations. If the outlines remained more or less
intact, the mood was no longer the same. Where there had been a calm
dignity, there was now an anxious frenzy; and where restraint with regard
to size, now a compulsion to the colossal. Yet classicism had not been
defeated. It had been given a violent shake, but the result was not a new
style. Rather it was a modification of the old. The line of continuity
waivered. Finally, however, there was no break. Even a quick look at a
Hellenistic monument or piece of sculpture informs us that there have
been important changes, but that we are nevertheless still in the presence
of the classical essences. Naturalism had been forced to put up with some
distortion. The muscles are now larger, the draperies more agitated, the
monuments more monumental, but this is still the Greek style. Yet it is a
style moving for the moment in a different direction.[6]

Then with the rise of Rome and the resultant establishment of a Roman
dominion over the Mediterranean world the Hellenistic reaction came to
an end, as the Romans presided over the restoration of naturalism, now
more or less free of the Hellenistic distortions. Early Roman art had been
the product of the amalgamation of two separate but similar styles. The
first of these was the Etruscan. The Etruscans, the early masters of Rome,
had absorbed the initial steps toward naturalism made by the first civilizations and passed them along to the Romans. The second style was that of
Greece, made accessible to the Romans by the proximity of the highly
developed Greek culture of southern Italy and Sicily.

It was true, then, that Rome had been trained in the naturalistic style
from almost its beginnings. And although there was never a conscious
effort to suppress the Hellenistic deviation and restore the older classical
tradition, nevertheless that is what happened as the Roman imperium
spread outward. The Hellenistic style had been somewhat decadent, or at
least postmature, and it had proceeded from a Greek culture that was no
longer fresh. But Roman culture was new and filled with the same enthusi-

asm that had marked Greek culture at an earlier point. This meant that when the Hellenistic convulsion had spent its force, Rome was ready to reassert the Hellenic tradition. Now throughout the West one could again find that rational, forthright, secular art that the Greeks had perfected.

To say that Roman art is the continuation of the Greek pre-Hellenistic tendency is admittedly not quite right. There were, for example, Hellenistic ingredients, such as the interest in size, that did not disappear. Also, the very fact that the Romans were as derivative as they were speaks against their production as authentic continuation. There were too many pauses, too many over-the-shoulder glances to see just how the Greeks had done it. In some ways, it was more copying than continuation. But Rome had no need for a new style. It would seem that the Greeks had done pretty much what the Romans would have wanted to do had they had the task of doing it for the first time themselves. If somewhat more practical and pragmatic, they continued to build where the Greeks had left off, figuratively and literally as well. The Romans copied, but not because they lacked the wit to do otherwise; rather because they were a second edition of the same civilizational effort. Thus with regard to style Rome was to reestablish the direction determined on at the West's first turning point. When Western art had moved from its primitive state to that of its first civilized expression, it had evolved, as said, from the abstract to the naturalistic. During the Hellenistic interlude that tendency had faltered. With Rome it was restored. And through Rome this classical style was now spread over a vast domain, west to Gibraltar and east into the Mesopotamian highlands, north to the borders of Scotland and south to the edge of the Sahara. For the Greco-Roman style had secured its hold upon the West just as the West had come to dominate its new empire.

THOUGHT

Shifting now to the first grand transition in the history of Western thought, we can observe at the outset that the outlines of the progression are much the same as with regard to style. It would be surprising, of course, were that not the case. As for the substance of the change, it was, briefly put, to move from supernaturalism to rationalism, or, said another way, from religion to philosophy. Primitive man had not been without faith in orderly structures, but within these and crucial to their continuation operated a myriad of gods and other spirits. Nature had no fundamental ordinances that could not be overturned. The work of primitive religion, then, had been to make the natural irregularity of things work to advantage, appealing first to this and then to that source of intervention.[7] The big change came with the advent of Greek philosophy, which reduced the many supernatural possibilities to a single set of natural rules, with access to these available not through special acts of manipulation, but through reason. Thus a system that had assumed discrete units of causation was replaced by one that insisted on homogeneity and interrelatedness. The direct approach to the gods and nature was put aside in favor of an effort to operate according to the rules of logic that were now taken to govern the world.[8]

Although the origins of this transition, like those with regard to style, lie in the Dark Age—we must assume that, since the tendency to rational explanation is already apparent in the earliest written documents that appear at the end of that age—still it took several centuries to arrive at an explicit statement of the new position. That came finally with the Milesians, Thales and his successors, beginning in the early sixth century B.C.. Again the initial civilizations had done much of the groundwork, first consolidating and ordering the spirits and then in their later stages producing religions of single principles that resembled philosophy and seem to have foreshadowed its coming. The Greeks appear to have absorbed the essentials of these developments during the Mycenaean centuries; and they were able somehow to keep the inheritance alive through the Dark Age. Whatever the explanation, once the Milesian breakthrough had been made, progress toward a thoroughly rational philosophy proceeded very rapidly. And by the middle of the fourth century B.C. things had advanced to the point where Aristotle was able to provide a lucid summary of the new thought.

What were its characteristics? In answering any such question, there are the twin dangers of generalizing to the point of obscuring the exceptions and, on the contrary, becoming so fixed upon those exceptions that no generalization is permitted to emerge. Taking a middle course, it would seem reasonable to conclude that there was indeed a Greek mind, although of course not all Greeks agreed with it; nor was it entirely static. But the bulk of Hellenic intellectual production points in much the same direction. It has already been said that the resultant thought was rational. To that characteristic should be added three more: a preoccupation with the secular realm; a sense that mankind's experience in this life could and would be basically a happy one; and a concern for the individual. These four assumptions, which we might loosely join together under the label *humanism,* were of course mutually supportive. Because there existed a logical order, it was possible to approach problems with a certain assurance; if it was reasonable to hope for a good life short of the grave, then there was no special inducement to look beyond it; and so on. Rather than succinct beliefs we find here an instance of what the historian Carl Becker called a climate of opinion: related and dependent ideas linked in the defense of a world view.[9] And, of course, if that world view reminds us of the modern one, the explanation is the obvious one: as we all know, the Modern Age has been in good part the ancient in new dress.

The Greeks, it should be said, and again like their modern counterparts, never entirely eliminated the irrational element from their thought.[10] Nor for that matter was their secularism thorough enough to bring on a purge of the remnants of religion; and their optimism was also not able to deprive them of their fascination with the tragic. Further, it is true that their individualism never overcame their civic loyalties. Still, it was their faith in these four—rationalism, secularism, optimism, and individualism—that set the Greeks apart.

This new Greek thought, however, after a time experienced a significant reaction, just as did style. Again, it occurred during the Hellenistic centuries, the fourth and third B.C. In the course of the fifth century B.C. the Sophists had demonstrated the limits of humanism. If man was the measure, they had argued, there were no essences. If there were no essences, then there was nothing to measure against. Values were merely opinions. Finally, said the Sophists, the last word would and should be provided by the only voice that could be heard amidst the roar of conflicting claims to truth, and that is the voice of force. The logic of humanism was leading it toward a position that was hardly in keeping with its original directions. It was against this line of reasoning that Socrates and even more so Plato rebelled: yet not in order to restore humanism, but to challenge it from a different angle. Rather than reassert the validity of an absolute morality within a secular context, Socrates and Plato looked again to the heavens. There, in the world of the perfect forms, one could find the absolutes that were lacking here on earth. Plato went on to spell out his conclusions from this reactionary insight: because the perception of truth was to be expected only of a few, only those few should rule. Thus the drift of Hellenism toward open and optimistic models had been brought to a halt and an alternative and distinctly contrary position nominated to replace them.[11]

But nothing in the history of thought is quite as simple as that. Plato's idealism was both too radical and too intellectual to make much of an impact at this time—too radical for most of the educated classes, who sought a modification of Hellenism, not its rejection; and too intellectual for the masses, more interested in the varieties of revived and imported religions. If philosophy were to continue in anything like its traditional role as the mainstay of Greek thought, it would need an appropriate modification, real but not extreme, to adapt to the new climate.

Aristotle would—oddly enough, given his deserved reputation—not provide it. What he offered was a highly articulate summation of Hellenic humanism, only somewhat compromised by the heritage of Platonic idealism. If Plato's innovations were too great, then Aristotle's were not great enough. Although he did what he did with brilliance and originality, his thought was nonetheless a leftover from the fifth century and scarcely in touch with Hellenistic trends. It was therefore left to Zeno and Epicurus, philosophers of the early third century B.C., to find the appropriate middle ground.

They did this, of course, in distinctly different ways. Zeno's Stoicism was religious and socially committed, while Epicureanism was agnostic and socially indifferent. Yet they shared an important message. And that was that while life could be made livable, it would not be easy. Gone was the optimism of the Golden Age, and in its place had come doctrines of persevering, appropriate to Hellenistic confusion. At the heart of these was an all-too-understandable search for inner peace in the midst of adversity. Stoicism offered the consolation that, however chaotic and threatening the world might seem, there was underneath the confusion a meaningful plan. Therefore one should go about one's duties and accept the inevitable disappointments as the unfathomable manifestations of a higher wisdom. Epicureanism took an equally sober, if quite dissimilar position, suggesting that if there were indeed gods they were no doubt preoccupied with their own problems; and that therefore man must shift for himself in a to-all-appearances purposeless universe. Only by a careful self-regulation could one attain the proper balance between pleasure and pain that would produce tranquility. These were not, we can agree, entirely bleak messages; but they are far removed from both the buoyant vitality of Homer and the more quiet optimism of Pericles. From the eighth century B.C. through the fifth, the Greeks had remained basically confident. Now they no longer were.[12]

What is one to make of Hellenistic science, technology, and scholarship? If the Hellenistic centuries saw a shift in the patterns of Greek thought away from those of Hellenism, what part did the increased interest and production in these areas play in it? That is not an easy question to answer. Science, technology, and scholarship are all peculiarly Hellenistic, and yet that fact is hard to reconcile with the image of the period as one of intellectual discouragement and renewed interest in the supernatural. There are two possible explanations. On the one hand, it is not unreasonable to assume that these three were natural extentions of Hellenic directions that had taken longer to develop and managed now to continue in a vital form. On the other hand, one can, borrowing from Spengler, see them as the work of a postcreative epoch: the Hellenic Greeks drew up the plans and laid the foundations, while their Hellenistic successors sought solutions to the technical problems and then catalogued the results. "Everything begins in prophecy," William Irwin Thompson once observed, "and ends in pedantry."[13] Unkind, perhaps, but true.

Hellenistic science, technology, and scholarship, then, were indeed continuations of the Hellenic effort to see the world as rational. And yet there is a hint of that onset of decadence that was mentioned in describing Hellenistic style. In certain crucial ways, then, they were after all typical of the period.

But, again as with art, Hellenistic thought was not the prelude to a general disintegration of the classical world view. With the coming of Rome, much of the spirit of Hellenic philosophy was restored; although again there was nothing like a return to the original quality. Here too the Romans borrowed a great deal. And they did so indiscriminately, taking from Hellenistic as well as Hellenic sources. Where, however, they took from the former, they made the necessary adjustments to return the substance to the spirit of the latter. Thus they received Stoicism enthusiastically, but modified it, removing much of the religious aura and stressing the call to duty in the service of the empire. Rome on the way up would seem to have had little use for oblique assurances. The preference was for pragmatic directness. Like Greece while Greece was also on the way up, Rome was not receptive to even the most qualified and rationalized pessimism. Rome looked for support for its secular pursuits, and it found it in the return to the Hellenic world view. Just as there had been no need to invent a new art, there was no need to invent new philosophies. Rome was able to borrow eclectically.

The results were less than profound, but nevertheless a fair reproduction of Greek humanism. Rome's great work with regard to thought was not to create, but to disseminate. And by the time the empire had reached the limits of its expansion in the early second century A.D., something like the Hellenic world view prevailed throughout the Mediterranean world—purer, ironically, in the Latin than the Hellenized provinces, for in the east Hellenization had been a two-way street, as the Greeks were exposed to the older traditions of the Orient. Hence Rome confirmed the directions taken by Greece upon its emergence from primitivism, which were then to remain the ones followed by the Classical Age throughout the greater part of its history. The Hellenic Greeks had developed a world view. The Hellenistic Greeks toyed with the possibility of major revision. The Romans rejected revision in favor of continuing along the original path.

So far, we have briefly reviewed the histories of classical style and thought, letting the outlines of their paths serve to reveal the course of classical culture as it moved from its origins in the prehistory of the Greek Dark Age first to its Hellenic forms; then on to the Hellenistic reaction; and finally to the reconstruction that Rome provided. With regard to style, we have seen the thousand-year evolution of naturalism as it proceeded from the relative abstraction of primitivism. And with regard to thought, we have seen the equally long evolution of a rationalistic humanism. We shall now undertake a similar review of the upward course of classical society, looking first at politics and then economics. The general purpose will remain the same: to try to get some sense of how it is that the West has moved from point to point, while at the same time confirming that during this first of its great transitions it adhered in all of its major divisions to but a single pattern—that is, primitive origin, Hellenic definition, Hellenistic contradiction, and, finally, Roman confirmation—and thus that the West acted here not as a loose collection of random parts, but indeed as a civilization.

POLITICS

As for the West's political structure as it progressed from its primitive condition to civilization, the most fundamental change had to do with the degree of centralization, that is, with the size and scope of the political units. Primitive society had been organized politically at the local level. There was no lack of government. It was very much present—rigorous, complex, and efficient. But it was severely limited, both geographically and demographically. Everything about the primitive condition—the absence of surpluses, the lack of easy means of transport and communication, the inability to keep sophisticated records, and more—militated against the development of governments that extended beyond the level of the clan and tribe. Thus the first turning point in the West's political history was reached when it became possible for governments to begin to make their authority felt over greater numbers and across greater distances. As with art and thought, the primary civilizations had already moved a considerable distance toward the new solutions. They had incorporated vast areas and great masses into centralized systems, although the compromises with local rule had had to be considerable, given the still limited facilities. What the West did that was new was to pass relatively rapidly from the decentralization of primitivism to the centralization of civilized government; and then to take that centralization to new heights and extend it finally over an even greater area.

Also, as with art and thought, the coming of the new centralized government occurred in three stages: to state it dialectically, there was first the Hellenic thesis; then the Hellenistic antithesis; and last the Roman synthesis. That may put the matter again too precisely; but as an overview it is basically correct. The Hellenic period produced the city-state. The Hellenistic period destroyed it and then tried to build an empire, but failed. The Roman period then succeeded in building the empire.

But we must return to the beginning, when the Greeks were still in the Dark Age. Prior to this, it should be kept in mind, earlier Greeks had infiltrated the Minoan civilization and had later established their own version of it on the mainland at Mycenae. Yet since ca. 1100 B.C. the rudiments of civilization had been lost, as the Minoan-Mycenaean creation fell victim to new waves of Greek barbarians. The political result was of course the abolition of all centralized control and the reversion to clan government, government in its most direct and local form. We start the story of the evolution of Greek politics from its primitive to its classical forms, then, with the Greeks thoroughly decentralized.

Beginning around 800 B.C., however, Greece moved rather directly toward greater centralization, as it put together its unique creation, the city-state network. We can assume a turning point within the Dark Age, here as with the cultural changes. Certainly the memories of the more sophisticated Mycenaean organization must have served as a catalyst. But at first these city-states were hardly distinguishable from the villages from which they had evolved. Still, they were soon to become true urban centers, ruling over the surrounding rural land. Although economic factors were not by any means exclusively responsible, obviously the growth of the cities was stimulated greatly by their development as centers of trade and, somewhat later, manufacturing, functions that distinguished them from their earlier, more purely administrative counterparts. We shall look at the economic developments shortly and here note only that, whatever the reasons, Greece was undergoing in the course of the three centuries that followed its revival at the end of the Dark Age (thus ca. 800–500 B.C.) an impressive political centralization. There was, to be sure, as yet no overall organization. However, the city-states had emerged triumphant over the much more decentralized rural clan structure. Further, certain of the city-states were developing as leaders, notably, of course, Athens.

Then, during the fifth century B.C., there occurred the long struggle to determine whether or not Greece would advance to the next level of centralization. Ultimately the answer was that it would not. The outcome came to depend on the nature of the Athenian bid for supremacy following the defeat of the Persians and the response to it of Athen's chief competitors. It could conceivably have worked out differently. But if Athens had an opportunity to create a Pan-Hellenic Greece, the harsh treatment of the allies and inability to look beyond the confines of city-state politics confirmed both friends and enemies in their jealousy and rejection. By the conclusion of the Peloponnesian War at the end of the fifth century, the Athenian effort had failed, and with it any possibility that the West would proceed immediately to greater centralization. The first period of classical political consolidation had come to an end. The Hellenic era had managed the transition from clan to city-state, but could not get beyond it. That was not necessarily wrong, of course. We are trying here only to record the evolution of a system.[14]

Before moving on to the political history of the Hellenistic era, there is a question that needs to be answered with regard to Greek democracy. Democracy was fundamental to the Greek political structure. If we are to view that structure within the context of evolving centralization, what part, then, did democracy play? Greek democracy should be understood as the product of three different influences. First, there was the world view: Greek humanism implied a politics something like that which was indeed achieved. If the individual by means of logic was capable of dealing successfully with a logical world, then the individual operating through the *demos,* the people, should be given the direction of affairs. Thus democracy was underwritten by common assumptions about the nature of things. Second, there was the matter of the contest between the aristocracy, which had survived from the time of the clans, and the rising commercial middle class (often, to be sure, recruited from the aristocracy, but now with different purposes). The entrepreneurs had found democracy—with, of course, a much restricted suffrage—a convenient weapon against the aristocracy, as the new rich progressively elbowed aside the old nobility. And, third, democracy, this time with a broader suffrage, also could serve the lower classes in their own struggle with the aristocracy and middle class.

The point here is that there was nothing in any of these three sources that might inhibit the tendency to political centralization. Modern democracy has so frequently been modified by the pluralistic conceptions of liberalism that it has come to be associated with government by compromise, with, that is, power hedged by various checks and balances. But democracy with the Greeks did not contain devices for hindering the direct expression of political power. On the contrary, it was intended to be used as a means of bringing a new power base together and eliminating the bars to its expression. It served, then, to complement the movement to centralization. Not only was political authority being removed from its diverse traditional repositories and given to the city-state, but also within that city-state it was being gathered increasingly into the hands of those who represented the innovative and expansive strata—of those, then, who would push for even more centralization.

We turn now to the Hellenistic period. And we can observe immediately that its politics shared with style and thought the search for new patterns. By this time, the city-state was no longer in a position to provide solutions. The failure of Athens to put together a workable empire did not return Greece for long to the world of independent *poleis.* That institution had had its day. It had suited well the early centuries of Mediterranean commerce and colonization. Now, however, both cultural and economic factors suggested some sort of political reorganization. Everything pointed to empire. Yet Athens had failed to provide one, and that left the classical world still groping.

Finding a workable imperial answer was not at all easy. Retrospectively, it would seem that the best place for a Western empire was the Mediterranean littoral and its hinterlands, very much the area that Rome would conquer. There the transportation was easiest and the competition from other powers least. But the Greeks had for some time dreamed of conquest to the east, into the still wealthy homelands of the older civilizations. And the Macedonians, who had come out of the obscurity of their northern hills in the middle of the fourth century to dominate Greece, inevitably inherited those dreams. The upshot was that Alexander did the right thing, but in the wrong direction: his bid for a permanent empire was appropriate to the circumstances of the post-Hellenic period, but by going east rather than west he took on a good many extra problems and gave up the one great advantage that the Mediterranean venture had to offer, the sea itself. The empire that he did create, extending as it did from the Adriatic to the Indus, was tremendously impressive but just as short-lived. It cannot be said that Alexander was without influence, for the Greek successor states into which the empire immediately dissolved upon his death in 323 B.C. endured until the coming of the Romans. The empire itself, however, had been only a thing of the moment.

When the real empire came into being, it was built not in a decade but over centuries; and not only was it based in the central Mediterranean, but also, perhaps even more important, that base was just far enough away from the Greeks to permit it to learn from their institutions and ambitions without being limited by them. In fact, there were two logical contenders for the job of doing what by this time was probably inevitable, for it would seem that Carthage had initially as much a claim to be the center of the new empire as Rome. In the course of the first two Punic wars, however, the issue was decided. Of the two competing imperialisms, Rome's was the stronger. Rome, not Carthage, would dominate the Mediterranean.

During the next three centuries—that is, from ca. 200 B.C. until ca. A.D. 100—Rome was able to acquire the more or less obvious pieces needed to complete the work of empire. As it did so, the composition of its domestic politics, to look again for a moment in that direction, necessarily began to change. Authority slowly shifted within the Roman government, as in those of the Greek city-states before it, from the old aristocracy to a new class of empire builders, likewise drawn in part from the older families but with much new blood. However, this time the result was not democracy, but rather the hereditary dictatorship of the principate and empire.

Yet the result was not dissimilar, for Rome's external aggrandizement was thereby finally paralleled by the internal consolidation that Greece had managed in a different way. Senatorial rule had suited the nobility of the Mediterranean city-states. Democracy had suited the middle and lower classes (not always at just the same moment). Now one city-state had prevailed and made an empire. And it was neither senatorial rule nor democracy—with which, indeed, Rome had occasionally experimented from the reform era of the later second century B.C. through the civil wars of the first—but rather a new authoritarianism that won out. It then endured. For it not only corresponded to the requirements of governing a large area with many different peoples, but also provided internal stability, built, as it was, upon a series of important domestic compromises. While the new arrangements—and it was Augustus who completed them—gave something to the surviving nobility, they gave even more to those who ran the empire, principally the equestrians (the men of business) and the army commanders. Like all successful dictatorships, Rome's placated the crucial classes.[15]

Hence from the late first century B.C., Rome was provided with a consolidation of power that permitted it to rule efficiently, if also sometimes ruthlessly, over the new empire. In this way the process of centralization that had been begun by Greece was now completed by Rome. And the long transition from the local, fragmented government of primitivism to the highly coordinated government of the classical high period had been finally made. To repeat: the pattern of the historical development of this political evolution resembled nicely that of the cultural. Hellenic Greece made the initial step. There next occurred in the Hellenistic era a period of interruption, during which a largely unsuccessful quest for a new order took place. Then Rome brought the original work to its conclusion. If that would seem to imply that there could not have been additional phases of expansion and centralization, then it is not meant to. There were to be none, however, for the political story almost from the moment that the Mediterranean world was at last subjugated is one of gradual disintegration. That disintegration, however, was a part of the West's second great change of directions. Before proceeding to it we shall review one more aspect of this first transition, that having to do with economic developments.

ECONOMICS

The changes that took place as the West progressed from the primitive to the fully developed classical economy were of course enormous. Merely to list them does them a certain injustice, but these were the most important: a transition was made from a barter economy to one that utilized currency; from an economy exclusively rural to one that incorporated huge cities; from one without significant machinery to one that made extensive use of it; from one in which the distinction between free and slave labor was probably as yet unknown to one that came to depend heavily on the latter; from one that was almost exclusively local to one that encompassed large areas; and from one in which distribution was accomplished without the market mechanism to one in which it predominated. And fundamental to all of them was specialization. The primitive economy had been almost without it. For the hand-to-mouth nature of the struggle for existence insisted that nearly every one of those hands be lent to the essential business of hunting and gathering food. Even after the coming of agriculture—a turning point in its own right within the long primitive age—it took millennia for the development of the art to the point where significant surpluses could be obtained. It was only then, and this moment saw the blossoming of those first civilizations that were both cause and result of the agrarian advance, that a differentiated economy was possible.

When the Greeks began to fashion their own economy as they moved beyond the Dark Age, the same sort of rapid development took place that can be observed in the other aspects of their civilization at this time. Again, the first civilizations had prepared the way. They had already made the preliminary innovations that were necessary to the development of the highly specialized classical economy, except for three. Surpluses, cities, large-scale commerce, the use of iron, the very conception of specialization, these were already in place. The ingredients so far lacking were currency, the market, and some sort of supraregional—that is, imperial—political organization that could facilitate economic expansion. Without these, there would be restrictions upon large-scale economic fluidity and consequently also upon the advance to new levels of specialization. Greece would supply the first two. But, as we saw, its attempt to manage the third finally ended in failure. Yet enough had been accomplished to make possible an economic revolution.[16]

If we credit the introduction of currency and the market to the Greeks, that is not meant to deny their earlier and non-Greek origins. Coins would seem to have been first used in Lydia in Asia Minor, and the market has a long protohistory that stretches back through Crete and Phoenicia to Egypt and Mesopotamia. The crucial implementation, however, was indeed the work of the Greek city-states and especially, although not only, Athens. Prior to this time—the development was just beginning in the eighth century and fairly complete by the fifth—the world's economies, both primitive and civilized, had been mainly distributive: what there was of a surplus from domestic production and whatever had been acquired by conquest or trade, very little in both cases before the advent of civilizations but of considerable quantity thereafter, was distributed among the population according to set prescriptions dictated by custom and authority.

The result, inadvertent or intentional, and probably something of both, had been to keep economic activity subordinate to other interests. Religion, the veneration of tradition, systems of privilege, and no doubt also concern for the long-term stability of society all took precedence over the free workings of a dynamic economy. Yet while the continued practice of the distributive system tended to hold back what seems to have been a natural tendency of the ancient world toward expansion, change did occur. And when the Greeks broke through the restraining wall of tradition, the new economy evolved quickly.

Why had the Greeks been able to make such a swift transition? Even though the situation was ready for it, it need not have happened when and where it did, and perhaps it need not have happened at all. Probably part of the answer lies in the fact that the Greeks were in a favorable position to serve as the merchants of the eastern Mediterranean, existing as they did in the middle of several trade routes. Also the ample coastline, coupled as it was with an interior that had its agricultural limits, was no doubt influential. However, the fundamental reason most likely had to do with the fact that the Greeks in their Dark Age had suffered enough of a collapse so that tradition—all tradition, but relevant here that of the distributive economy—could be put aside; and yet at the same time the collapse was not so complete that an entirely new beginning was necessary. Whatever the explanation, the economic system that the Greeks devised in those centuries made a distinct break with the past and carried to new levels of specialization and exchange first Greece and environs, and then the whole of the central-eastern Mediterranean region.

If, however, the Greek advances with regard to the use of currency and the market economy were able to create a new economy and social structure, their political conservatism made it difficult for them even to conceive of the administrative organization that would facilitate building upon what they had already built. But it was not just a matter of not conceiving. They were concerned to preserve the unique Hellenic world that they had made and now, as it turned out, were doing much to destroy. They chose, in effect, the city-state over empire; then, not unnaturally, tried to have it both ways. And when Athens, by this time predictably, failed in its bid for leadership—here we are thinking of economic leadership, but politics and economics at such points are difficult to sort out— no other Greek city-state, least of all Sparta, was able to replace it. The defeat, then, of Athens in the Peloponnesian War had more than political consequences, for it brought to an end as well an economic venture, or rather two. Athens had tried to put itself at the center of a Greek market economy that was rapidly putting itself at the center of an eastern-Mediterranean market economy. The failure of the first spelled the failure of the second as well. Still, the West's economy did not collapse. Greece lost its function as the centerpiece, but the Western energies now fanned out in a lateral pattern. This was the period of the Hellenistic pause, as visible in economics as in the other areas.

The essential economic work of the Hellenistic period was to bring the Greek market economy with its increased specialization and derived social upheaval to new peoples, but without, of course, the overall imperial structure—Alexander's accomplishment, as noted, was almost too brief to have been an exception—that would have permitted the ascent to an even higher plateau. Yet the movement outward provided something of a substitute for that ascent, for it too brought growth. So the Hellenistic economy managed to sustain a certain vitality even while failing to take what would seem to have been the next logical step. Probably the volume of trade actually increased. Certainly the Hellenistic cities flourished. There was also some technological improvement, especially in milling. Nevertheless, the creation of the larger unit was lacking.

The new organization, in economics just as much as in politics, was the doing of the Romans.[17] It was they who provided the third and final element necessary to complete the transition to a specialized supraregional economy: for they created not only the *Pax Romana,* but also managed to pull together under a single administration the economy, in fact, economies, of the entire Mediterranean basin. There is little in the history of Rome's early expansion that would indicate a contemporary insight into its economic significance. Certainly Rome until the later republican period was far behind Greece in the development of the market economy. It is also true that its initial economic contribution after establishing Roman political hegemony in the eastern Mediterranean was negative, as it intervened to prevent others from asserting their leadership. But gradually a new economy with Rome at its center emerged. It would be wrong to suggest that Rome was an economic hub in the same sense that Athens had been, also to ignore the survival of the regional economies as the basic areas of exchange within the empire. Yet Rome became the administrative, military, and financial center of a vast new market system; and, if not a center with regard to manufacturing, at least one with regard to consumption, as the wealth of the provinces was used for warfare and building, welfare and dissipation.

If one views from the vantage point of economics the domestic history of Rome during the period of the growth of the empire, it would seem that the central problem was that of adjusting to the larger entity that the city had created. So far there had been no plan. Rome had sought victories, not economic preeminence abroad, and certainly not economic change at home. But conquest brought new circumstances, and radical adjustments became necessary. In 146 B.C. Rome razed both Carthage and Corinth and was now dominant. Thirteen years later began the revolutions that were not only to destroy the republic, but also to bring to power the new groups that would integrate Rome into the larger market economy over which it now presided. At first, it must be admitted, the intention of those revolutions had been to turn the clock back, to restore the republic of small farmers and simple virtues. That would seem to have been the purpose of Tiberius Gracchus. However, with his younger brother Gaius entrepreneurial elements appeared within the reform coalition. From that moment, the antisenatorial, innovative forces were pointed in the direction of the market: toward adapting to the more sophisticated external economy and benefiting from Rome's new mastery of it. A little over a century later Octavian completed the work of transition, having established the principate to replace the old republican system. Rome now had put itself firmly at the head of the empire, not just politically, but economically as well. In this new world of specialization, it was Rome's part to manage. That it did reasonably well, and for a long time, until the late second century A.D. Then things began to change once again.

This time Rome did not have the answers, and the Roman imperial economy entered on the long slide that would end with its obliteration. But if that economy was not destined to go on forever, still it had provided the structure within which the economic development begun by Greece had continued to a logical culmination. Again, there is no reason to insist that this was the only possible outcome, nor that the Roman economy could not have passed on to yet more specialized levels that would in retrospect make it seem to have been only a stage along the way to a still later culmination. Yet with that acknowledged, it is nevertheless clear that Greece had begun an economic venture that she was unable or unwilling to take beyond a certain point; and that Rome, finding things in a state of semidisarray, seized the opportunity provided by its chance military conquest of a natural economic system, the Mediterranean basin, and thereby brought the Greek venture to completion—before, to be sure, letting the whole thing slip away.

This quick summary of the transformation of the ancient economy from its primitive to its classical form completes the review of the first great transition in the West's history. We have seen how in all of the major areas the Greeks provided an initial construction distinctly different from the primitive; how that construction then began to fall apart; but also how before the falling apart was very far along things were put back together again, as the Romans continued the work begun by the Greeks. This was as true for the two basic components of the West's culture, style and thought, as for the two basic components of the West's society, politics and economics. It would seem, then, that the West was developing as a single unit, with its parts experiencing together the common effects of expansion and contraction, innovation and reaction. The individual periods into which this history naturally divides were not merely periods with regard to this or that category, but rather with regard to all, with regard, therefore, to the civilization itself.

A second point: although it would appear that the changes were, at least compared to the pace of history prior to these times, relatively swift, still the passage from the precivilization of the Dark Age to what we might view as the completion of the classical impulse took the better part of a millennium. The changes that we rattle off so rapidly in fact were stretched out over centuries. To the participants themselves, they were scarcely perceivable. Only at the more dramatic junctures did contemporaries get any sense of the civilizational history that they were experiencing. Civilizations, the largest of mankind's creations, are also necessarily the slowest.

The pace of this transition from primitivism to classicism was, then, even if breathtaking by previous standards, nevertheless quite deliberate. And that raises a question that was touched on in a general sense earlier: if it indeed happened gradually, then just when was it as the West evolved from its first turning point in the Dark Age toward it various classical forms that the Classical Age began? Put too finely, the matter is trivial. But there is a more profound inference: we are asking, in effect, when it was in the course of these events that the essence of primitivism was replaced by the essence of classicism. When did the new ways become clearly accepted over the old, and when did the new institutions come to replace their predecessors? The question is not often asked. Historians have been very concerned to establish the end of the Age of Antiquity, but have neglected the matter of its beginnings. Perhaps that is because classicism is not assumed to have had beginnings in a proper sense. It obviously had an end. It is clear that medieval custom at some point replaced classicism. There is a point at which we must say that we are no longer in the presence of antiquity, that this is something else, these acts, styles, and thoughts are more like the medieval history that follows than the classical history that came before. But with the beginnings of classicism we have perhaps not been as much interested in defining a comparable point because we have not been inclined to recognize in primitivism a mode of existence of equal validity. The Greeks, we have more or less assumed, did not pass from a distinct life-style to classicism, they merely emerged. And therefore classicism is coeval with their appearance on the scene.

If we see in primitivism, however, a distinct society with a distinct culture, these as it were in opposition to those of antiquity, then the question with regard to the point at which classicism replaced primitivism takes on more significance. Having broached the matter, I should add that I have no ready answer. Yet there are a few things that are obvious, given our usages here: Classical Antiquity, if we mean by that a certain coherent historical entity, certainly did not begin with the appearance (ca. 2000 B.C.) of the first Greeks in Crete, for they were absorbed into Minoan civilization. Second, Classical Antiquity did also not begin when the Greeks established a version of Minoan civilization at Mycenae (ca. 1600 B.C.), for Mycenae was just that, a version of Minoan civilization. Nor does Classical Antiquity date from the Dark Age (1100–800 B.C.). There we assume a turning point to have occurred, but to begin a journey is not to end it, nor is it, more to the point, to be halfway. For we are looking for that halfway mark at which the lay of the land starts to look more like the future toward which we are going than the past we have left behind.

What of, then, the years immediately following 800 B.C., when we credit the Greeks for the first time with being civilized; or perhaps 500 B.C., the beginning of the Golden Age (not, to be sure, an "age" by our standards)? Here we come down to impressions, but the first would seem too early, and the second, although it was used in our simplified model,[18] is certainly too late. By 800 B.C., too little that was essentially classical had appeared, but by 500 B.C. there was little to add. Sometime, then, between 800 and 500, the West's Age of Antiquity, the Classical Age, began. If we need to be more precise, let us choose, admittedly arbitrarily, the middle of the seventh century B.C. This age began to take shape around 1000 B.C. But primitivism was not disposed of easily. It remained the predominant force until its hold was finally broken around 650 B.C. From that point we date the new age. It continued to develop, following with occasional interruption (notably during the Hellenistic era) the lines set at the original turning point. Finally, it could develop no more. During the second century A.D., and even earlier there had been ominous signs, this age at last reached its limits. The classical impulse had run its course. To be sure, the structures that it had created were to endure for another several centuries, and with them the Classical Age itself. But the line of development had been broken, and a new line was beginning, one that would carry the West beyond late classicism to its medieval formulations.

Why? Why did the one impulse, the one line of development, come to an end and another begin? To ask this is not to ask why Rome fell. That is a much easier question. Rome fell because the dry rot was finally so extensive that it simply toppled over, like a long-neglected barn. Seeking after the origins of the dry rot is, however, more difficult. For those origins would appear to be not only far removed from the fall, but also entirely unspectacular. It is a subject, even if there can be no firm answers, that is worth pursuing. We shall do that directly, as we move to a review of the West's second great turning point and the history that proceeded from it.

From the Classical Age to the Middle Ages

From the late second century A.D. onward, Rome was never out of trouble. Even before that, beginning with the civil wars of the first century B.C., there is much that seems to point toward some sort of coming breakdown. In retrospect, we can see that here, in the century and a half after the end of the republic—and to be more precise is not important for our purposes—the classical world had arrived at a turning point. It is also clear that the new course that the West now set out on would last a long time, again, as with the original course, for the better part of a millennium; and that the ultimate result would be to give the West a new look and a new substance as well. A new semiabstract style would replace the old naturalism. A new world view, fundamentally religious, would replace the old rationalistic humanism. A new political order based again on local units would replace the old centralized empire. And a new economic order—both local and agrarian, and hedged in by the stipulations of revived distributive mechanisms—would replace the old imperial system of coordinated specialization and open markets.

What, then, was the West doing? Why was it heading off in a new direction, and that just at the moment when one might think that it would linger to enjoy what it had been building over the centuries since it embarked on the path to civilization. Here we return to the speculation made when we were considering the general nature and possible function of these turning points, that is, that civilizations may occasionally redirect themselves in order to survive. If applied to this change of directions, it would suggest that Rome called a halt to its expansion because it had begun to sense that to proceed further meant the destruction of what it already had. The classical essence was being dissipated. If Rome became yet greater, it would no longer be Rome. And perhaps it had already gone too far. But to begin to slide in the other direction? Rome did not want that either, of course. It would only edge back a bit from the abyss, undoing some of the excesses, repairing some of the lost morality, and perhaps also withdrawing from one or two of the more remote and less defensible provinces. And then Rome would indeed linger awhile, consolidating after so many centuries of growth. Yet it turned out that it was not possible to linger. History would not stand still. Therefore Rome and the West were forced to undertake what would finally reveal itself as the long trip to the Middle Ages. What was to have been a minor strategic withdrawal slowly turned into a major rout. Rome perhaps had miscalculated. It had been correct, however, in its initial intuition: growth had gone so far that if the attempt had been made to continue it, one of two things would have happened. Either that attempt would have failed, at the same time expending energies that would go unregenerated; or it would have been successful and as a result Rome and the classical world carried so far beyond their point of origins that they would have become something else. From these equally undesirable alternatives, then, Rome recoiled. In that recoil we can now perceive the unleashing of a new impulse.

Such suggestions may appear rather problematical beside the traditional explanations, which rely on the firmer facts of military defeat, currency shortage, political rebellion, and the like. Yet it must be remembered that we are trying to account not for particular redirections of aspects of a civilization, but rather for the general redirection of an entire civilization. Further, our explanation needs to be directed at the relevant centuries. Again, we must note that the processes that brought Rome down had their origins in the three centuries that lie between Tiberius Gracchus and Marcus Aurelius. So many of our histories of Rome's decline focus on the next three centuries, those that extend from the time of Marcus Aurelius to that of Romulus Augustulus. And they typically address themselves only to parts and leave the whole neglected. These remarks, however, are more a complaint than a refutation. The suggestion that the fall of Rome resulted from a change of directions designed to protect the civilization—from itself, as it were—must remain only that, a suggestion and nothing more. Its merit is that it provides for a big question a big answer; its fault is that it is, like most big answers, entirely beyond refutation, as impossible to disprove as to prove.

Proceeding to the story of the long devolution, we are on firmer ground. It is always easier to say what happened than why. History has a way of revealing everything except what we would like to know. But otherwise it would be very dull: with all revealed, we could only learn and never wonder. In any case, what happened was this: Rome and with it the development of the West's classical impulse peaked sometime in the late republic or early principate. Thereafter, they began to drift in a different direction. The earliest clear manifestation of this was the period of confusion that began with the death of Marcus Aurelius and the succession of his unfortunate son, Commodus, in A.D. 180 and continued until the later third century. At that point there occurred the first of a number of attempts at reviving classicism—empire, economy, and culture. These stretched from the reign of Aurelian (270–75) through those of Diocletian (284–305) and Constantine (311–37); and even beyond to that of Justinian (527–65). There were, then, approximately three centuries of revival. Although scarcely coordinated and often interrupted, they can be looked on as forming a unit, a period on the downward slope of the classical journey not unlike the Hellenistic on the upward slope. The Hellenistic era provided a pause on the way up. The era of imperial revival provided a pause on the way down. As we shall see, it made itself visible in style and thought as well as politics and economics. It was, then, like the other major movements with which we have been concerned, civilizational in its sweep.

The imperial revival clearly did not work in the long run. For, as we know, the downward course continued. After Justinian, the Western world increasingly lost its classical character. And it acquired simultaneously a new character, that which we have come to refer to as medieval. As for when the Classical Age came to an end and the Middle Ages began, we would choose the point at which the medieval elements became the more influential.[1] We would, that is, if we could find it, which we cannot. Historians disagree, and with reasonable cause. There are too many factors to measure and our means of measurement too inexact. The traditional 476 is certainly too early. It would be better, it would seem, to put the line of demarcation at some point in the late sixth century. Until then, the aura of late classicism is still present. But beyond that time it is only a memory.

Wherever we put that line, however, the larger fact remains clear: between the fourth and the seventh centuries the Classical Age was replaced by the Middle Ages. Classical culture and society gave way to medieval culture and society. Again, it is not so important here to say just when. The point is the obvious one, that after moving in one direction for a very long time the West gradually bent to move in another direction. Then, after that new movement had had time to make itself sufficiently felt, the old views, customs, and institutions were shed, and there emerged a different set.

This, then, is the outline of the West's civilizational history as it proceeded from its turning point in the midst of the Classical Age toward the radically different constructions of the Middle Ages: there occurred initially a period of chaos during which classicism in all its aspects was given a violent shake; then a period of attempted revival; and then the final collapse of the West as a classical entity and its reestablishment along medieval lines. We shall now turn to the business of elaborating this overview through a look at the development of culture and society during these time periods.

Before we do that, however, there is one more piece to the outline that should be put in place. It has to do with the Carolingians, but also, of more significance for this essay, with the matter of giving a final date for the end of the West's long descent. There is a difficulty here. The Carolingians appeared in the eighth century and reorganized Europe. Suddenly there was a new empire. Had the long process of unraveling come to an end? Yes, but not for long. By the later ninth century what they had begun had been pretty thoroughly demolished. It was not until the later tenth century that the West began to grow again, moving slowly along its third great line of development toward the Modern Age.

What, then, was the significance of the Carolingian era? What was it at its core, and just how does it fit into the larger context that we are here concerned with? There are three possibilities, and they stand in contradiction, forcing us to choose: first, we can accept the Carolingians' own view of their mission, which they assumed was to restore Rome. And there were elements of restoration, to be sure. We shall touch on the more obvious in a moment. If we accept these as the most important achievements, then we can characterize the period as the last of the imperial revivals. But, second, there is reason to link the Carolingians with the new growth that was, after an interlude, to follow. We speak rightly of a Carolingian Renaissance, and it foreshadowed, if dimly, the twelfth century Renaissance, which in turn foreshadowed the fifteenth century Renaissance. If we look hard enough, we can discover some of the embryonic forms that were to reach maturity in the Modern Age. Yet we must look very hard indeed.

The third possibility seems best to characterize the period: the Carolingian era was essentially neither a classical revival nor a prefiguration of modern times. Instead it should be seen as primarily a culmination of late-classical and early-medieval development, of, that is, the medieval impulse, that disintegrative impulse that had been at work since the last turning point. That is not to say that the Carolingians pushed disintegration to new levels. They did not. What they did was to begin the work of formalizing it. We shall see just how in the course of our review and here only note that we should not mark the end of the West's movement away from it classical high to its medieval low at the beginning of the Carolingian era but at its end, in the tenth century. For it was then that the disintegrative impulse itself disintegrated, with the result that the West's orientation again shifted, this time toward the modern. From turning point to turning point there had been, then, once more roughly a thousand years— from about the first century to the tenth or eleventh. That is unfortunate. It makes our account seem rather too deterministic and too ominous. But, with apologies, a thousand years is roughly what it was.[2]

STYLE

With regard to style, the long movement from the classical to the medieval was characterized by eight fundamental changes. It can be argued that in fact there was only one. But if that is the case, still it is hard to describe that single change except with reference to its parts. And the parts are these: there was the replacement, first, of classical naturalism by medieval abstraction; second, of classical symmetry by medieval irregularity; third, of classical simplicity by medieval complexity; fourth, of classical stability by medieval dynamism; fifth, of classical horizontal emphasis by medieval vertical emphasis; sixth, of classical enframement—that is, the tendency to suggest earthly finite limits—by medieval lack of enframement, the tendency to suggest the incompleteness of the secular work; seventh, of classical external orientation by medieval internal orientation; and eighth, of classical explicit presentation by medieval implicit presentation—put another way, of a style derived from and expressing logical assumptions by one derived from and expressing supralogical assumptions. Just as all manifestations of classical style did not demonstrate all of the classical characteristics, all medieval manifestations did not conform to all of the medieval. Nevertheless, when we speak of the prevalence of the classical style, we mean that most manifestations were demonstrating more classical characteristics than not; and the same with regard to the medieval.

How radical were these changes? As stated here, they would seem to have been very radical indeed, taking style in each instance from one extreme position to its exact polar opposite. But that impression needs a certain correction: succinctly put, it is that these changes were as radical as they could be without, and the reservation is important, breaking the line of civilizational continuity. For the West's style throughout this long history was never without a certain classical remnant, even when the medieval conventions had clearly achieved ascendancy. And we can note here that the same observation can be made with respect to all of the major aspects of the West's history during this transition from the classical to the medieval forms. Western civilization, that is to say, was thoroughly transformed; but it remained Western civilization. Whether we are observing style, thought, politics, or economics, there is no doubt that even when the medieval West was most intensely medieval it still remained the heir of the Classical Age. It was not merely a matter of the survival of languages and institutions, important as those were. It was also a matter of essences. The medieval West never entirely escaped from the essential preoccupations of the classical West, try as it might.

It should come as no surprise, then, when we inquire into the sources of medieval style—not the reasons for it, which presumably have little to do with style per se and are rooted in the movement of the civilization, but rather the models from which the new style derived its specific content— to learn that the classical style itself was one of those sources. If we were first to put in chronological order a very large number of photographs of artworks selected from the time of Caesar and Augustus until, let us say, the Norman Conquest, thus covering the thousand years of our transition, and then to pass through them quickly, we would see that those features present at the start would to some degree be there at the finish.

But we would in addition see something else. Not only would the classical features be joined by others, but also they would suffer from a progressive clumsiness that finally reached startling proportions. For to the extent that the artists of later Rome and the early Middle Ages sought to maintain the vitality and deftness of the classical style, they simply failed. From the second century on, there is apparent a certain awkwardness, a crudity of style, that is obviously the result of failing competence. Probably it can be attributed to shifting priorities. The fact remains, however. No matter how we explain it, when the later Romans attempted to produce classical art, they did it poorly.

Yet they attempted to do it rather consistently; and even when we can no longer speak of Romans, the effort continued. Thus when C. R. Morey produced his masterful summary analysis of medieval style he could list the classical as one of the three major influences.[3] However lacking in skill, the early Middle Ages went on trying as it worked to develop a style of its own: it never gave up entirely on the classical tradition and succeeded finally in incorporating it, although in an admittedly decadent condition. It was this persistence of the classical tradition as a significant and immediately recognizable remnant that accounts for the smoothness of the transition. On the path from high Roman to high Romanesque, from first-century style to eleventh-century style, there are no great gaps. Change blends into change. Where there are lacunae, they are due more to a breakdown in the production of all art, especially with regard to monumental architecture, than to sudden radical stylistic innovations.

Still it is clear that medieval style was not merely the classical style become decadent. There were also important new sources of inspiration. Morey, describing the evident as all good summaries must, pointed to two more: the Northern, or barbarian, style—that is, the style of Europe's northern peoples, at this time mostly Celts and Germans—and the Near Eastern style, that latter-day amalgamation of the several ancient styles of the civilizations of Egypt, Mesopotamia, and Asia Minor, helped to a certain homogenization by the infiltration of late Hellenism. It was these two sources that gave medieval style its distinction. If the Roman influence kept it within the Western tradition, the Northern and Near Eastern traditions provided the unique elements. And the effects of the latter two were certainly all the more pronounced due to the fact that they had so much in common: both tended to the abstract, both were open-ended and unframed, both thrived on complexity, and both lent themselves to the creation of an aura of the mysterious and transcendental. They were, then, styles that reflected the religious as opposed to the philosophical mind. And because religious was what the Western mind was becoming as it shed its classical for its medieval world view—we shall be reviewing that process in the next section—the reception of the Northern and Near Eastern forms was especially warm. The West took to the new styles because it had arrived at a point in its own history where it found them entirely compatible.[4]

So far we have listed the changes that occurred as Western style made its way from the classical to the medieval world; and we have mentioned the three major sources from which the specific ingredients were derived. We now need to relate these developments to the general periodization already given. To repeat, Western civilization in this millennium of devolution (roughly the first millennium A.D.) went through three phases: first a period of collapse (the first, second, and third centuries); then a period of attempted revival (the fourth, fifth, and sixth centuries); then a period of renewed classical collapse and simultaneous medieval stabilization (the seventh through the tenth centuries). As we bring this periodization to bear on the history of style, we can provide it with a rough chronology.

The first phase began at that very imprecise moment when classical style started to slip in another direction. The changes were subtle and would perhaps escape our attention if we did not know the end of the story. But during the first and second centuries A.D., Roman art and architecture revealed new aspects. At first there were only nuances. Confident realism disintegrated into realism-for-effects. Republican restraint was replaced by imperial excess. Strains of the erotic and the neurotic appeared. And as time went on there occurred an occasional preview of the medieval orientation toward the interior and the vertical, of the first, for example, in the Pantheon (early 2d century), and of the second in the remarkably Romanesque-like halls of the Baths of Caracalla (early 3d century). Also present in this first phase were those first signs of decadence already referred to. The further we move along, the more striking they become, until by the later third century one can speak of fundamental ineptitude. The classical style at this point seemed to be threatened not so much by rejection but rather by death through neglect and indifference. Old skills were being unlearned, and there were few new ones coming forward to fill the gap. The Roman tradition was not being destroyed from without, by external assault, but from within, by internal disintegration.

Then in the fourth century, things changed, and in an odd way. For the first phase, the phase of devolution and decay, was brought to an end, as classical style participated in and in a sense benefited from the general attempt at restoration that we have already referred to as the classical revival. But to say that the revival resulted in the restoration of the classical style during this second phase is incomplete and leaves out what is perhaps the more important part of the story. What happened was this: the immediate result of the revival was indeed a restoration of classical style. One can see it in its clearest form in Diocletian's Palace at Split, built in the very early fourth century. However, if we are to take the whole of the following three centuries as a more or less continuous revival, then clearly there is much more to the history of style in this period than classical restoration. By the fifth century new influences were drifting in from the east, and in the sixth the Byzantine style made its appearance. So it was that by the end of the period of classical revival, classical style had assimilated a huge portion of the Eastern tradition. In the process, Roman art and architecture had become something very different. Now the style was no longer purely classical, but a classical-Eastern mix. Apparently, the efforts at revival had initially sent Rome scurrying back in search of its fundamentals. But those had soon been revealed as somehow inappropriate to the new mood. And at that point the floodgates that had been holding back the eastern tides were opened. The result was the literally brilliant Byzantine achievement, as West and East merged.

By this time the West was halfway to its medieval style. Two of the essential three ingredients, the Roman and the Eastern, had been brought together and joined. To complete the work, there remained only one more thing to be done, and that was to assimilate the Northern. This was the accomplishment of the third phase. It began with the final collapse in the late sixth and seventh centuries of the classical revival in the West—and now by West we no longer mean to include Constantinople and the eastern Mediterranean, which henceforth developed independently—and extended until the eleventh century, when a new trend set in. During these centuries, it is obvious that the civilized elements within both Western culture and society were reduced almost to the point of extinction. Western civilization might well have ceased to exist. Certainly had there been a rival civilization with any capacity for expansion—Byzantium proved to everyone's satisfaction that it was not one—the West would surely have been destroyed. It was its good fortune to be overrun by barbarians. And they were ultimately absorbed. The West lived on. But not as before. Although the barbarians became Western, they superimposed on the higher culture many of their own ways. This was especially true with regard to style. Their decoration, their interest in abstraction, their tendency toward the vertical and infinite, and, one might add, their bent to fanaticism, all now became a part of the developing medieval style. Thus the art of the Middle Ages was a fortunate creation. It brought together elements of three very distinct cultural traditions and joined them together to produce something new.

With the addition of the barbarian influence, this medieval style was, so

to speak, complete. The result was initially the rather restricted production
of the Carolingian period and then later the more considerable output of
the Romanesque era. And it was in the Romanesque that the West found
its essential medieval stylistic expression. It was a truly Christian art:
severe, pious, otherworldly, introspective, and humble, the aesthetic counterpart of the medieval Church during the period of its greatest intensity—
just after, that is, it had been rescued from the local lords by the great
monastic reform movement of the tenth century and just before it began to
lose itself in the new secular world emerging rapidly from the twelfth
century on.[5]

But what of the Gothic? Was it not the Gothic rather than the Romanesque that was the nearest stylistic equivalent of the medieval spirit? No, it
was not. We have been deceived. And that almost inevitably, for the
Middle Ages that the Modern Age inherited directly and came to know
best had been rebuilt during what we refer to as the High and late Middle
Ages on the foundations, often literally, of the early Middle Ages. The
earlier and more purely medieval style was obscured. Romanesque was
relegated to being the bottom layer on the many-layered Gothic cake.
Because that is how we have been forced to see it, it is assumed that that is
what it was intended to be. Yet such was not the case. The Romanesque
may have turned out to be the first step toward the Gothic, but it was in its
own right the end of a long line of evolution, the most complete example of
the medieval style. It is not that the Gothic style was not also medieval. Yet
is was medieval in the process of becoming something else. It would seem
that it in fact tried very hard to remain medieval, but its protomodern
features were difficult to conceal. The Gothic was less a style of rural piety
than of urban pride.

By the Romanesque period, then, the stylistic evolution from the full
classical to the full medieval had been completed. There had been three
sources—late Roman, Near Eastern, and Northern. And one can think of
the influence from these being brought to bear respectively in three
phases: during the first phase, the predominant mode remained that of
classicism, and the changes that occurred were the results not of the
impact of outside influences but of the unfolding of internal processes.
High Roman was metamorphosing into late Roman, following the impetus
of its own internal evolution. This phase, to repeat the chronology, lasted
from the first century through the third. Then a second phase began,
during which Near Eastern styles penetrated the classical world and fused
with the late Roman to produce the Byzantine, this coinciding with the
general efforts at classical revival that ran from the fourth century through
the sixth. Finally, there was a third phase, one that saw the spread of
barbarian influence and the resultant amalgamation of the Northern style
with the Byzantine, this happening gradually over the long period that

stretches from the seventh to the eleventh centuries. The culmination was the Romanesque. The overall effect was to replace the naturalistic, logical, finite, and humanistic style that Rome had inherited from Greece with a style that was semiabstract, supralogical, infinite, and theocentric. A new age had found a new style.

THOUGHT

In sketching the history of style it has been difficult to avoid saying something about the history of thought. One cannot entirely separate them. Thought is the articulation of style, style the shorthand of thought. Therefore as we turn to outline the major changes in the Western mind as it ventured from its classical to its medieval world view we find that we have already adumbrated the underlying change, the conversion from philosophy to religion—from, that is, the secular, optimistic humanism of the Greeks and Romans to the securely pessimistic Christian theocentrism of the West in the early Middle Ages. Whereas classical thought had posited a natural world operating by laws that insured its regularity, medieval thought now developed a view, equally consistent, that assumed the frequent intervention of God, in the presence of Whom all rules vanished; and with the departing rules also went mankind's chances for controlling its own destiny. The Deity necessarily replaced man as the motive force, and, just as logically, heaven replaced earth as the presumed final locus of human activity. No longer could reason serve as the guide. It could operate only in a natural world, free from divinities and their miracles. In a world open to supernatural interference, to seemingly arbitrary interruption of necessary cause-and-effect relationships, reason offered no more than a sometimes-useful method for ordering religious insights. And faith—piety, humility before God's absolute power, and trust in the wisdom of His judgments—took over as the new means to improvement, seen henceforth as preparation for eternal salvation.[6]

If, then, the fundamental change in style as it evolved from the classical to the medieval was the conversion from the natural to the abstract—from, we might say, a style of earthly representation to one of heavenly or supranatural abstraction—the fundamental change in thought was the exact counterpart: from a system designed to acquire secular knowledge by secular means to one designed to receive divine revelation by religious means. *Nihil est in intellectu quod non prius fuerit in sensu.* Nothing is in the intellect that was not first in the senses.[7] This had been the principle around which classical thought—Plato very distinctly excepted, of course—had been organized. We must proceed, it said, from the things around us through our senses as assisted by the rational process to truth.

Medieval thought's great contribution was to reverse the order: nothing can be in the senses that was not first in the intellect. For the only source of truth is God revealing Himself to man—and not man in nature, but man apart from nature, man as soul. Thomas Aquinas and the Schoolmen would begin to turn things around once more and thereby open the door yet again to temporal knowledge. But that was much later, and the Middle Ages from its beginnings until the developments of the eleventh, twelfth, and thirteenth centuries held to its original convictions.

To compare further the classical and medieval minds it makes an interesting exercise to explore their positions with regard to monasticism. Although monasticism had its origins in the West during the Classical Age, it remained a peripheral phenomenon until the early medieval period. But at that point it became the archetypical model for life in this world as it should now be lived. Not that medieval men and women sought to emulate the proffered ideal with any consistency. They seem to have lived out their lives under the influence of those same pragmatic attitudes that dictate how life is lived in all ages. Yet it would be wrong not to take their veneration of monasticism seriously. For by it they gave testimony to their opinion regarding the way things ought to be. Therefore if one takes the five admonitions of the Benedictine rule—to poverty, chastity, obedience, piety, and labor—it can be assumed that we have before us a distilled version of the medieval mind, fit to be contrasted with a comparably distilled version of the classical mind.

To begin with poverty: to the classical mind, poverty was anything but an ideal. On the contrary, for the Greeks as well as the Romans it was the image of the good life that was held up to be admired. But the medieval mind, sure that rewards in this world only obscured the true path, elevated austerity. And it was much the same with regard to chastity: while to the Greeks and Romans sexual enjoyments were for the most part proper, the new Christian West condemned not only licentiousness but all sex; although, wisely, the Church assumed that sinners must indeed be permitted to sin, and only a few heresies took the matter to its logical conclusions. But either way the point is the same: for the medieval mind sex detracted from holiness. At best it was a necessary evil.

As for obedience, its significance as an ideal is crucial. For the classical mind, obedience certainly had its place, but it was only to be tolerated in the interest of higher purposes. Although one might willingly submit to the rules of family, community, and state, the starting point was freedom. For the medieval mind, however, submission to God's will was the starting point. Just as knowledge proceeded from the top downward, from God to man, so did authority. The Greeks and Romans participated. Medieval man obeyed.

With regard to piety and labor, here too the contrast is vivid: the classical mind had originally been pious to a degree, but as it shed its religious past, devoutness was replaced by humanist pride. And the transition from pride to piety amounted to a complete reversal of positions. Christian piety reduced pride to a sin. Confidence in mankind's abilities was replaced by humility as an acknowledgment of impotence. And labor? The Greeks and Romans had despised it. There was no benefit inherent in work. It was stultifying. Only by finding release from labor—and the classical solution was to pass much of the burden on to slaves—could the individual be freed to become fully human. But medieval man did not wish to become fully human, or rather he sought very hard to avoid the appearance of flaunting his secular side. Therefore labor: to assist in the suppression of the desires and for the glory of God. Long hours in the fields, long hours at the copy desk, long hours at prayer—this was a life that was the precise antithesis of the classical ideal.

And yet if the monastic model goes a long way in describing the medieval mind, it does not go the whole way. There was another element present, one difficult to summarize. The attitude of thought in the early Middle Ages was never wholly Christian, for medieval thought like medieval style was the result of a putting together of the late-classical, Eastern, and Northern-barbarian heritages. It is thus unlikely that a perfect consistency of any sort could have been the outcome. Still, it is true that the first two of these, the late-classical and Eastern traditions, did flow together to produce very nearly a homogeneous entity: late classicism had been condensed into Neoplatonism, and its variation on the theme of otherworldliness coalesced so easily and completely with the Eastern variation that the end-product was close to being a perfectly joined whole. Neoplatonism was a trifle more otherworldly than the Eastern position as defined by the early Church, and those who insisted on sticking to the finer points, especially with regard to the Neoplatonic doctrine on the unreality of matter, risked being declared heretical. For the most part, however, the two traditions became almost one. Certainly the process of amalgamation was made even less difficult by the fact that the most profound of the Church fathers, St. Augustine, retained in his theology much from his earlier Neoplatonism.[8]

It was the third element, the Northern, that was never quite brought into agreement with the other two. In many ways, to be sure, the Northern influence reinforced the tendencies of the late-classical and Eastern (now Christian) blend. Both the Celtic and Germanic world views were in good part religious, and neither people was much given to revering humankind. The representation of humans is almost wholly absent from their art. And although the few barbaric sagas that have survived point to an obsession with the warrior-hero, these heroes are not the personalities of humanist literature. For they are denied a personal development. There only to die, they are sacrificed to the requirements of destiny. Their individuality is not important. Thus the barbarians can hardly be accused of harboring a subversive humanism in defiance of the late-classical-Christian anti-humanist concord. Yet there was another side to the Northern outlook that presented something different. For example, the Celts and Germans had been in their preconversion innocence neither ascetic nor chaste nor pious. Their appetite for work was suspect, too. They were, in fact, very ebullient, life-affirming peoples, if also at times gloomy and prone to the disdainful final gesture. In short, they brought to the medieval mix a certain reckless assertiveness found in neither of the other traditions. The new medieval mind, then, was pious and God-fearing, but never completely. It was Christian, but not always.

With regard to the steps or periods in the history of the transformation of classical thought into medieval thought, one can delineate, following the pattern already suggested for the history of style, these three: first an era of classical devolution, then one of revival, and finally one of simultaneous breakdown and reconstruction along medieval lines. We shall look briefly at each in turn.

It was during the first period that the Latin world slipped from the patriotic confidence of the late republic and early principate to the jaded cynicism of the post-Augustan years and then beyond to an experimentation with Neoplatonism and the full variety of Eastern mystery-religion imports. Thus we move here from the Rome of Livy (d. A.D. 17), with his still confident histories; to the Rome of Tacitus (d. ca. 120) and Juvenal (d. ca. 140), with their criticism of the present and nostalgia for the past; and on to the Rome of Neoplatonic otherworldliness, where Plotinus (d. 270) could believe that "in this world itself all is best when human interests and the memory of them have been put out of the way."[9] Not that the entire empire had taken to Neoplatonism, of course; but in the peculiar and sometimes overdrawn way that leading intellectuals have of capturing the mood of their times, Plotinus gave expression to the vastly changed Roman climate of the third century.

The first period, then, which can be thought of in round numbers as having lasted from year one to 300, saw Roman thought proceed from an optimistic humanism to despair and onward even to a rejection of the secular condition. This it did mostly on its own, for, although Eastern modes were beginning to infiltrate, Rome was still Rome and the attacks on classicism came mostly from within. But that was not true of the next period, which extended from roughly 300 to 600, for it was during these next three centuries that, intellectually speaking, the East moved West.

For the West now experienced the joining of late classicism and the Eastern tradition, the latter conveyed by the spread of Christianity. As suggested, bringing late classicism and Christianity together was not particularly difficult. The journey from Plotinus to Augustine was hardly jarring, for Neoplatonism, as noted a moment ago, could be and was readily converted to Christian purposes. It was mostly a matter of upgrading matter and the world from unreal to merely sinful—if that is a promotion—and transforming the ideal of the Good into the Judaic-Christian God, putting, as it were, a humanlike countenance over the Platonic abstraction. "The Platonists saw truth," wrote Augustine, "but they saw it from afar."[10] Augustine would bring it home. Nor was he the first Christian to be influenced by Neoplatonism. The entire Greek-speaking, Hellenized East had been affected increasingly by it for several centuries prior to Augustine's conversion; and because Christianity from Paul on had been part and parcel of that Hellenized milieu, Christian doctrine had almost from it beginnings been subjected to the influence of Neoplatonism's more sophisticated and ready-made opinions. As then Christianity absorbed and overtook its older competitor, one can perhaps be forgiven for suggesting that the new religion's chief appeal lay in its ability to personalize and popularize Neoplatonism. In any case, that is the simple part of the story of this second period, and if it has been made to seem otherwise, let me restate the essentials: in the three centuries following 300, late classicism, which had already exchanged its humanism for Neoplatonism, was merged with Christianity, which had itself been influenced during its development by Neoplatonism. Hence the relatively effortless combination of two similar ingredients.

The truly complex part of the matter derives from the fact that exactly these centuries that saw the fusion of East and West—or, better, the Easternization of the West—were also times of classical revival, of, that is, a conscious attempt to restore classical values and institutions to a working condition. The result with regard to thought was that both Christianity and Neoplatonism were alternately employed by the empire: Constantine was the first to use Christianity, doing so in the early fourth century; then Julian the Apostate tried Neoplatonism a few decades later; and finally Theodosius made Christianity the sole official religion toward the end of the century. But what good could these messages of worldly renunciation do for governments trying to rejuvenate? Not much. Yet as Christianity and Neoplatonism in turn became official, they began to fudge on worldly renunciation. Or perhaps it was merely the upbeat mood that accompanied the revival. For whatever reasons, earthly rewards, especially noticeable with regard to Christianity, were offered for good behavior. If the Romans did things for the Christian God, then the Christian God would do things for the Romans. Constantine accepted the new religion and thereby defeated his rivals at Milvian Bridge. For the moment, good old-fashioned Roman pragmatism was reasserting itself against the Eastern importations. Even a hint of revived humanism can be seen in Constantine's Nicene

Creed, where the efforts at secular renewal won a significant victory. The Eastern interpretation of Christ's nature refused to grant that He could be human and divine at the same time. It could not admit that a body that was human and thus sinful could be also a piece of God. In short, the East had said that man was so depraved that he could not in his human form be reconciled with God. Nicea—and the position was repeated over a century later at the Council of Chalcedon—said that he could be.

The result of all of this was that the Christianization of the West did not initially have quite the meaning that one might have anticipated. Certainly Christianity, and the same would have been true of Neoplatonism had it won out, was an awkward doctrine for a revived Rome to work with. Because Christianity has been used for so many worldly purposes since those days, it is easy to forget how little suited this religion originally was for its new role. Yet the adaptation was made. Therefore Rome's becoming Christian did not indicate that it had given up defending its secular realm, but, on the contrary, that it had decided on defending it even more vigorously. That not all Christians were unconscious of the dangers inherent in the Church's new concessions to a reviving secularism is evidenced by Augustine's prolonged efforts to keep Church doctrine free of the heresies to which its new status as a state religion exposed it. However, by this time (Augustine died in 430) the cooperation was beginning to prove unsuccessful, for the classical revival was failing. If that had not been clear for other reasons, the sacks of Rome by the Visigoths (410) and the Vandals (455) made the point explicit. And it was Augustine who announced the restoration of the independence of Christianity from Rome: the Heavenly City, that is, the community of the saved, would travel along with the Earthly City for a while longer, but their paths would, he insisted, soon part. Rome's eventual defeat again became good Christian doctrine. Although collaboration in the future was never ruled out, Christianity and Rome were separated, thereby freeing Christianity to return to its secular pessimism. Finally, then, the Christianization of classical thought in the middle period of this grand transition brought Eastern otherworldliness to the West, but not before the West had for a time successfully resisted, turning the religion to its own secular purposes.

The other notable characteristic of these centuries derived from the efforts to put together collections of surviving works, with the obvious hope of preserving something of classicism in the face of the impending collapse. This attention to preservation fits the theme of classical revival, but it gives testimony, too, to the extent that late Rome understood its predicament. It copied furiously as the sea of miracles rose higher and higher. But it wrote the miracles into the record, too, for the ability to distinguish had already been lost. By the end of the sixth century, the classical world view had all but disappeared.

At that point, ca. 600, the history of the transition of thought from its classical to its medieval state entered upon a third and final period, one that was to last until ca. 1000. Again, a caution: with ideas there are few dividing lines in the fine sense, and, for that matter, there was never a single, agreed-upon classical or medieval mind. We are talking of tendencies and averages of a sort, and because it sometimes seems otherwise, it is well to remind ourselves occasionally that while these generalizations that we are using are convenient, they run roughshod over the many exceptions. With that in mind, then, we can describe this last phase in the formation of the medieval world view. Thus far, that world view was, as we have seen, the product of the combination of the late-classical and Eastern world views, both otherworldly and antihumanist. Now in this last phase the Northern, barbarian tradition became important. As suggested, for all its fatalism there was a certain vitality within it that seems to have been retained even as it was blended into the more literate high culture of late-classical and early-medieval Christianity. But we are now in the Dark Ages, and even the literate high culture was not very literate. There was but a single original thinker in the whole of the period, and that is John Scotus Erigena (d. 877), an Irishman who established himself at the late Carolingian court of Charles the Bald. John was remarkably innovative in his efforts to continue the reconciliation of Neoplatonism and Christianity, but because he had neither predecessors nor successors it is not easy to accept him as a spokesman for his times.[11]

Here is a genuine predicament: almost half a millennium for which we have only one creative thinker—those who are contemptuous of intellectuals, and there are many, can look back on these centuries as a kind of golden age—and we cannot take him as typical. But so be it. For a time without writers we must look elsewhere, to personalities about whom we have some information. And here one comes quickly to Charlemagne himself, one of the few figures from the Dark Ages who can be partially understood as an individual. What we find is a man struggling, caught between two attitudes: between, on the one hand, a deep sense of sin and desire for redemption and, on the other, a rather persistent inclination toward those standard barbarian enjoyments noted a moment ago—certainly wine and women, and possibly song as well. If Charlemagne, then, was at all representative—and that he was is apparent from contemporary folk literature—then it would seem to reinforce the impression that the Northern influence included a persistent secularism, one that even when Christianized refused to go away. After all, the barbarians had little to mope about. It was not their culture that was waning, and for them the fall of Rome had been one long series of victories. They were very much on the way up. If they were not an optimistic people, at least their pessimism lacked the elaborate refinement of the later Romans.

But the point to be made here is that what we know of the climate of thought in the Dark Ages does not quite match the picture one receives from the few formal statements of theology. It would appear that the admixture of Northern vitality during this last phase served to brake the West's slide toward secular renunciation and helped to prevent the development of a true ethic of contemplation and acceptance. The West, for better or for worse, retained something of its dynamism. It failed to succumb entirely to the East. Ironically, it would seem that it owed its salvation in part to the Northerners, who brought along with their bent to destruction a certain stubborn refusal to be humble. To be sure, they would become Christians, but they could never stop threatening to kill everyone who would not follow their example. Clovis's comment when he learned of Christ's crucifixion was typical: "If only I had been there with my Franks!" Indeed, what a splendid battle there would have been.

These, then, were the three periods in the transition of Western thought from the classical to the medieval: an initial one, consisting of the first three centuries A.D., during which classical humanism first went sour and then gave way to Neoplatonism; then a second, lasting from the fourth through the sixth centuries, in which late classicism merged with the flow of ideas from the East, at last accepting Christianity; and finally a third, from roughly the seventh through the tenth centuries, which saw the influence of Northern barbarism brought to bear upon the late-classical-Christian fusion. The result?: a body of thought still somewhat conscious of its Greek and Latin heritage, but now crucially affected by the cooperation of the very most otherworldly aspects of that heritage with Eastern otherworldly theology,[12] all this then further transformed by contact with the untamed and somewhat brutal *Lebenslust* of the North. Such, more or less, was the mind of the West at the end of its thousand-year devolution.

POLITICS

The corresponding thousand-year political devolution from empire to feudal decentralization is the next subject for review. It is a story that continues to fascinate us. There is indeed something uncanny in the collapse of the Roman imperial structure. The transformation of the West's politics was not particularly rapid—this is not the history of a sudden catastrophe—but it was so thorough that one can only wonder at the remarkable ability of human societies to take on new shapes. By the time of the early medieval centuries these came in several varieties, but not so many that one cannot recognize a common condition: for they were all particles, relatively small and independent units of political organization. It can be said, then, that as the West moved from its classical political form to its medieval counterpart, the significant change was from a politics of empire, in which society was given its order from a central core, from, that is, a single locus of sovereignty, to a politics of particularism, in which society was reconstituted in many distinct and relatively independent loci. The tendency of classicism to centralization was now replaced by the early medieval tendency to decentralization. Put another way, an imperial machine that could no longer function was being exchanged for lesser units that functioned very nicely.

The process of conversion was, as with all such histories, slow and irregular; yet the outlines are surprisingly clear. As with the parallel histories of style, thought, and, as we shall soon see, also economics, there was a three-fold division: first a period of imperial decline; next a period of revival; and then a final period of collapse, during which the West responded rapidly by giving full articulation to the countersystem that had been developing as an infrastructure within the decaying empire. The chronology is that with which we are already familiar, the first decline lasting from the first century through most of the third, the revival from the late third through the sixth, and the final fall and reconstitution from the sixth through the tenth.

It would be very reasonable at this point to ask if it would not have been better to treat the several components of civilization together, period by period, rather than tracing separately the progress of each of them along what turns out to be the very same course. That is, after all, what many general histories do, and there is obviously much to be said for it. But there is, we need to remind ourselves, another purpose being served here, and that has to do with the attempt to understand those same components in the present as parts of a civilizational history. And that is not easy. The point was made earlier, and I shall repeat it here: we grant a coherency to the past that is refused to the present. We can readily grasp the significance of the parallel movements of style, thought, politics, and economics in the past, so readily that to belabor the point by taking the time to treat each of these threads in isolation indeed risks appearing pedantic. To be sure, we concede, they are all parts of a single civilizational movement and behave accordingly. But when we come to our own times there is a reluctance to make the same assumptions. The connections even when we can find them are mysterious and hard to analyze. Also the portrayal of the strands of present developments as parts within a civilization continuum would seem to admit to a certain lack of control over them, which may be true but seems to defy common sense.

Nevertheless, that is the ultimate intention here: to see the various aspects of our contemporary experience as components within a civilizational history—to suggest, that is, that not only has the West behaved as a civilization in the past, with each of the categories conforming to the fundamental directions, but that also the West in the present is behaving as a civilization, and that, further, it is likely to continue to do so. Style and economics, politics and thought, thought and economics, style and politics—these will presumably go on unfolding together as parts of a civilizational whole. If it seems unreasonable to link changes in areas remote from one another, indeed to anticipate innovation in a certain field because of prior innovations in only vaguely related fields, then we should be able to reply that this is the way it has happened in the past. Therefore the separate histories. They are so displayed in order is to establish the similarity of their only superficially independent courses.

To return to Roman politics: at the beginning of the first period, that is, at the turn of the millennium, Augustus was engaged in the work of giving Rome a new system.[13] During the first two centuries B.C., Rome had undergone a remarkable expansion. Now it must adapt its institutions to the results. The requirements were two in number: first, it was necessary to provide for the defense and administration of the empire. And, second, the appropriate internal adjustments would have to be made to accommodate the new groups that had risen from the ranks, as the various opportunities created by the expansion turned a conservative and rigid society into one inspired by a vision of upward mobility. The first task was not a difficult one. It had been for the most part already accomplished, done on the move, step by step in the course of the long period of conquest. The domestic readjustment was, however, another matter. Since the days of the brothers Tiberius and Gaius Gracchus in the late second century B.C., Rome had been struggling with a problem. Reduced to its simplest terms, it was this: how to include in the power structure those who made their living running and supplying the empire. These were the equestrians. As mentioned earlier when describing the culmination of the classical political evolution, it was an essential part of Augustus's compromise to bring them into the circle of the new imperial establishment. The result was to add to the old senatorial class of large landowners a middle class of entrepreneurs. Rome had not indeed become bourgeois, but it did now have something like a substantial bourgeoisie participating in the operation of the empire.[14]

By the first century A.D., the classical world had been given a new shape: Western Europe, the North African littoral, and much of the Near East—in short, the Mediterranean basin and huge portions to the east and north—all these were now governed from Rome. And Rome was governed by the emperor, who had built his authority upon a forced reconciliation of old men and new, of traditional agrarian aristocracy and rising bourgeoisie. The classical world at its political peak consisted, then, of an external centralization resting on a crucial internal compromise. The one reinforced the other. Hence the story of the initial descent from the peak can best be described by reference to the progressive disintegration of both. For both the efforts at external centralization, based as they were upon the ability to continue to exercise imperial authority throughout the empire, and those aimed at internal reconciliation, based in turn upon the ability of the imperial establishment to continue to incorporate the middle classes without provoking other classes to revolution, entered upon their times of trouble together; and this in the course of the first three centuries A.D.

The beginnings of the failure of the external structure of the empire are visible already in the early second century A.D. No sooner had Rome reached the limits of her expansion than the process of contraction began. In the first century, Rome had still been able to add significant territories. In the second century, however, began the retreat. Trajan's armies failed in the effort to defeat Parthia. Hadrian, his successor, withdrew and, ominously, built walls along the imperial frontiers. Rome was no longer moving outward—rather, it was now concentrating very hard on trying not to be pushed back.

But it did not work, at least not for long. Marcus Aurelius (ruled 161–80) kept things together only by constant fighting. And in the long period that followed his reign, confusion prevailed. Emperors came and went, mostly murdered (every one from Caracalla, killed in 217, until Claudius II, who put an end to the pattern in 270 by dying of the plague); and when Aurelian turned to the matter of restoring order in the later third century, he found it advisable, most ominous indeed, to wall the city of Rome itself. Gallienus had just before already taken the crucial decision to defend not the frontiers, through which the barbarians were penetrating with increasing frequency, but rather bastions. The effort at saving the whole had not succeeded, and the army was forced to salvage what it could.

Running a similar course to the deterioration that afflicted the territorial limits of the empire, and of course exacerbating it, there was the process of internal decay. That balance achieved by Augustus gradually became unworkable. Next the senatorial order was further reduced in power, as the equestrians, the men of tax contracts and business, became even stronger. Under the Flavians in the late first and early second centuries, they formed a sort of favored class. Rome indeed for the moment was bourgeois. But only for the moment. Soon the freedmen and then the army were replacing the equestrians. The freedmen could be absorbed without damage to the existing system. However, that was not at all true of the army, which with the decline of the cities had now become the chief support of imperial authority. "Look after the soldiers and scorn the rest," Septimius Severus (193–211) is supposed to have said.[15] By the third century the Augustan compromise, essentially an alliance between old agriculture and new business, had been destroyed, and to the advantage of neither of its components. The winner in Rome seemed to be the army; but because the army was more and more composed not of Romans but rather of barbarians, there was in fact no winner in Rome.

Then in the late third and early fourth centuries began a long period of reform and restoration. The initial steps had already been taken by Gallienus and Aurelian when Diocletian, one of the most effective of these reforming emperors, ascended the imperial throne in 284. It was his task to give substance to a new idea born of a new sense of urgency: that if Rome were to be saved, radical measures would be required, and immediately. His political reform consisted of four parts. First, he brought the army under control. If the army had been meant to make the imperial office stronger, it had recently begun to do just the opposite, as the legions competed in countless wars to place their candidates on the throne. Diocletian separated the command of the army from its ties with the provincial governments, making it less likely that the governors would use the military to further their own ambitions. Second, he reformed the domestic structure, completing the long evolution of Rome from senatorial republic to oriental despotism. The emperor was now to be an absolute dictator, with all the trappings of divine appointment. Third, Diocletian sought unity through division: by creating four regions of administration rather than one, he would give up the fiction of rule from Rome in exchange for order. And, fourth, he linked this new division to a system of selecting an heir that was to eliminate the now-inevitable civil wars that accompanied each succession. These were the essential political measures—there were to be economic reforms, too, but they will be considered separately—by which Diocletian intended to halt the spiral toward imperial dissolution that had characterized the last century.

Following quickly upon Diocletian's reform efforts came those of Constantine. The succession mechanism had failed spectacularly at its first test, but still the empire emerged from the fighting intact, more intact, surprisingly, than before, with Constantine after his Eastern victory in 323 in firm control. He was able to take two immediate steps to consolidate power: he ended the rifts within the Christian Church, which, coupled with his conversion, bought for Rome the crucial political support of this rapidly growing religion. And he founded New Rome, a replacement capital that would, he hoped, permit the East to rule the West as once the West had ruled the East. Administered from this new city, which was situated on the Bosphorus in the midst of the still prosperous Eastern commercial network, the reconstituted empire could perhaps survive. Constantinople—as it soon came to be called—would do for Rome what Rome could no longer do for itself.

Taken together, the reforms of Diocletian and Constantine represented a profound attempt at transforming the political nature of the empire. A new authority, a new army, a new city, and a new religion were intended to provide a new life. To what extent were they successful? The core of the Eastern empire that we know as Byzantium was to last for over a millennium, a remarkable achievement. Yet the Roman Empire itself was restored but briefly. To bring greater cohesion, Constantine in 335, just two years before his death, once again divided the empire. It worked, however, no better than before. By the end of the fourth century, the split between East and West had become final, Justinian's brief sixth-century reunification excepted. And the West itself was now increasingly subdivided into Gallo-Roman and German kingdoms. The march to a decentralized political order had been only interrupted.

Nor did the search to find a substitute in the army and the Church for the old collaboration of a prosperous agriculture with a flourishing commerce prove successful. The combined effect of militarization and Christianization was, it is true, to make rebellion less likely. The real problem came increasingly, however, to be not rebellion, but evasion. The empire had been financed by plunder and taxes. With plunder no longer available, taxes had become oppressive and thus evasion a way of life. But the difficulty was even more severe: the empire had been operated by people engaged, and both in public and private capacities, in the business of making profits. By the third and fourth centuries there were only losses to be had. The result was a general retreat from responsibility at all levels, causing widespread damage to the machinery of administration. The army found it difficult to find a solution. It could hardly fight a war against the empire's civilian population. And Christianity's response, founded as it was on only a passing commitment to life on earth, could be at best ambivalent.

Yet the Roman way of life hung on. Political order, while weakened and fragmented, did not disappear. If the process of decay had not been stopped, at least its rate was now slower. Not only in the East, but also in the West, Rome although divided had managed to hold on. But then in the later sixth century the final blow was delivered, and that from an unexpected source. It originated in Justinian's dream of reunification. This was to be the last bid, launched from Constantiople, to restore the original Roman Empire. Its chief victim was the German kingdom of Theodoric in Italy. Theodoric had tried to maintain the old order. But Justinian's destructive wars of reconquest unraveled the fabric of classical civilization. Nor could his brief period of authority in the West repair the damage. With the next wave of German invasion, led by the Lombards, Rome went under for the last time. Ironically, the final attempt at classical revival had brought an end to the West's Classical Age, which the barbarians, another irony, had been desperately trying to preserve.[16]

The political history of the fourth, fifth, and sixth centuries records the search for a solution that did not exist. The circumstances that had permitted Rome to dominate the Mediterranean world and simultaneously solve its domestic problems could no longer be duplicated. For whatever initial reasons, Rome had by this time moved too far in another direction. The political history of the seventh through the tenth centuries, however, records the gradual adjustment to the inevitable, the search for a solution that did exist. And when it was finally articulated, it became a new ideal. That ideal, broadly conceived, we know as feudalism. Feudalism is a system for partitioning power in which the individual units, while not conceded absolute authority, are nevertheless favored at the expense of the whole. It is, in short, a design for decentralization—but, it should be added, for a decentralization that stops well short of anarchy. Such a system was badly needed by Europe at this point: something that could halt the slide toward complete political fragmentation while at the same time acknowledging the impossibility of reviving the empire. Slowly and without a plan, the new structure was put together.

Quite naturally, it was constructed out of materials already at hand, and therefore the forms of Western feudalism can be traced to their origins in late Roman and German customs. Specifically, the new order was a hybrid shaped by the joining of the Roman *beneficium*, land tenure on easy terms granted in exchange for some future expectation, to the German *comitatus*, a Latin name for the group of loyal barbarian warriors adhering to a leader. When in the early Carolingian period the vassal—that is, the aristocratic warrior of the *comitatus*—received for his promised services a fief, or *beneficium*, the basic parts of the feudal system had been assembled. It is not difficult to become the captive of the assumption that the heritage was responsible for the creation. But since other feudalisms have come into existence in other societies without the help of the specific institutional history found in the West, it would seem that it was the requirements of the times rather than the presence of ready-made parts that served as the chief inspiration. This system of decentralization arose to fill a need. Had it not been the feudalism with which we are familiar it would have been something very much like it.[17]

There were, of course, other contributing agents in the creation of feudalism, but their effects would not seem to force us to change our conclusion that the true cause was the need itself. The arrival of the stirrup in the West at this time is sometimes held up as a cause: because the stirrup made the mounted knight a more effective fighter, and because mounted knights were expensive, it is argued that the stirrup occasioned the granting of the fief, which was in turn designed to enable the vassal to maintain himself—the only way, in a society without other resources, that he might be expected to do so. No doubt the stirrup did make a contribution. But when the evolution of feudalism is put within its larger context, it would seem unlikely that it was a major factor. So also with the threats from the Arabs, Vikings, and Magyars. Their invasions certainly prompted the West to look quickly for ways to defend itself. Yet if in the areas between the Loire and Rhine feudalism was the result, to the east of the Rhine it was not, and there feudal institutions were only imported after the era of the invasions had passed.

No, feudalism was not the fortuitous product of the amalgamation of certain traditions, and neither was it the work of technological innovation nor transient dangers. All of these surely helped give it its distinctive features. They did not, however, cause feudalism. The cause, that is, the essential cause, was the collapse of imperial authority, for which feudalism finally came to provide an adequate, if very different, substitute.

Here the Carolingians have been mentioned in connection with feudalism, and yet nothing has been said of Charlemagne's empire. That is, in a brief account such as this, as it should be. The more lasting political contribution of the Carolingians, as already remarked, was to the decentralization of Europe, which their assistance to feudalization helped to formalize. But their efforts at establishing a lasting superstate were entirely unsuccessful. There was nothing unusual in that failure. The West was not ready for a new centralization. Necessarily, Carolingian administration, even under Charlemagne, remained remarkably primitive; and at no time was there any thought of a unified succession, the realm remaining subject to division among all surviving sons at the death of the emperor. Perhaps the real purpose of the imperial trappings was defensive: Charlemagne became emperor not so much to found an empire as to declare that the West was not to be considered as a part of an empire, that is, the Byzantine.

Whatever the intentions, it was during the later Carolingian period, in the second half of the ninth century and the first half of the tenth, that feudalism became at last the characteristic political form in the heartland of medieval Europe. In that relatively narrow but crucial area—northern France, the Lowlands, and westernmost Germany—feudalism now took hold and would next spread, as did so many of the West's medieval ways, outward to much of Europe. And, once arrived, it would stay a long time. Therein, however, lies a source of confusion. Because the forms of feudalism were so enduring, lasting in some places even into the twentieth century, they have come to be associated with political traditions that were irrelevant and even antithetical to their original purposes. This began to happen quite early, as feudalism was employed increasingly after the year 1000 not to disseminate political authority but rather to retrieve it, especially to serve the purposes of the developing monarchies. Both in the England of William the Conqueror and in the Germany of Frederick Barbarossa, for example, feudalism was encouraged in order to provide a framework upon which to rest royal authority. Indeed, feudalism in the twelfth and thirteenth centuries was chiefly associated with the cause of increasing ducal and monarchical power. Later we can find it operating, if reluctantly, in the service of absolutism. And later still one can even speak of a perverted association with fascism. It was, after all, the former vassal of the Prussian king, Paul von Hindenburg-Beneckendorff, who appointed Hitler chancellor. In all fairness, it should be noted that feudal elements were also well represented in the resistance to fascism.

This later history of feudalism should not be permitted, however, to obscure its original function. The West accepted feudalism during this final period in the process of devolution from classical centralization because the West, not just politically but also with regard to all aspects of its activity, was fundamentally fragmented. Between 600 and 1000, it sought and found a structure of government that matched its condition. The Roman Empire had broken down, and in the West neither kingdoms nor dukedoms nor even counties were capable of providing order. Adequate governance and protection could be obtained prior to 1000 for the most part only at the level of that local lord sufficiently affluent to build a castle. It was the great virtue of feudalism to lend to the reality of local power a sufficient appearance of unity. The kings kept their crowns. But the barons ruled the land without a serious rival, until, that is, after 1000, when the West began once again the business of gathering authority into central offices.

To summarize, the West's political course during the millennium of descent from the classical peak of centralization had seen, first, a period of three centuries, to about 300, during which both the original internal balance and Rome's ability to control the empire were gradually destroyed. Then between 300 and 600 (more accurately, 284 and 565) occurred a series of dramatic revivals, which produced a temporary, if forced, restoration. Finally, from around 600 until 1000, came the final collapse of the remnants of Roman government and simultaneous establishment of a new system founded on the decentralizing mechanisms of feudalism. It had taken a thousand years for the West to transform itself, but it had been accomplished: in place of the great empire that had arrived at a point at which it could neither move forward nor stand in one place, there was now a network of very small but politically viable pieces.

ECONOMICS

The corresponding economic story is just as extraordinary. The West in these same ten centuries passed, first, from an imperial economy that worked to an imperial economy that threatened not to work, next to an imperial economy that was forced to work, and then to an imperial economy that was finally beyond repair, that would not work at all. At that point, a new economy came into existence, local, self-sufficient, and operable even in the worth of circumstances—the very antithesis of the imperial economy, as particularistic and unspecialized as the classical had been ecumenical and specialized. If this economic transformation almost exactly mirrored the political transformation, then the question inevitably arises regarding the relationship between the two—and not only between these two, but between them and the equally similar histories of style and thought. Here once again we are confronted with the challenge of economic determinism: did Rome's economic collapse, in short, cause the other parallel histories? One can only say that, while it is conceivable, the evidence nevertheless remains impossible to evaluate. The problem is the one mentioned earlier, that which involves the establishment of an appropriate chronology. Neither the economic deterioration nor, for that matter, the final medieval economic stabilization can be said to have preceded the other histories. At times economic influence, especially upon politics, is obvious. At other times it was the other way around. And the ties to style and thought are at best implicit. The only reliable conclusion is that the economic history was an intimate part of the civilizational history, making its extremely important contribution but being affected as well by the consistent pressures created by the changes in culture and politics. Probably the best answer to the riddle posed by the question of economic influence is that there is no such thing, that economics as an entity separate from culture and politics—from, that is, the total civilizational milieu—simply does not exist.

Certainly the importance of noneconomic factors for the course of economic developments becomes apparent whenever one tries to account for the latter in purely economic terms. It is perhaps not so hard to explain other histories by reference to economics; but it is indeed difficult to explain economics by reference to economics. One begins to suspect that everything is economically determined except economics itself. Precisely because of its significance it is far more than just a product of its own mechanisms. It inescapably becomes the subject of a culture's superstitions, prejudices, and ideals. And since economic activity is so thoroughly integrated with the other civilizational components, it is not remarkable to find that it is seldom left alone to pursue a course determined by purely economic considerations. Certainly the reciprocal effects are obvious here, with regard to Rome's fall. Rome's economy had first contributed to and benefited from the prevailing harmony; and then it also conformed as Roman culture and politics edged toward their final disintegration.

But whatever the relationship between economics and the other parts of the civilizational experience, there remains a discernible economic history with regard to Rome's fall. We can begin it with the observation that the healthy economy of the first century, still healthy through most of the second, had become very disturbed by the third. What, from an economic standpoint, had gone wrong? Nothing and everything. That is, there would seem to have been no single major catastrophe to which the decline can be attributed. Yet there were a large number of minor catastrophes, so many that one suspects that they were results rather than causes: had the Roman economy continued to be prosperous within a flourishing civilization, each of them could have been endured. As it happened, none of them was, and their collective impact finally became enormous. To be sure, some were even in themselves quite damaging. The plague that arrived in the second century was especially destructive. So was the ever-present inflation, aggravated by the government's progressive devaluations of the currency. As the coinage became increasingly worthless, Rome discovered the hard way that devaluation as a means of paying the increasing costs of empire in the long run would not work. Without a dependable medium of exchange, trade was hindered. Set upon from all sides, the classical economy began to grind to a halt. As that happened, Rome could no longer provide the services it had formerly rendered. And without the services—essentially the maintenance of the *Pax Romana,* the orderly empire—Rome had nothing to offer, for, as noted earlier, it had never become an economic center in its own right.

There were also problems centering upon the imperial cities. A number of things were working together to drive farmers from the land and into the urban centers: production was shifting outward toward the frontier, specialized entrepreneurial farming was replacing peasant farming, and free labor was being exchanged for imported slaves. Thus there was a flight to the city. And in the city there was nothing to absorb the new arrivals, for Rome never hit upon the solution of an industrial revolution. As a result, it became increasingly necessary for the city governments to provide food and amusement, the infamous bread and games of Rome's declining centuries. These obligations then became increasingly onerous as the economy produced fewer and fewer surpluses.

But perhaps the most difficult economic predicament that Rome now was forced to deal with was the gradual loss of its supply of energy. Slaves were the fuel of the classical world. Mining the silver of Attica, they had done much to make Athens rich. Now they supported the Roman Empire. Viewed only economically, they were a perfect resource, cheap and abundant—so abundant that Rome never bothered having its slave population tend to the matter of reproducing itself. But that was not an important oversight, as long as new conquests supplied new adults for the system. In fact, it was not an oversight at all, it was an economy, for the costs of sustaining the next generation while it was still unproductive were simply transferred to others, to those who were about to be conquered. The difficulties began when Rome ran out of victims. And when the conquests came to an end, the resupply system broke down. Rome then tried to create slave families in order to encourage procreation. However, it was too late, and it did not work. The older patterns, perhaps, were too habitual. In any case, Rome lost its source of cheap and abundant energy.

And there were still more problems: specifically, the soil-depletion problem, the barbarian-disruption problem, the imbalance-of-payments problem, the leadership problem, and, mentioned in connection with politics, the evasion-of-responsibility problem. Of course during the period of classical revival Rome tried to deal with these, as with the other economic difficulties and everything else that needed restoring. The central conception permeating the economic reforms of these centuries (again, we are referring to the fourth, fifth, and sixth) was order by means of decree, backed by the authority of the restored army. Prices were at last stabilized by imperial dictate, the flight from positions within both the economy and the civilian administration was forbidden, and new, stiff taxes were levied. Even the military recruitment needs were taken care of by decree, as soldiering was made hereditary. In the short run, such measures might be effective, but only in the short run. If the population wished to avoid participation in an economy that it had already found hopeless, then it would now avoid the enforcement measures, and taxes as well. It would have taken more power than any ancient government ever possessed even to begin to make the economy work by commanding it to do so. There was as a result little restoration, only delay. Although the efforts at reform dragged on, they met with minimal success. What there was of it was in the East, in the increasingly separate Byzantine sphere. By the seventh century, the urban and commercial economy of the Classical Age had all but disappeared in the central and western Mediterranean.[18]

Just what happened next, as the West during the Carolingian period began to settle into its medieval economic patterns, is still a matter for debate. It has been maintained that the economy declined even more, and this due to the Arabs, who cut northern Europe off from the Mediterranean. But it has also been asserted that, on the contrary, the economy revived slightly, again due to the Arabs, who stimulated trade. Another school has argued that the economy did indeed worsen, although not because of the Arabs, but rather because of the Carolingians, who destroyed the still-lingering monetary system of northern Italy when they defeated the Lombards. And, finally, others say that the economy improved somewhat—yes, because of the Carolingians, who did in fact provide new levels of stability for a time.[19] Which of these suggestions is correct is not so important here, for the significant larger development is inescapable: Europe from the seventh through the tenth centuries was very busy putting in place the various pieces of a new economic system, one that went beyond being merely what was left after the removal of the urban-commercial element. The new economy was emerging in its own right as a well-organized, working entity, built now upon a largely local and self-sufficient agriculture.

This local agrarian order, exactly like the new political order that it so closely resembled, was a more or less obvious response to the requirements of the age. For whatever reasons, the Roman economy had collapsed, leaving few choices. If the framework that had encompassed the network of specialization and traded surpluses could not be restored, and it could not, then the West either might have done what it did, that is, turn to locally self-sufficient agriculture, or sunk still further to an even less sophisticated economy based on hunting and gathering. The West responded in time, and with an impressive organization. This may have been a dark age with regard to learning—without surpluses and trade there could be little cultural production—but we should not think of it as a dark age with regard to economics. The economy was a rather quiet one. Nevertheless, it was in place, and it worked. And not only did it work, but also it was nearly indestructible. True, individual units could be destroyed, as they so frequently were by the raids in the later Carolingian period of the weakened West's many enemies, but because these units were not interdependent the whole survived.

If the general characteristics of the medieval economy were the result of a predictable response to the new circumstances, so too were many of the specific forms. For example, it was probably inevitable that slave labor be replaced by serf rather than free labor. Very small farms with a free peasantry would have been hard to protect. Largish farms, the manors, worked much better. Serfs were in a sense slaves whose status had been improved sufficiently to make it worthwhile for them to have children. Therefore serfdom or something rather like it was a likely development. The linkage of the manorial structure to the feudal structure was also logical. Likewise, each of the technical innovations was more or less foreseeable. The heavy plow that permitted the cultivation of the richer valley soils; the three-field method of crop rotation, with the accompanying introduction of new protein-rich vegetables; the more extensive use of fertilizers; and the three aimed at replacing the slower ox with the horse, that is, the horse shoe, collar, and tandem harness—all of these were the reasonable by-products of a society now devoted almost exclusively to agriculture. Although perhaps not individually predictable, the innovations were clearly prompted by the new circumstances.

By the year 1000, then, a medieval economy had been created that was capable of providing, if not elegantly, for Western society. It was in a sense almost the exact opposite of the classical economy that it had replaced. In this regard it was very much like the other major parts of the West's civilization that had evolved with it. Style, thought, politics, and economics had moved together from their classical to their medieval forms. As we have seen, in the course of doing that they had radically altered their features. The West had exchanged naturalism, humanism, imperialism, and specialization for abstraction, theism, localism, and self-sufficiency. And now the long process of devolution had finally been brought to an end. This was the West's second great transition, and like the first it had taken roughly a millennium, from the first century through the tenth. Also like the first, the transition had been temporarily interrupted: the period of classical revival had tried to bring it to a halt. But it could not. In no regard had the West been able to manage more than a temporary return to the classical forms. Soon it had continued in its evolution toward the new order, which was finally achieved during the centuries of the early Middle Ages. This early medieval period and thus the Middle Ages themselves we can date from the point in the evolution at which the West had become more medieval—that is, abstract, theist, local, and self-sufficient—than classical—that is, naturalistic, humanistic, imperialistic, and specialized— therefore sometime in the sixth century.

What had been accomplished? A great deal. Rome, which had become something of a monster, an imperial ogre resting on the backs of a vast slave population with an ever-larger army able to provide ever-less security, had been replaced by a system that provided greater equity, probably better average nutrition, and more protection, if not always for the individual at least for the civilization. The West had descended to a level where it had found survival certain. Obviously a great deal had also been lost. The Classical Age had about it much that was undeniably attractive. And the good had gone with the bad. Yet there were reasons to be satisfied with what had been achieved by the end of the first millennium A.D. Perhaps the best testimony to the positive aspects is the fact that at just that moment a new phase of civilizational growth began. What late Rome had not been able to accomplish the early Middle Ages could. For it was at this point that the third great transition began. From the tenth and eleventh centuries until the late nineteenth and early twentieth, when its momentum in turn would fail, the modern impulse would run its course.

4

From the Middle Ages
to the Modern Age

For some time now medievalists have been arguing that both the culture and the society of the Modern Age did not make their appearance suddenly at the time of the Renaissance, but rather that their early forms can be found in various stages of development beginning in the eleventh century. Of course it is also correct to point out that medieval forms lasted well beyond the Renaissance.[1] Obviously the process of transformation was a lengthy one. Further, like the two grand movements that preceded it—the first, again, took the West from the primitive condition to the classical and the second from the classical to the medieval—it did not evolve smoothly. The creation of the modern world out of its medieval predecessor was accomplished only convulsively, in fits and starts. Periods of growth and advancing modernism, usually of considerable duration, were followed by shorter but often violent ones of reaction and retreat. To be sure, the gains were never entirely offset by the losses, so that the work of building the modern forms went on, despite the uneven course. And eventually the new came to prevail over the old, from which point, around 1500, we date the beginnings of the Modern Age itself.

If we preview these alternating periods of development and regression, then they can be said to run roughly as follows: there were first somewhat more than three centuries, starting around 1000, of remarkable innovation. This period of growth was then followed by what is usually referred to as the crisis of the fourteenth century, which had become acute by about 1350 and endured until perhaps 1450. Then another period of renewed growth followed, from ca. 1450 to ca. 1550, this one tipping the balance and occasioning a new age, which is only to say that in retrospect it would seem that from some point in this century the West can be said to be no longer more medieval than modern, but now rather more modern than medieval—just as a millennium earlier it had reached a point at which it was more medieval than classical. This expansion was in turn followed by the crisis of the seventeenth century, during which once again the West experienced across-the-board reversals.

Although severe, these were not finally sufficient to prevent for long modern cultural and societal conventions from continuing to expand. The latter part of the seventeenth century already saw a revival, which continued through most of the eighteenth century. There then occurred yet another period of reversal, one that lasted approximately half a century, from ca. 1780 to ca. 1830, known with regard to its cultural content as the Romantic era. Next came yet another period of expansion. This one endured for most of the nineteenth century and has continued in many regards into the twentieth—and no doubt its traces will be found even in the next century. As we noted earlier, however, the late nineteenth century brought a new, much more serious attack on modernism. For this one swept aside its culture and now would seem to be inaugurating a corresponding reconstitution of society. In short, the twentieth century gives every appearance of bringing to an end the long modern journey upward. The force of expansionary, creative modernism has been at last dissipated. The Modern Age will no doubt continue until it is replaced. But the turning point, it is being suggested here, has been reached.

These, then, are the chronological divisions into which the West's march toward the modern can be broken down. The civilization as a whole conformed to them. This is not to imply, however, that Western history during this long evolution was all of a piece, adhering always to these generalizations. There have been many variations on the theme. For example, the major national states, whose histories have generally been consistent with the periodization as outlined here, have nevertheless reached their respective peaks of power at very different times, Spain in the sixteenth century, France in the seventeenth, Britain in the nineteenth, and Germany, Russia, and the United States in the twentieth.

Also, the several categories into which we divide the civilizational story might be said to have reached maturity independently. Thus style with regard to painting, sculpture, and architecture had made the full transition from the medieval to the modern by the sixteenth century. It could thereafter not become more modern without declining in quality. It had peaked. The modern style in music, however, did not peak until the early eighteenth century. And modern thought did not reach a comparable point until the mid-eighteenth, modern political forms until the nineteenth, and the modern economy, at least with regard to size, until the twentieth. The various strands, then, took turns at the center of the stage. Still, the general rhythms prevailed.

Perhaps it should be added here that neither this essay's efforts at generalization nor its conclusion, which again, is that our modern world is now entering upon a period of decline, should be permitted to obscure the modern accomplishment. There is indeed something magnificent in this rising from the ashes. No matter how appreciative one is with regard to the early medieval creation, the story of the working out of the modern impulse has a heroic element. We need not deny that, even when we regret it. With that said, we can turn to a history of style, the first of the four categories into which this review has been divided, as style found its way from its medieval to its modern forms.

STYLE

The overall change in the West's style as it proceeded from its medieval to its modern essentials is clear enough: it was a matter of replacing the relatively abstract and vertical tendencies with naturalism and a new horizontal principle. Yet the very first period, that beginning around 1000, was unique in that it tried hard to move in two directions at once. With the advent of expansion, these centuries in all areas represented indeed the first step toward the modern. Yet the immediate interest was in working toward a further refinement and more articulate expression of the medieval ideals that had only so recently been fully embodied. The result was a peculiar mixture of elements. One can see it especially clearly with regard to style. The new Gothic conventions that began to appear in the eleventh century were in many ways essentially medieval, the logical culmination of the development of a religious style. Certainly they represented the continuation of the tendency to the vertical that is visible since the later Roman centuries. But, as we have already observed, there was also a good bit of the new, countermedieval tendency active in the Gothic. It may have been an art aspiring to God, but the effort was a very calculated and rational one, the work of a powerful, protohumanist mind imposing its order on God's world. Also the Gothic was an urban product, a creation of the newly important towns, in direct contrast to the rural Romanesque. There were even a few secular buildings, mostly guild and town halls, among its production. The most notable of these prefigurations of modern style, however, was Gothic Realism. For the first time since the days of Greek and Roman naturalism, the human face was sculpted with a high regard for its personal features. The result is somewhat uncanny, as these modern, realistically portrayed men and women stare out at us from their places within the medieval Gothic cathedral.[2]

That the Gothic was not wholly a medieval style, but rather a medieval style that was taking its first steps toward the modern, made it entirely appropriate to the other lines of the West's development between 1000 and 1350. The West was moving again, and that fact was reflected in every area.

But then, beginning in the fourteenth century, indeed, in some places even during the second half of the thirteenth, the growth came to an end. Europe was now to be forced to endure some remarkable setbacks. The most dramatic of these reversals was with regard to the demographic curve, as the Black Death, which began in 1347, reduced Europe's population severely. While we shall be concerned later with other manifestations of this crisis, here our focus is on style. And one can only say that a distinct style, fitting this century of confusion and only this century, did not appear. Instead, one finds a late form of Gothic along side increasing signs of the new naturalism of the coming Renaissance, the latter of course especially noticeable in Italy.

But if there was not a distinct style, certainly there was a distinct mood, a mixture of frenzy, decadence, and despair.[3] Ornamentation became overly elaborate, overripe, as it were, and death as a theme figured prominently, as in the very explicit depictions of putrefaction that were now among the habitual subjects. No doubt this morbidity can be explained by the horror of the Plague. And yet there is more to it than that. The medieval way of life was disintegrating. Those solutions worked out with so much difficulty in the millennium before 1000 were now found to be hindrances. They were being rejected in favor of yet newer solutions. Tension and anxiety were inevitable in this time of transition. Even without the Black Death, Europe, and of course its art, would have reflected these.[4]

Soon enough, however, the crisis was over, and the West returned to the work of building the modern world. The aesthetic result, apparent from the middle of the fifteenth century, was the style of the Renaissance. At first much more visible in Italy, by the early sixteenth century it would dominate northern Europe as well. In neither painting nor sculpture nor architecture was there of course a true renaissance, that is, a rebirth of the very same classical forms. Still, a great deal was borrowed, and certainly this new style was of the same spirit. Greek and Roman style had been naturalistic, and so was that of the Renaissance. The Greeks and Romans had focused on the human individual, and so did the new artists. And of course the architecture of the Renaissance was tremendously indebted to its classical models. The overall effect in all aspects of Renaissance style was to establish the new art as a revised edition of the old. It is surprising how little of the medieval heritage finally survived. It had been very much apparent in early Renaissance style. Western painting, for example, from Giotto through Botticelli had reflected an integration of new and old. However, once the style of the High Renaissance had been achieved, it meant the almost total expulsion of the medieval remnant. The arrival of the mature Renaissance forms occasioned nearly a clean break—although again not, to be sure, the total break that would have signified the end of one civilization and the beginning of another—with the dominant style of the Middle Ages and its replacement by the style of the Modern Age.

In the course of the discussion of the crisis that style has experienced in the twentieth century, the outlines of the history from this point on, from, that is, the coming of the Modern Age, have already been briefly described. To the extent that they are reproduced here, it is in order to place the development within the larger context of the evolution of the modern style from its medieval starting point. By roughly 1500, then, the Modern Age with regard to style had begun. But no sooner was the modern style established than it was distinctly altered by the distortions of the mannerist, baroque, and rococo periods that together captivated the late sixteenth century and much of the seventeenth. These were the stylistic manifestations of the general civilizational convulsion that afflicted the West just then. High naturalism gave way to sensual and psychological, even mystical, attitudes. And there was again a sudden passion for the ornate. The forthright approach of the Renaissance was being for the moment bent to the purposes of complexity, subtlety, and obfuscation.

This mood, however, was also to pass. The modern impulse was too strong, it could not be more than interrupted. Classicism again won out, toward the end of the seventeenth century, this time to be known as neoclassicism. As such it became the basic style of modernism. Until overthrown by the great stylistic revolution of the twentieth century, it remained the prevailing style of the West. The Romantic decades of the late eighteenth and early nineteenth centuries did not, as noted before, do much to alter it. There was a certain blurring of the naturalistic outlines in painting. Perhaps more significant, even menacing with regard to the prospects for modernism, one could observe an occasional experiment in architecture with imported, non-Western forms.[5] But Romanticism did not, any more than had the baroque, attempt a real revolution against modernism.

Music is here something of an exception. Its Romantic works were clearly more extreme than the corresponding visual stylistic expressions. But in general music had been slower to develop, and perhaps that accounts for the fact that when it at last did react against classicism, it was with more vigor. It had not had much of a baroque reaction, for the baroque in music, as Aldous Huxley once noted, is simply the mature form of the musical innovations made during the Renaissance—their complexities apparently required a longer period to develop.[6] Thus the baroque phase produced not a reaction, but instead ushered in the greatest modern period. When, then, music entered upon its Romantic phase, the reaction was more profound than in painting and sculpture. Such anomalies again remind us of the difficulties inherent in any effort to draw firm boundaries with regard to civilizational history.

Yet whatever the effects of Romanticism on Western style, they are hardly perceptible beyond the Romantic decades themselves. Romanticism made a lot of noise for a while and then quit. And the middle of the nineteenth century saw an almost full restoration of neoclassicism. This was the time when the effort to make the West's cities over in the classical image was at its most impressive. Tremendous building programs, extending from Europe to America and even beyond to those parts of the non-Western world upon which the West was now impacting, carried on the programs of the Renaissance and Enlightenment. There could be no better testimony to the respect that this rejuvenated classical world had for the old. For a time the West's cities—contemptuous of their medieval past and not yet ready for postmodern innovation—were to become truly neoclassical, with classical sculpture and buildings adorning classical boulevards that were delineated by classical grid plans.[7] If it was difficult to improve on the quality of the revived forms as the sixteenth century had first defined them, it was certainly possible to extend the quantity to reshape entirely the urban scene. Athens and Rome, as once before, were reconstructed in the provinces, this time on the banks of the Spree, the Danube, the Seine, the Thames, and the Potomac, and on and on into the interior.

The middle of the nineteenth century also saw in painting and sculpture the return to a full naturalism. Nature in three dimensions, sharp and clear, and the human face and figure as they look to the eye, these were the subjects of this period of realism that was to be the last phase of a purely modern art. But it is true, as noted earlier, that realism's rather off-center interests suggested that naturalism might be nearing its end. Also, the inclination of realism to begin to wonder about higher realities was dangerous to its basically secular assumptions. Philosophical realism, which argued that the idea of the thing is necessarily of a higher reality than the thing itself, was beginning to replace as the thought behind the style the naturalistic realism that had been content not to look beyond this world. As that happened, artists began to seek some sort of sign of that higher reality within the subject matter—for want of any better notion, a ball or a cube or perhaps a cone—and thus their portrayals came more and more to resemble the abstractions themselves. Thus naturalism began to suffer from the very efforts that were to make it more vital.

This contrary effect can likewise be seen with regard to the pursuit of an exact rendition of light and its effects. Light—in art as in physics the subject of the ultimate quest, the attempt to fit in the last piece of the modern puzzle—was carefully inspected to find out just how it worked.

Did it appear in nature with imperceptible shadings or in distinct blotches? and so on. As the questions resulted in theories and then as the theories became more dear than the naturalistic style that they had been intended to enhance, a new style started to develop within the old. Realism, then, seems to have contained the seeds of its own destruction. Yet in the middle of the nineteenth century it still prevailed, and along with it, of course, naturalism and the modern tradition. Outwardly, at least, the Renaissance was intact.

But the changes once they began to emerge occurred very rapidly. Consider the evolution in painting: in the half-century from 1860 to 1910 the West dropped realism for impressionism, then briefly took to expressionism, and finally settled for cubism, the first school in which the essentials of postmodern style gained the upper hand. For with cubism painting crossed the fuzzy line that separates the naturalistic from the abstract.

Impressionism and expressionism, we should make clear before going on, had only been halfway houses. One, to be sure, would not wish to ignore their contribution to a new art. Both had been testing grounds for those theories that inquired into the nature of light and the reality beyond reality. Both had been radically innovative, meddling considerably with the natural outlines. The impressionists by their insistence on blurring shapes had done more than any school since the victory of the modern style to alter naturalism. Neither the baroque nor the Romantic had gone so far. And expressionist experimentation with distortion then went even further.

Yet these two movements belonged to the modern tradition. One could still say of their faces, figures, and landscapes, yes, I know that person, I recognize that view. It is true that the advice of Stéphane Mallarmé (1842–98) to the new generation of writers spoke of the charms of evocation, allusion, and suggestion.[8] The direct approach to the natural world was giving way to one oblique and hinting. It was still, however, the natural world that was being approached.

But with cubism we are in a different world. Here the abstraction came first, and its relationship to the natural was tenuous, even unnecessary. Cubism, like all of the abstract art that was to follow, broke with the commitment that the modern style—the style, that is, of the Modern Age—had undertaken to portray nature. A new postnaturalist style was born, one that has provided the single most consistent element in the art of the twentieth century.

With regard to architecture, the new antimodern style had developed its basic forms well before World War I, but its occasional manifestations had as yet done little to alter the look of the West's cities. Then, during the interwar years, there was a rush to innovate. And by mid-century Western architecture, as said earlier, had been revolutionized. The neoclassical city was rapidly disappearing behind the rising skyscraper, with its clean, postmodern facades, and every mall and complex rushed to assume the new look. Suddenly the West had taken on a radically different appearance. From the strip pop-architecture of the sprawling suburbs to the gleaming towers of the inner city, the new style now prevailed.

Thus the modern style in all areas came to an end. After almost a millennium of development and half a millennium of dominance, it had been replaced by a very different style. In painting and sculpture, naturalism had succumbed to abstraction. To the extent that the human figure survived, it either had had its parts rearranged or was shot through with holes.[9] In architecture, the neoclassical columns, capitals, and friezes had been removed and replaced with the smooth steel, concrete, and glass surfaces of functionalism. And the horizontal lines of the older city were now broken by the new verticalism. In music, the rhythms and harmonies of the fifteenth through the nineteenth centuries had given way to new conventions in which there were few guidelines. And although the talk here has been mostly of art, in literature style also had undergone its own revolution, having passed, as noted in chapter 1, from rational order to the rejection of rational order.

Why had a tradition of such long duration been so suddenly dispensed with? And not with regard only to this or that field, but across the board, in painting, sculpture, architecture, music, and literature, and throughout the West as well? One can be more certain of the wrong answers than the right. It is, for example, obviously wrong that the revolutions in each area of style were arrived at for internal reasons. They all came together and therefore almost certainly are the work of something outside themselves. Nor is it likely that it was the doing of style itself, because there is nothing there either to act or to act upon: style has a history, but only a history. As it unfolds it is in the hands of its components. One becomes a painter, sculptor, architect, or musician. One cannot become a stylist. Perhaps if critics were given the function of creating, then we would have stylists, but they are not. When we speak of the style of a period or an age, we mean only that there is a common essence that can be observed in the several disciplines.

Was, then, this new style the product of the new thought? No, it could not have been. The chronology is not right, for while the significant changes happened generally contemporaneous to the revolution in thought, they were as often before as after. Further, the events in the corresponding developments in thought were too muddled to have dictated such a consistent conversion of style. And only toward the end of the process did a few very insightful intellectuals, Ortega y Gasset and T. E. Hulme among them, begin to comprehend what was taking place—that is, that the style of the Modern Age was making its exit.[10]

Then what of society and its effects? Were there changes in the societal structure that occasioned the revolution in style? Certainly nothing as fundamental as these sweeping changes could escape the influence of society. Yet how could the West's societal history, up to this point essentially continuous, account for something so lacking in continuity? If there were in the modern centuries up until this time interruptions with regard to economic growth, these were, as we shall see, always surmounted, with growth finally continuing; and if there were political revolutions, these almost invariably attempted to advance the modern conception of society. There is no easy answer. Again, the suggestion here is that the revolution in style that wiped out the old modern and replaced it with something radically new records a turn in the direction of the civilization itself, one that may be noticed earlier in some areas, usually the cultural, but is taking place and must certainly eventually be recorded in all areas. In a sense, style is like a seismograph, finely sensitized, set to monitor volcanic activity. The needle flurries long before the slides hit the bottom of the mountain. Seismographs, of course, do not cause erruptions. They are only able to record here above the surface the dynamic activity taking place far below. And these particular rumblings appear to have been caused not by the continuing work of the thousand-year modern expansion, but rather by something more profound, the powerful contractions that are bringing that course to an end and reversing it. The revolution in style can be said, then, to be related not to the changes in society that have so far caused revolutions—those, again, have been the revolutions of modernism, of the Modern Age—but to those dislocations that are apt to provoke the revolutions yet to come. To put it another way, one could say that today's stylistic conventions are not the product of today's dominant societal modes, but rather the product of tomorrow's, already present but not yet mature and still subordinate.

THOUGHT

Taking the history of thought during this same millennium, that which extends from the tenth century to the twentieth, what can be said with regard to an overview? The fundamental transition is again obvious: the West's world view evolved from otherworldly humility to humanism, from, that is, the religious, salvation-oriented concerns of Augustinian Christianity to the secular-oriented concerns of optimistic modernism. And then eventually, toward the very end, that humanism failed. For all the meanderings, these were the essential changes, their development evolving in the same pattern of ebb and flow that is found in all modern phenomena: to repeat, first a period (ca. 1000–1350) during which the modern elements were introduced; then a reaction (ca. 1350–1450); next a period (ca. 1450–1550) during which those modern elements became predominant, thus marking the advent of the Modern Age itself; then another reaction (ca. 1550–1650); then a long phase of modern ascendance (ca. 1650–1900) punctuated only by the Romantic interlude (ca. 1780–1830); and finally the onset of the destruction of the modern elements in the late nineteenth and early twentieth centuries. Such a summary leaves out the many exceptions, of course, and is helpful only in so far as it is used as a guide to the prevailing patterns. But one can apologize too much for insisting on such a periodization.

The first of these periods in the history of the West's transition from medieval to modern thought, that which corresponds to the era of the Gothic, was occupied with the heroic effort to reconcile reason and faith. Faith was the inheritance from the early Middle Ages. It had been accepted as a means of knowing in defiance of reason. The Christian message was inherently antirational. "I believe because it is impossible" had been something of a motto for these centuries: the greater the assault upon reason, the greater the testimony to an unassailable faith.[11] Only by treating secular knowledge—that is, insights about the natural world obtained by the senses and analyzed by reason—with the greatest skepticism could this supernatural system be preserved.

And preserved it was, for more than six centuries, from the time of St. Augustine until the first effective challenges after 1000. In the annals of thought, that is a remarkable record. But of course the durability of these assumptions was much assisted by the level of literacy. To mount more than a passing assault on a prevailing world view, one must be able to write, and few could. Also of course the static nature of early medieval society favored a static theology. For a long time, various factors conspired to insure a relatively stable intellectual climate.

Then with the turn of the millennium thought, along with everything else, began a search for new ways. The West was no longer satisfied with the old answers. Faith's exclusive monopoly of knowledge was found to be—well, unreasonable. It should share with the rational approach the burden of explanation, and not just for the trivial secular truths, but for the fundamental questions concerning the existence and nature of God as well. No subject was now too sacred. Reason had been given to man to use, according to the new theory, and use it he must, or God would be offended. That did not mean he was to use it wrongly, and to arrive at any conclusion not sanctioned by the main tenets of dogma was to demonstrate obvious error. After all, God-given reason and God-given revelation would necessarily always agree. Reason was not being introduced to challenge faith, but to reinforce it. There was to be no harm done to Christianity, it was only to be enriched. Thus for as long as this Scholastic Synthesis (as this joining of reason and faith by the Christian scholastics of the twelfth and thirteenth centuries is called) was able to hold together, there was no significant damage.

However, the bringing of the two into the same camp was a risky experiment. There is certainly something admirable in this attempt at reconciling mankind's two major systems of knowledge, the intuitional-religious with the rational-empirical, but the former was extremely vulnerable to the extent that it had made its truths explicit.[12] And by this time, of course, so many centuries after the Church fathers had begun the work of dogmatization, Christian faith had become very explicit indeed. Why, therefore, did the Christian West undertake reconciliation? Again, as with so many of the big questions, we do not seem to be able to provide a conclusive answer. One possibility is summed up in the contemporary phrase, *"Stadtluft macht frei"*. Town air makes you free. It was not just runaway serfs who found freedom in the growing towns of this period. The towns represented the forces of change within the old order and tended to opt for novelty; and reason was novel. Also, it has been said, businessmen had a greater need for logic and calculation, in short, for reason, than did the lords of the manor. Perhaps. Once can also note that reason at just this time became more available—reason, that is, as a formal methodology—as contact with the Arabs increased. The Arabs had throughout the early Middle Ages maintained a higher level of culture and had even managed to preserve more of the Western philosophical tradition than had the West itself. Now the Arabs instructed the West in its own Aristotelian heritage.

But regardless of the specific channels whereby reason reentered the West after its long absence, it was no doubt almost inevitable that it would do so one way or another as Europe began to revive. Given the continuities that bound the early Middle Ages to its classical past, it would have been remarkable had the rejuvenating West ignored Greek and Roman thought. Since the Church was the chief guardian of that tradition, and that despite its quarrels with it, it is not surprising that rationalism first made its appearance within theology. These explanations have, however, an awkward quality, for they smack of tautology. All we know is that the West did reintroduce reason; and that, yes, it was a risky experiment. For once reason had been reintroduced, it would be very difficult to control, especially if the social changes that were apparently favoring the employment of the logical approach continued.

Before long, however, there occurred a period of interruption. No sooner had St. Thomas Aquinas (d. 1274), building on the work of Anselm, Abelard, and Albertus Magnus, put the final pieces of this fragile synthesis in place than an attack was mounted on it. The fourteenth century was destructive, as much so with regard to thought as to everything else.[13] The challenges came from opposite corners: from, on the one hand, a new enthusiasm for the mystical approach to God, which disdained the presumption that Divine Truth was accessible to reason; and from, on the other, a more careful attitude to secular knowledge, which demanded that assumptions be dependent not on faith, but rather on experience. Europe was witnessing at the same time both a revival of the earlier antiintellectualism and the stirrings of the scientific world view. It was a confusing era. Medieval faith and modern empiricism seemed to join hands to defeat the scholastic use of reason; and yet there was very little agreement on with what to replace it. In previous centuries, the papacy might have been expected to have made a choice and been fairly effective in enforcing it. But not in the fourteenth, distinguished by its papal disintegration, with the papacy first the captive of the French kings (1309–77) and then hopelessly divided during the Great Schism (1378–1417).[14]

Then in the fifteenth century, especially toward the end, a new pattern began to emerge as the Renaissance and its new modern thought came to prevail. In the discussion of the crisis of thought in the twentieth century we have already reviewed the essentials of the modern outlook, and that in order to show that the West is now moving beyond it. Here, as with style, we have arrived at our subject from the other direction, from that of its origins. And this offers an opportunity to say something more about it, putting it in the context of its medieval past. Only within that context can some of modern thought's complexities be explained.

This is true especially with regard to the popularity of Neoplatonism in this first period in which the modern spirit in thought can be said to have prevailed. The modern mind, again to summarize it, has been secular, rational, and humanist, a new version of the classical mind—that dominant classical mind, that is, represented by Aristotle. Therefore the Renaissance, one would think, should have continued the Aristotelian revival begun by the Schoolmen. It found itself, however, in opposition to Scholasticism. And because of that it seems to have seen in Plato a more proper classicism, unadulterated by the tamperings of the medieval theologians whom the Renaissance humanists despised. In the search for an authentic classical philosopher, the Renaissance came to Plato, ironically the least classical of classical thinkers. Yet if Plato was not in all ways the perfect model for the humanism of the Renaissance intellectuals, they managed to find in him what they wanted. There is in fact a legitimate humanist element in his concern for the secular life. Plato's true philosopher may yearn for the death that will free him to soar to the immaterial world of forms, but The Republic, after all, is devoted to planning for the here and now.

Another interesting confusion in early modern thought is to be found in the new science. The more we learn of medieval scientific efforts, the clearer become the connections of Renaissance science to its immediate past history. If this modern scientific interest in the natural world's inner workings was a part of the revival of classicism, then that revival had been gradually taking place since at least the eleventh century. When the astronomy of Copernicus, the anatomy of Vesalius, and the mechanics of Leonardo finally burst upon the world, they had had a thorough preparation. But in the course of it they had also inherited much of the medieval world view, as can be seen, for example, in Copernicus's arguments for the heliocentric theory: putting the sun at the center simplified things, and God preferred simple solutions—hardly a scientific conclusion.

The entire modern intellectual fabric was shot through with similar contradictions. Still, there is no mistaking the predominance of the themes that we traditionally associate with the Renaissance. For all of the lingering influence of the Christian heritage, there was an obvious concentration on the natural world and a new confidence that it could be known and controlled for the benefit of mankind. These attitudes were especially apparent with regard to education, the goal of which was now taken to be preparation for an active participation in the arts and politics. A sound mind in a sound body replaced service to the Church and salvation of the soul as the purpose of schooling. If there was a blemish upon human nature left behind by Original Sin, then, as Milton could promise, education would remove it.[15] Likewise, the medieval preoccupation with theology was gradually transformed into a concern for ethics. Dogmatic considerations in general were becoming less important, as the Erasmian emphasis on moral behavior took hold.

These were, of course, revolutionary changes. Even if the modern ideas were not sudden creations, their essential features had been during the period of their initial development obscured and nicely contained within the prevailing Christian schemes. Now that they were out in the open and operating independently, they formed a threat to the old order that not all were willing to let pass without resistance. Even at the peak of the Renaissance in the first half of the sixteenth century, voices were raised in protest. The most prominent of these was Martin Luther's.

For Luther was an opponent of modern thought. He argued against free will, condemned reason and science, and opposed the spread of secularism. And as the reaction he both inherited and did his best to exacerbate became more acute, the West's intellectual mood changed once again. For a century, from roughly 1550 until 1650, Europe experienced wave after wave of religious counterrevolt.[16] Nor, as it turned out, was it only the Protestants who objected to the Renaissance. There was a Catholic reformation as well, and although the strength of its protest was diluted by the commitment to Thomism—that is to say, because Catholicism had accepted Aquinas's joining of reason to faith, it could not follow Protestantism in its return to a full Augustinian fundamentalism—nevertheless Catholicism backed out of its previous alliance with humanism in order to reaffirm its religious priorities. As further evidence of the multidenominational nature of the reaction, there was the witch-craze, which now captivated all of Europe. Protestants and Catholics could unite in their common conviction that witches were all around—and, it went without saying, that those unregenerate should be burned.[17]

The interest in witches was of course only the homely aspect of an era in which the paramount importance of the supernatural was again an ardently held belief. The fourteenth century had witnessed the phenomenon, and now the seventeenth also did. At both times the West had recoiled from its modernist strivings, and the results were very similar, as a general return to supernaturalist assumptions for the moment interrupted the movement toward the fully modern position. It would seem that in both instances the pace of change was suddenly felt to be too rapid and thus too damaging. If the aversion to modernism was even more acute in the seventeenth century than in the fourteenth, it is no doubt due to the fact that just before the fourteenth the modern position had for the first time been clearly defined. The twelfth and thirteenth centuries had tried to pretend that nothing was happening; but the fifteenth and sixteenth centuries had boasted that everything was happening. The West could not accept so much so quickly.

This seventeenth-century reaction, in this regard also very much like its fourteenth-century counterpart, was not, however, effective beyond its time. After the seventeenth century, or, more accurately, after the period that ran from the late sixteenth century through the middle of the seventeenth, the West began to incline toward secular humanism once again. Not everywhere, to be sure. There were areas, especially those remote from the cultural core—which at this time extended roughly from Rome northwest through France and the lower Rhineland to London—in which the reaction lingered on well into the eighteenth century. One thinks, for example, of Puritan New England, and there were many others: Presbyterian Scotland, Counter-Reformation Spain, Orthodox Russia, and more. But within that core, where the debates that the rest of the West would somewhat later emulate were taking place, the intellectual disposition was now, from about 1650 on, once again more clearly to modernism. Just as the West's style at this point moved beyond its baroque reaction and went on to a revival of classicism, Western thought now put aside its doubts regarding the humanist world view and entered upon the final stages in the process of its assimilation. It is from the later seventeenth century that we date the Enlightenment, which appeared first in England, where John Locke was its great advocate; and it was the work of that movement to spread the doctrines of secular humanism among the West's intellectual leadership.

The Enlightenment, despite its English and late-seventeenth-century origins, is generally associated with France and the eighteenth century, and rightly so. For it was there and then that modern thought revealed itself most articulately. The Italian Renaissance had put forward a rough draft. The German Reformation then attacked it. The English proto-Enlightenment of the late seventeenth century, overcoming the religious objections, began to give modernism its final formulation. It was left to the French Enlightenment of the eighteenth century to complete the work. And a prodigious work of completion it was. Not since the fifth century B.C. had there been such a flood of writing devoted to understanding and evaluating mankind and the natural world. The doubts that had still beset many of the thinkers of the second half of the seventeenth century—"on thy knees, powerless reason," Pascal had defiantly commanded—were now all but swept aside.[18] The enthusiasts of the Enlightenment instructed a West that was increasingly ready to learn. "At once the gadflies and representatives of their age, the philosophes," as Peter Gay has put it, "preached to a Europe half prepared to listen to them"; and, we can add, to an America as well.[19] Even those groups which originally resisted were for the most part in the process of becoming converted, and would largely succumb in the course of the nineteenth and twentieth centuries—with the last holdouts surrendering, to be sure, just as new waves of intellectuals started to make known their disenchantment. For the time being, however, the Enlightenment's world view was vastly appealing, a modern dogma for a modern age, a program, again to quote Gay, "of secularism, humanity, cosmopolitanism, and freedom, above all, freedom in its many forms—freedom from arbitrary power, freedom of speech, freedom of trade, freedom to realize one's talents, freedom of aesthetic response, freedom, in a word, of moral man to make his own way in the world."[20]

And that way would be made in good part by relying on reason. The world was natural, not supernatural, and reason was the key to understanding it. Not faith in the unique nature of the Christian world, but reason applied to the regular and undeviating natural world would yield up what there was to be yielded, those rewards of this life beyond which the Enlightenment was not inclined to press. The Renaissance had not been particularly excited about the prospects for reason, no doubt following the same logic that had led it to Neoplatonism: opposed to Scholasticism, it found the rationalism that the scholastics had done so much to revive merely stuffy. But reason, crucial to classicism, could hardly be permanently left out of a classical rebirth. Probably the fact that the religious reformers had had so little appreciation for the rational method—Luther spoke of "that Whore Reason"—helped the eighteenth century accept it. Anything so repulsive to the Reformation could not be all that bad.[21]

So the eighteenth century became the Age of Reason. Skeptics remained, even among the more prominent enlightened thinkers. David Hume, for example, carefully explained why the natural order upon which reason depended was not after all so very dependable: within an infinity of possibilities, our expectations, based as they must be on experience drawn from only fragments of the infinite, cannot have any certainty about them. If there is a natural order, we cannot perceive it whole, and therefore our knowledge of it remains severely limited. But such honest confessions of the limits to reason deterred no one, not even, it has been noted, Hume himself.[22] Reason and its scientific extension were the sole means to power over the world conceived as a purely secular affair. If God did not intervene, as the philosophes of the first half of the eighteenth believed, or if there were no God, as the next generation tended to argue,[23] then there could be no other means. If this would seem to imply that the significance of passion was denied, then that is not the case. Passion was a part of the natural world and, balanced by reason, it was a necessary contributor to the human comedy. In a sense, passion took the place of faith in a new synthesis, this time with both parts secular.

There is another aspect of Enlightenment thought that is worth noting: from the establishment of modern thought with the victory of humanism in the fifteenth and sixteenth centuries on through the seventeenth century, the golden age to which the present looked lay in the past, with the original classicism of Greece and Rome. In the eighteenth century, however, the view swung round and was directed toward the future. The convention of assuming that the contemporary states of culture and society could be at best inferior imitations of those which had gone before was being replaced by a quite different assumption. Now the present was coming to be seen as a step toward a better future. It has been suggested that the Modern Age took the Christian expectation of a glorious life after death and merely secularized it. That may be true, or it could be that such an outlook was an outgrowth of the modern expansionist tendencies apparent in all areas. Certainly the idea of progress, to paraphrase the old General Electric ad, was to become one of our more important products. For the sense of building toward a better future has been a, perhaps the, crucial motivator of modern man.[24]

If modern art, as said a moment ago, was done in its purest form during the Renaissance, then it was during the Enlightenment that modern thought reached the corresponding point in its evolution. Coming fresh from Newton's pulling together of the work of the earlier modern centuries (the *Principia* was published in 1687), the faith in science among the philosophes was intense. The new thought, following its empirical-rationalist principles, would reshape society to lasting advantage. If there were now also moments of despair—Voltaire's *Candide* (1759) was the product of one of these—nevertheless the prevailing mood of these thinkers was one of optimism.[25] Among the West's intellectuals the modernist position would never again be as consistently and as vigorously represented.

For already in the latter decades of the eighteenth century Western thought had begun to veer in another direction. A reaction against the Enlightenment became increasingly pronounced, and by ca. 1790 it had gained the upper hand. This was the Romantic Movement, the first of several major attacks upon the mature modernism. Until ca. 1830, those conclusions that had been more or less agreed upon by the Enlightenment thinkers were fiercely rebutted: dedication to reason gave way to a preference for feeling, the yearning for order to a new enthusiasm for disorder, and the commitment to enlightenment via clarification to an appreciation of the delights of the ambiguous. The Romantics turned away from the common-sensical world of the philosophes and tried to recapture some of the mystery that modern thought had dispelled.[26]

At the same time, there were significant attempts to order that mystery, that, for example, of Rousseau. Rousseau, who can be described as either the last of the philosophes or first of the Romantics, is often thought of in connection with his condemnation of the civilized society of the Modern Age, and condemn it he did. However, it should be remembered that he did not stop there and went on to try to show how a proper civilized society might be reconstructed, so that it might take into account not only mankind's rational potential but also his intuitional-emotional capacity. And far from being the unfettered creation of a free spirit, the result turned out to be surprisingly tightly structured. There was a certainty about Rousseau's general will, the final summation of the authentic desires of all individual wills, that lent itself to authoritarian, even conservative usage.

Kant also made a contribution to setting limits to the Romantic drift toward the chaotic. There were those who were ready to pick up where Hume had left off by denying that any knowledge of the secular world was possible, even questioning the existence of the physical matter that the mind seemed to observe. But Kant was not disposed to such radical views. Rather, he turned the Romantic interest in the subjective element into a device for restoring a measure of certainty about the objective world, insisting that the individual brings with him to the act of perceiving nature inherent standards and categories that permit him to form a coherent picture of reality. Whether it is a true picture is another matter, but it is at least one that is logical and effective. Kant put modern thought back in business. He found in the Romantic critique of the Enlightenment a way to negate some of the damage done by the Enlightenment to its own hopes for reason. Kant took a step beyond the world view of the philosophes in order to preserve its essence: the ability of the human understanding, unaided by divine help, to make sense of the natural world.

Hegel likewise contributed to the demonstration that Romantic inclinations need not be destructive to order. Proceeding from a fundamental Christian Neoplatonism, that Augustinianism that had remained strong throughout the history of German Protestantism, he argued that world history was nothing less than the unfolding of a divine process. But the final result was not a life beyond death, but the realization of a secular perfection, as reason, God's instrument in this world, achieved supremacy. Just to make the work even a little more orderly, Hegel pointed out that the Prussian state was ideally suited to preside over the evolution of this happy scheme. With God and country both in harmonious collaboration, whatever was was right. And yet, consistent with the Romantic challenge to the classical-modern notions of stability, Hegel had his own alternative programs: for history moved dialetically. Not only was the present endorsed as part of God's plan, but so also were the forces that were undoing it to create a new present, even if they moved, as they must, in a different direction. This was a conception of progress, but one no longer mechanistic and linear, as with the philosophes. Instead, it was organic and cyclic. Thus Hegel, in keeping with the mood of his times, took something from the Enlightenment but put it to new purposes.[27]

If one asks about the lasting effects of the Romantic reaction upon modern thought, it should be said that in the long run they were tremendous. Twentieth-century thought is permeated with Romanticism, so much so that one tends to overlook it. But it is ubiquitous, and would appear to be providing the initial elements of the postmodern world view that is replacing the modern. When we look, however, for the results of the Romantic reaction upon the period that immediately followed it—upon, that is, the middle decades of the nineteenth century—then they are not overly apparent. The Romantic attack might hold within it a tremendously destructive potential with regard to modernism, but it would seem that the immediate impact had been blunted by the extreme variety of Romantic thought. For every revolutionary, there had been a Hegel; for every antirationalist, a Kant; and for every wild-eyed Rousseauian, a Rousseau, more sober by half and not unconscious of the circumstances of power.

So the modern outlook survived the Romantic Movement. And during the half century that began around 1830 modernism enjoyed another of its periods of earnest confidence. In many ways it was the eighteenth century restored, and Franklin LeVan Baumer has very appropriately named it the New Enlightenment.[28] In some ways it even surpassed its predecessor. Undoubtedly with regard to quantity it was more impressive. There were now more schools devoted to inculcating modernist principles and everywhere more neophilosophes at work spreading the new version of enlightenment. Also significant was the fact that the bourgeoisie was increasingly making itself felt as a cultural force, for in its enthusiasm for modernism it had no peers. Then too one can note that the belief in progress was now being carried to new heights. Science, henceforth to be applied to the study of society without apology, would by abolishing ignorance provide at last the foundations upon which a secular utopia could be constructed. And the benefits were now more direct: for it was just at this time that science was bringing remarkable medical advances and revolutionizing transportation and communication. The golden future seemed to be drawing nearer by the day. The sudden acquisition of power over nature was indeed exhilarating.

Yet lurking not too far beneath the surface of this mid-nineteenth-century optimism—we noted a parallel development with regard to mid-nineteenth-century realism—there were signs that all was not well with modern thought and its world view. Not only was there a handful among the prominent men of letters who frankly opposed the Enlightenment heritage, figures such as Schopenhauer, Baudelaire, and Dostoevsky, but there were also, more significant, strains within the conceptions of the predominant secular optimists themselves that hinted at the collapse of the modern position that was soon to occur. Again, we are speaking here of the intellectuals, those who took it upon themselves to attempt to articulate the moods that would only later become apparent among the broader populations. For the bulk of the upper and upper-middle classes would seem to have harbored few doubts concerning the humanist program until well into the twentieth century, by which time humanism had become stylized as a mass culture, only then to begin to wither. Nevertheless, we need to remind ourselves as we review these changes that the main body of intellectual production almost always proves to be eventually representative of that of the entire society.

Although these early manifestations of growing dissatisfaction with modernism among its proponents appear only here and there and as fragments, they can be reduced to an essential two. First, there were the subtle changes that were taking place in the relationship between the modern world view and science. In the eighteenth century, science had been the instrument of that world view, and there had been no conflict. But in the nineteenth, science, now the producer of so many miracles, became an object of adulation in its own right. The course of empiricism could no longer be controlled. Modernist humanism and science had not parted company just yet, but clearly the latter was breaking away from its moorings and drifting out toward a foreign channel. The effects were not as obvious as they have become in the twentieth century, but they are there.

An instance is to be found in Darwin's biology. For it challenged not only traditional Christian beliefs, but also humanism itself. Even if in other regards Darwinism bolstered secularism and the idea of progress, still the theory included an unfortunate message for humanist optimism. Humankind's stature was reduced by being identified as merely one branch of life among many; and further, still worse, it must suffer from the confrontation with both its inelegant origins and uncertain future. Empiricism unchained was already beginning to demonstrate its now familiar ingratitude.

Second, there were the broader implications of evolution, which as a concept was employed far beyond the realm of biology. There had been a certain stability inherent in the modern view of things. Now that firm picture was being disturbed. Evolution meant flux, and flux returned a mysterious element that *philosophe* mechanism had sought to remove. The world was not after all like a machine. Rather, it was like a plant. And therefore it was transient and vulnerable. This insight did not overwhelm the nineteenth century. The positivistic hopes for solid, permanent improvements of the secular condition remained prominent. But at that moment at which modern imagery exchanged the closed system of physics for the open system of biology, another new idea had been set loose that would prove just as abrasive to modernism as uninstructed empiricism. Just as the West's stylistic transformation was beginning to blur the sharp outlines of the natural world as rendered on the painter's canvas, Western thought was altering its own conceptions, moving away from the precision of the Enlightenment toward something less easily defined.

The New Enlightenment nevertheless remained in most ways a true copy of the original. The better part of its representatives remained remarkably loyal to the Enlightenment's precepts, and that is especially true of both its most typical thinker, John Stuart Mill, and its most profound, Karl Marx.[29] Mill preached liberalism and Marx socialism, but the assumptions behind their respective dogmas were much the same: once the restrictions barring the way to freedom were removed, the good life here on earth would follow naturally. Mill, oddly enough, saw the need for somewhat more socialist intervention than did Marx. For Marx's vision of society after the final withering away of the state is little else than an eighteenth-century laissez-faire utopia. But both men agreed on man's essential goodness. The Enlightenment had been right. The individual was to be trusted. The West's intellectuals in these middle decades of the nineteenth century still believed in him. Even if he failed momentarily to do the right thing, there was Darwin's omnipresent natural selection—one could find in Darwin material for all sorts of arguments—to provide any needed corrections and assure progress. Clearly at this point modern thought, the product of a thousand-year evolution, was still entirely vital.

Then began the great crisis that was to destroy the assumptions upon which modern thought had built. It is difficult, as we might expect, to give a precise date for the onset of this profound change of mood. During Mill's lifetime (he died in 1873), one would have had to look closely to notice the new strains, although, as we have seen, they were present. But by the time Darwin and Marx passed from the scene a decade later, the dissent was more visible. And by the outbreak of the First World War, the bulk of the West's intellectuals seem to have convinced themselves that modernism, that world view of the Modern Age that had reached its zenith in the Enlightenment, was somehow no longer appropriate. Following the lead of the great early figures of this new movement, the most significant of which was probably Nietzsche, the attack on the modern beliefs had become stronger and stronger until modernism was swept away. Since it has been so often suggested that the war itself was the cause of the changes, it should be noted that by and large they had already occurred prior to its beginning. As Gay has insisted in commenting on the culture of the Weimar Republic, where the attack on modernism was concentrated during the twenties, the essential objections had already been made well before 1914.[30] Nisbet has made the same point with regard to the collapse of faith in progress: there has been little in the pessimism of the twentieth century that was not already articulated by the leading intellectuals of the nineteenth century, particularly Schopenhauer, Tocqueville, Burckhardt, Nietzsche, Max Weber, and Henry and Brooks Adams.[31]

We need not repeat here the discussion of the crisis in twentieth-century thought except to review the conclusions: first, modern thought has been indeed destroyed. The faith in human dignity, efficacy, and responsibility has been crushed. The priority of the secular life has been put in question. The confidence in a growing body of knowledge that would result from a rational mind working upon an orderly world has all but disappeared. The world is no longer perceived as necessarily orderly; moreover, the mind is not taken to be dependably rational. And the conviction that ongoing progress was a more or less inevitable result of the West's strivings has faded away, replaced by a general skepticism verging on despair.

But, second, the situation with regard to the creation of something that might be said to be a long-term successor to modern thought is, to say the least, ambiguous. The disappearance of modern style has been accompanied by the appearance of a distinct postmodern style. We do not with regard to style lack a substitute for the departed modern. However, one cannot as easily point to a new, postmodern world view. Modern thought is dying—with regard to the West's intellectuals, one would say dead—but the heir has not thus far come forward. Yet one is expected, and if not immediately, then in the foreseeable future. The eclectic disillusionment and sense of futility of the West's present climate of opinion will probably not last for long. Civilizations, our own certainly included, need guidelines, seek guidelines, and will find guidelines. It is interesting to speculate on just what these might be, and in the final chapter of this essay we shall do just that. Now, however, we turn to the history of society in its transition from its early medieval to its modern forms, first taking up the course of political development.

POLITICS

If we search for an underlying process in this millennial-long transition of the West from its medieval to its modern political condition, one that can match the progression to naturalism and to secular humanism in the corresponding histories of style and thought, it is no doubt to be found in the steady creation out of particularism of the institutions of centralized power. It is this theme, the process of centralization, that would seem to underly all those others—including the movements to egalitarization, emancipation, liberalism, and democracy—that we rightly associate with the coming of the Modern Age in politics. Liberty, as it happened, was in good part a derivative of power. Since the two are somewhat antithetical, there is an implicit paradox in that relationship. But the explanation is not hard to find: it was the power of the central authority that was instrumental in bringing about freedom, that is, in throwing off the restraints of the older political hierarchy. Also, to the extent that the new state was able to preside over a society that generally approved of what it was doing, an open system of government with no more restrictions than absolutely necessary—liberalism's least government is the best government—served that state's purposes very effectively. Freedom and central government finally proved to be entirely compatible.

There was little of the insidious in this. It simply meant that the new majorities finally came to speak with one voice, if in fact usually through the representatives of two or more all-but-indistinguishable parties. And they spoke with one voice because at their core was the new bourgeoisie, which, as the fulfillment of the modern dream, was more than just a class. For it expanded in the course of the Modern Age to become nearly the whole; and it was best able to continue to expand within a growing economy that thrived on the absence of regulation that only central government could insure. Far from being in opposition, then, the movements to political centralization and to political freedom complemented one another. Centralization cleared the way for freedom; and because society became progressively more of a piece it used that freedom to strengthen the tendency to centralization. Not everyone was pleased, to be sure. But complaints, whatever their source, were not in the long run destined to be successful, not, that is, while the modern political structure continued its evolution. Centralization and liberalization were underwritten by the rising bourgeoisie. Time, as we say, was on their side.

Yet as with style and thought and all things civilizational, the work was not done quickly; and we find as we trace the outlines of the development the usual pattern of alternating periods of action and reaction, so that it is but gradually that the modern political constructions emerge. Not only was the pace slow, but also the process was complex, for every move forward rather than making a new beginning built on what was at hand, however ill-suited to the new purposes, while every countermove destroyed some of the new and old together.

The complicated nature of this history is illustrated already in the very first period of political revival that began to reverse the thousand-year devolution from Roman centralization to medieval particularism. For the first effort to restore a degree of centralization, the first attempt, that is, to push off in the new direction, was based, as noted earlier, on the very feudalism that had been designed to give substance to the fragmentation of political authority in the early medieval centuries.

How could a new order be wrested from the feudalized decentralization? The method was simple enough: by merely emphasizing the lines of obligation that led upward from the lowest vassal to the prince—sometimes in fact a count, sometimes an archbishop, a duke, or a king—an entire feudal system could be manipulated to produce a considerable centralization. Certainly more than a vestige of the old particularism remained. Further, there was constant tension and much fighting, as the increasingly disadvantaged lesser nobility tried to protect itself from the new leadership. But from the latter part of the eleventh century, the princes managed gains fairly consistently. The result, which has been called princely or monarchical feudalism to distinguish it from the earlier variety, gave the West a new form of government: rather than a network of more-or-less sovereign local units, there were now several largish polities, the more distinguished recognizable as the early forms of the national states that would eventually become the characteristic vehicles of Western politics in the Modern Age.

But the Modern Age had not yet arrived. The West's politics was on its way toward its modern forms, yet still distinctly medieval. This princely feudalism, with its odd mixture of medieval and modern elements, was only the first in a series of experiments that would lead from the medieval to the modern. It was the political combination corresponding to the Gothic amalgam of abstraction and realism and to the Scholastic Synthesis of faith and reason. And it too would fall apart, also the victim of its inner contradictions, before it could evolve further toward the modern solution of a more thorough centralization. But for a time, roughly during the two centuries following 1000, princely feudalism seemed to provide a workable system, with neither too much nor too little exercise of central authority. The princes provided enough cohesion so that external enemies could be repelled and internal warfare kept within bounds. More than that these medieval societies did not yet need. This was indeed a period of expansion, and the economic, social, and intellectual ties that induce local communities to bind themselves together into larger entities were growing stronger; however, those ties were not yet significant enough to warrant a still more centralized state.

Yet the princes, ambitious and willful, could not be restrained from seeking greater centralization. Early successes encouraged them to try for more. But they soon went too far and thereby brought about their own downfall. In England, for example, we can see the process clearly at work: for a full century following the Norman conquest, the kings made intelligent use of the feudal structure. Then they were tempted to go another step, one that might bring them nearly exclusive authority. Scornful of the risks, the monarchy pushed forward. And under Henry II, it made its ambitious bid to control the English church. The result was Thomas à Becket's stubborn resistance. Becket's murder by the king's men solved nothing. It provoked a popular reaction that proved to be the first in a not unrelated series of setbacks, one that would lead finally to Runnymede, where John was forced by his barons in effect to acknowledge that the long expansion of royal power had come to an end. This proved to be a concession from which the English feudal monarchy would not fully recover until almost three more centuries had gone by.[32]

The German kings—since 962 they had also taken to calling themselves emperors—made a similar bid for greater centralization, and with similar results. They too wanted to control their church. One must remember that in each of these protonational states the church was a great landowner, capable of raising a considerable feudal army, and thus the concern to reduce its independence. In the German instance, the easiest way to that end lay through Rome: if the German kings could dominate the papacy, then obviously they would have little trouble from local clerics. And dominate the papacy they did, and with it central and northern Italy and Burgundy as well. But in the end they found themselves overextended. Piece by piece, the product of their remarkable effort at centralizing middle Europe came tumbling down. The monarchy first lost control of the papacy, a victim of its success in revitalizing the institution; then it lost control of the German church, as the revitalized papacy intervened north of the Alps; and finally, without the church to rely on, it lost control of its own aristocracy. The resultant lapse into a new decentralization was then little disturbed for the remainder of the Middle Ages. The German monarchy's efforts at drawing the various particularist elements together into a central state had proved even less successful than those of the English monarchy.[33]

France's experiment with princely feudalism ran a similar course, first being made to work and then failing. Although it had got off to a late start—feudalism had been too well-developed north of the Loire for the earliest Capetians to oppose it successfully, nor could they for some time find the means to use its hierarchy to their advantage—the French monarchy was ultimately successful in building a solid feudal state. Here the battle against the church went in the king's favor. The late start proved very fortunate, for it matched the period of French monarchical ascent with a period of papal decline—a decline that Philip the Fair (1285–1314) encouraged when he brought the papacy north. By the fourteenth century, with the popes safely held captive at Avignon, little, it must have seemed to some, remained to be done.

There was still, however, a considerable problem: even at the peak of its feudal power, the French monarchy had begun to unload some of its geographic responsibilities, recognizing the difficulty in trying to impose a central order upon a society still in good part locally self-sufficient. The method chosen to redistribute authority involved granting regions to the sons of the king, to be ruled in the royal interest. But these endowments, or appanages, were made in perpetuity, and thus tended to drift away from the monarchy after the first generation. The French feudal monarchy was, if in a quieter way, experiencing the same losses that its English and German counterparts had earlier experienced. When put to a test in the form of a series of English invasions during the Hundred Years' War (1337–1453), it revealed very quickly its internal weaknesses, as France rather suddenly passed from strong government to fragmentation.

The papacy itself also saw its efforts at centralization first succeed and then fail during these first several centuries following the turn of the millennium. No sooner had the popes escaped from the overlordship of the German king-emperors than they began to assert themselves throughout the West, and with increasing success. But just as they were making their greatest bid for secular power, they were struck down, first the victims of the French kings and then of a succession of internal divisions. The conciliar movement tried to put things back together again, but it could not and ultimately had the opposite effect. It would seem that the papacy, very much like the feudal monarchies, was also being forced to pay the price for having tried to impose on Europe a higher degree of centralized government than the traffic would bear. Ironically, this attempt might have done better had there been even less call for centralization: without the opposition of the kings, Rome well might have enjoyed greater secular power. In any case, the papacy was no more able than the protonational monarchies to consolidate and extend the gains that it had made.

We see, then, that after two to three centuries—the process had begun in some places (e.g., Germany) as early as the tenth century and lasted in others (e.g., France) until about the middle of the fourteenth (where there was an earlier start there was also usually an earlier finish)—this initial attempt to re-create a system of centrally controlled politics lost its momentum. The West at that point (one could say the fourteenth century, but in specific instances even earlier) began to slide backward toward the old particularism. This retrograde movement, away from centralization, was of course but another aspect of that general civilizational contraction that lay between the high medieval growth era and the coming of the Renaissance. And, as with all segments of the West's history at this time, there was with regard to politics considerable turmoil. It was not just a matter of veering smoothly in another direction for a while, but rather of moving unevenly in several directions at the same time. Both rural and urban rioting were not uncommon, and warfare was constant, especially from the middle of the fourteenth century. The Hundred Years' War, just referred to in connection with the collapse of royal authority in France, is only the most prominent of the wars and rebellions that disturbed Europe's peace in these decades.[34]

Then came the new period of construction. In the second half of the fifteenth century, Western politics again returned to the path that led toward centralization. The outlines of the units within which this new consolidation would take place, the national states, had during the intitial period already been sketched in, determined gradually by a mixture of language, culture, geography, conquest, and chance. Now, after the century or so of confusion, those states reappeared rather abruptly as the centers of power. Their authority was this time so extensive, the balance between the feudal remnant and the new monarchy so overloaded in favor of the latter, that we rightly choose this moment from which to date modern politics. The feudal monarchies had been as much feudal as monarchical. Their roots in the era of particularistic feudalism were too clearly visible. These early modern states, however, while obviously having benefited from the medieval attempts at greater centralization, managed to move well beyond them.

With regard to every crucial facet of politics, the national states now spectacularly advanced their authority. National courts replaced local courts; a national standing army replaced the feudal host; new taxes replaced the now inadequate traditional collections; bureaucratic offices expanded to supervise the new tasks of government; weights, measurements, and currencies were given a national standardization; a national navy was created to protect the recently acquired national colonies; and finally the church, so often the stumbling block in the search for greater centralization under the feudal monarchies, was finally brought under the direction of the king. These changes were most evident in England and France, but they can be found occurring from Portugal and Spain to Russia. Even where the evolution of the nation-state found itself cut off prematurely, as in Italy and Germany, very similar developments can be observed taking place within the city-state and duchy.[35]

Accompanying this remarkable reorganization of Europe into new centralized political units came the equally remarkable rise of the bourgeoisie. The towns had not been without a role in the putting together of the feudal monarchies, although at that time they had remained a peripheral force. Now, in the move to the national monarchies, they were much more important. Larger, wealthier, and more confident, the West's urban centers contributed where they could to the growing power of the kings. The motive was straightforward enough: the aristocracy had tried to prevent the bourgeoisie from bettering its political position as the latter's economic power increased. There had been exceptions, in particular where more power for the bourgeoisie might mean less power for the kings, thus leading to instances of bourgeois-aristocratic collaboration. But generally the aristocracy and the bourgeoisie had found themselves on opposite sides, with the aristocracy retaining the upper hand as long as the medieval pattern held. Therefore the bourgeoisie at this point chose the new monarchies to aid it in its struggle against its traditional enemy. A small minority even within the early modern population, this ascending middle class could hardly offer to lend armies. It could, however, offer to pay for them, and that is what it did. The bourgeoisie in effect paid the kings to reduce the influence of the aristocracy. And for the moment the bourgeoisie was satisfied enough with that favor that it would ask for no additional compensation other than freedom for the towns to govern themselves internally.

The aristocracy did not, of course, disappear. Indeed, in some ways it became more prominent than ever before. But it was an eminence enjoyed in the service of the monarchy, not on its own behalf. The new state had a new purpose, and if the old nobility was allowed to occupy the places of authority and dominate court life, then that lent itself to a deception as to directions that made the transition all the easier. As long as it was possible to bask in the light reflected from the king, the aristocracy's prestige was left it, even if its original function was not. And if it could continue to hold its head up, then it would not take the occasional calls to reaction too seriously.

Or at least it would not until in the latter part of the sixteenth century Europe entered upon a new period of contraction. Beginning then and lasting through much of the seventeenth century, the aristocracy took its revenge. In a series of revolts, it tried to set the clock back, now assisted by help from every quarter as dissatisfaction with the gains that the national state had so recently made appeared at all levels of society. The national state would in fact seem to have come near to being destroyed. Once again warfare—motivated this time by religion, class antagonisms, and both regional and national rivalries, usually in combination—put it to a severe test. Even when the fighting for the moment abated, the ability of the crown to keep order was often in doubt. Urban crime, a relatively new phenomenon, made the cities unsafe, while highwaymen, and this was their heyday, did the same for the countryside. The institutions of the national monarchies were being pushed to the breaking point.[36]

Yet they did not break. In the latter part of the seventeenth century the political crisis, like the other crises, came to an end. The national monarchies had survived. In the long run this could only benefit the bourgeoisie. For the time being, however, the aristocracy was still important. Its reaction had failed. But it could not yet be cast aside. As it was, it had even been able to extend its hold on the higher administration. Still, its privileges were now more than ever before precariously dependent upon a somewhat fortuitous circumstance. Medieval politics had been inconceivable without the aristocracy. It had provided the essential linkage. This early modern system, however, was all too conceivable without it. The national bureaucracy and the new armies and navies could just as well be run by others. Nor was it necessary that court life be left to a monopoly of the nobility. Even the great estates might as easily be managed by someone else, for they were by this time becoming more and more only parts within a national economy and no longer self-contained realms within the realm.

So it happened that by the late seventeenth century the aristocracy was being put in an increasingly difficult position. The economy was continuing in its drift toward commerce and industry, to the obvious advantage of the bourgeoisie. If the superficial levels of Western society seemed to attest to a revival of aristocratic influence, this appearance, then, was misleading. After the crisis of the seventeenth century, modernism was again on the march, and the aristocracy was being quietly compelled to provide the leadership for the creation of a polity from which, and necessarily, it would eventually be ousted.

Compelled may not be quite the right word, for the aristocracy's cooperation was freely given. Yet its choices were more and more restricted, as the possible lines of retreat, those that led back to the medieval world, were cut off. Not that it did not still consider once more attempting some sort of reactionary coup. And, interestingly enough, the last serious effort at turning back provoked instead the next push forward. Our focus is here on France, where the great revolution that began in 1788–89 served to delineate more clearly than in other countries the various facets of the West's politics at this moment. On the eve of the revolution, France was ruled by a theoretically strong but personally weak monarch, assisted by the usual aristocracy. When the state, still reliant upon its traditional sources of income—now much debilitated through centuries of grants of exemption—found itself unable to meet the increasingly large expenses of modern government, it sought reforms. The sanction of the aristocracy, crucial because its membership performed the direct tasks of national government, was made conditional on being given real power. The aristocracy was now insisting that it should not only execute the laws, but determine them as well. It would no longer work for the monarchy; in the future, it hoped, the monarchy would be made to work for it.

Thus the aristocracy once more challenged the modern state. Political authority had been centralized within that state in the course of the last three centuries. Next it must be decided to what purpose and to whose benefit. The modern state was being forced to declare its true nature. What would it opt for? Finally, during the middle and later decades of the nineteenth century, it would conclude that its true nature was to be bourgeois—liberal, democratic, and republican (Queen Victoria's contribution was to permit the creation of a de facto republic within the English monarchy). The centralized state would be put at the disposal of a large, single-minded, growth-oriented middle class that would find the convenient balance between freedom and authority. When one reflects upon the French Revolution it is difficult to understand it apart from these later developments, to which it certainly contributed.

But the Revolution itself, as distinct from the results of the movement of which it formed a part, was a rather more complicated phenomenon. Viewed alone, it would seem to have provided a variety of models, only a few of which would be implemented in the next several generations. The rest would either be forgotten or reappear at a much later date. For along with the forms for the bourgeois liberal-democratic state, the French Revolution offered a foretaste of both socialism, a modern but non-bourgeois political solution, and fascism, which was to be bourgeois but not modern.[37]

The point here is that the French Revolution, very much like the contemporary Romantic Movement that in some regards would appear to have been its cultural counterpart, was not of a piece. And it failed finally to make the transition from the monarchical national state with its aristocratic supporters to the liberal-democratic state with its bourgeois supporters. This step, in fact a series of steps, was taken only, as said, in the course of the following century. What happened between 1789 and 1799 was that the French, forced to act by the refusal of the aristocracy to make the necessary accommodations, groped for a new solution. And they found none. Rather, they tried out a number of possibilities—constitutional monarchy, moderate republicanism, radical republicanism, radical authoritarianism, and finally moderate authoritarianism—in quick succession, without having much success with any of them, until, that is, Bonaparte discovered that domestic concord could be achieved best by a policy of military conquest.

Once the French emperor was put aside and safely settled on St. Helena, Europe could set about answering the question of who would rule that the Revolution had only been able to put. Would it continue to be the king, and, if so, supported by whom? Could the aristocracy be expected to cooperate any better than before? And what of the bourgeoisie, whose willingness to rule directly the French Revolution had for the first time revealed. As it happened, the mood everywhere was conservative. Certainly that was natural enough after the upheavals of the last quarter of a century. Further, this drift was reinforced by the reactionary strains within Romantic thought, which, given the circumstances, proved more politically influential than the equally evident radical strains. The result was an attempt to restore the old alliance between the monarchy and the nobility. Because the latter had been chastened by the total failure of its attempt in France to go it alone, it did indeed lend itself to the next effort at cooperation. Europe in effect was returned to its condition before the Revolution, with the important exception that nothing that had happened would be forgotten. If that fact at first favored those who wished to prevent change, it would eventually work to the advantage of those who sought it. For the memory of the Revolution could be used not only as a bogey, but also as a platform. And as a platform it was certain to have a constantly increasing appeal, for the urban, commercial, and industrial sectors of society were continuing to grow, with regard not only to size but also to political consciousness. Post-Napoleonic conservatism with its renewed association of monarchy and aristocracy was therefore not destined to last long.

Beginning around 1830 the bourgeoisie began its final ascent. Almost every government of France from that date on has been either supported or operated directly by the representatives of the business and professional classes, beginning with the bourgeois monarchy of the liberal Orleanist, Louis Philippe. In England this was the era of Whig-Liberal predominance, which resulted in the clear option for a modern urban middle-class society. To be sure, in central Europe and America the changes were being made somewhat slower, but they were occurring there as well. The revolutions of 1848–49 had only limited success, but they made clear that their demands could not go unnoticed even in the most autocratic regimes. And when Bismarck drew up his complex constitution for the new Germany, he was careful to give to the bourgeoisie a Reichstag with significant budgetary and legislative rights. Nor was it without meaning when he chose the quintessential bourgeois party, the National Liberals, as his first ally. In the United States, the bourgeoisie won a much more decisive battle when it first provoked the aristocracy (Southern and unpatented, but aristocracy nonetheless) to rebel and then crushed it. It is true that in Russia and most of eastern Europe bourgeois influence was not of great importance, but within those key Western areas in which industrialization was transforming society, the direction of the national state was quickly passing into the hands of the middle classes.

As noted before, there was little in the liberalism of the bourgeoisie that would lead to opposition to the centralization that had replaced particularism. If liberalism had its origins in the attempt to defend the corporate structure of the Middle Ages against centralization, still the bourgeoisie learned soon enough to use the liberal tradition for its own purposes, bringing the principle of egalitarianism to bear against corporatism. Liberalism became the theoretical foundation for that open society that benefited most the bourgeoisie, who became the skilled practitioners of freedom. Noble ideal that it was, liberalism also clearly lent itself to the enrichment of those who best knew how to employ it. At its worst, liberalism turned the notion of the open society into a means for opening doors to middle-class exploitation. But at its worst or best, it chose to continue the centralization process that had characterized the evolution of modern politics. Now in command, the liberal bourgeoisie went on to add to the mechanisms of central power.

Nevertheless, the adaptation of liberalism to the purposes of centralization required it to make significant adjustments. That was not true with regard to democracy, the other bourgeois principle of politics. Democracy from the beginning implied a centralized government. The only difficulty with regard to its implementation by the modern state was the matter of defining the *demos*. Just who the people were was far from obvious. The original opinion as modern democracy came of age in the early nineteenth century was that the people, that is, the politically operative people, should be the adult males of property. It occurred to few that females might also be extended the suffrage, and that question was not at issue. The debate hung upon the matter of how much property. The upper-middle class had pressed for democracy, an excellent argument with which to destroy hereditary privilege, but it had intended to restrict the vote to its own ranks. By mid-century, however, the middle-middle class was agitating for inclusion. And by the later decades not only the lower-middle class, but also the peasantry and urban proletariat wanted the same rights. The old order was forced to give way.

It is remarkable how quietly it did so. The bourgeoisie, that is, the haute bourgeoisie, the middle class of substance, had surrendered not everything—it still controlled the economy, the press, and the judiciary and also retained considerable political advantages—but yet a great deal. The gates had been opened and the masses permitted to enter the political arena, the very same hordes that Marx had designated the heirs to the bourgeoisie, a prophecy that the intended victims took at least as seriously as the intended benefactors. It would seem that the bourgeoisie was being pushed to surrender its recently won ascendance, both by the momentum of the rapidly progressing economic and social changes brought about by the further spread of industrialization; and by the force of its own logic, now turned against it. If all men—and, from the early twentieth century, all women, too—were equal, then that fact must be given political form, and not just negatively, in the courts, but positively as well, with regard to ability to control the government. But how much actual harm did the extension of the suffrage to the entire adult population do to the old bourgeoisie and the national state that it had come to dominate? Immediately, it did very little. The modern political party was organized to channel the energies of the new voters, and it did so with impressive skill, offering a little welfare, a little imperialism, and a lot of oratory. The old elites had read the developing situation very quickly and were soon competing for the honor of awarding the ballot to the next stratum. Occasionally, a particular party miscalculated, as did the English Conservatives in 1867, when those enfranchised by the Conservatives subsequently decided to vote for the Liberals.[38] But generally the transformation from a liberal to a democratic politics was made with hardly a hitch. The bourgeoisie made the concessions that it thought that it had to make. These were tremendous. And yet nothing happened: for the bourgeoisie remained in control of the state.

That fact takes some explaining. The masses had been given the means to control the state and yet held back from making full use of them. They in part went on voting for bourgeois parties; and when they devised proletarian parties these showed remarkable restraint, even when Marx's gospel of revolution was accepted as official policy. The desire for revolution, contrary to expectation, more or less disappeared as the nineteenth century wore on: 1789, 1830, 1848, 1871—those are the West's great revolutionary years. After 1871, which saw the ill-fated Paris Commune, there was much talk but little action. The First World War provoked the Russian Revolution, of course, but the revolutions that it did not provoke are the more notable. The suppressed masses supported the war from the outset, enduring the slaughter and privations that followed with hardly a protest. And when there were mutinies, these addressed themselves chiefly to the most obvious grievance, death to no purpose. One can assume, then, that the alienation between the bourgeoisie and the classes below it was by the decades of the late nineteenth and early twentieth centuries not especially profound. The hope of social progress, at the moment being partially fulfilled, was apparently enough to turn the masses away from their intention, to the extent that there had been one, of ousting the bourgeoisie. It no doubt seemed more appropriate merely to join it.[39]

The monarchy, then, replaced the aristocracy, and the bourgeoisie in turn replaced the monarchy; but the proletariat failed to replace the bourgeoisie. Power in the modern state had come to rest. And there it remains. The triumph of the bourgeoisie turned out to be just that—not the prelude to a new upheaval, but rather the end of the line, the final stage in the evolution of modern politics. Yet in history nothing is really the end of the line. Even the most stable constellations soon begin to shift. Here a few subtle changes would seem to have produced some considerable effects. Little in our recent past is ever entirely clear, but what appears to have taken place is that the introduction of the masses into politics, that is, the democratization of modern politics, turned out to matter after all. For the masses became bourgeois only in the sense that they sought and attained the higher standard of living; but they did not become bourgeois with regard to the desire to impose a set of ideals, a class leadership, or, if you will, a class exploitation. They have tended to have no ideals, for they have been sincere when they insist that they are not interested in leading anyone anywhere, indeed, are not interested in politics in any form; and they have been equally disinclined to go to the work of exploitation, either at home or abroad. This new bourgeoisie that is scarcely bourgeois is dedicated to but a single purpose. It wishes to consume, unmolested, in isolation, touched as little as possible by the old bourgeois culture, society, and state. As for ideologies, it has proved consistently indifferent. It had never known the conservatism of the aristocracy, can not be aroused by the moral appeal of socialism, and has turned liberalism's demand for *Freiheit* into the quest for *Freizeit*, not freedom, but free-time, leisure with which more fully to explore the pleasures of consumerism and the individualist life-style.[40]

Thus the nineteenth-century victory of the bourgeoisie has been thwarted by the twentieth-century incorporation of the masses, who have subverted middle-class society much more thoroughly by imitating it than they ever could have by overthrowing it. Democracy under the circumstances has not been able to rise above the level of interest-group politics: the state and society are first edged a bit in one direction by a more-or-less random coalition of groups with specific and restricted interests, only to be later edged in another direction by a different but similar coalition. The result is to transform the general disinterest in politics into a general contempt. The suspicion grows that contemporary national politics has nothing to do with planning for a better society, but that it is merely a device for facilitating corruption: it serves only to keep free the channels through which the spoils are distributed.

There have been two attempts made in this century to provide the West with a new system, one that might give it direction, end the alienation from politics, and restore vitality. Both have arisen at times and in places where the old system, for reasons of economic depression, military defeat, or both acting together, had either been made to look ineffective or ceased to operate altogether. The first of these was Leninism, Marxist communism as interpreted and put into operation by Lenin's generation in Russia beginning in 1917. The second was fascism, which hit the West only a few years later with an even more alluring appeal.

Leninism, successful precisely where, in contradiction to Marx's original prediction, the bourgeois state had not yet been achieved, tried by means of an elitist party operating through an authoritarian bureaucracy to industrialize without industrialists and distribute the results of the production without distributors, without, that is, the help of bourgeois middlemen. How well did it work? An evaluation is difficult. The Soviet Union has indeed industrialized and in turn successfully asserted itself as a power among nations, but at a considerable cost to its citizens. And when Leninism was applied to central Europe, it had to be modified to the point where one hesitates to describe it as the same system.[41] In fact, even in the Soviet Union the evolution of Leninism into yet another variety of the welfare-state economy, complete with deep dissatisfactions and its own version of a rebellious youth culture, makes a comment on the viability of the original model difficult. The final test will come when Soviet society, like the West, must confront the end of growth. Because Leninism has been predicated as much on the ideal of continued growth as has capitalism, there is little in it—except perhaps its necessarily learned ability to suppress consumerism—that would seem to suggest a worthy alternative politics for the West as a whole. Nor has it so far been popular in the area of the older West.

Fascism on the other hand was for a while extremely popular in the older West. There were two conditions necessary for its success: first, the bourgeois state needed to have evolved to the point where it was assuming responsibility for society's fortunes, where, that is, its promises of modernization and the good life were taken seriously; and, second, those promises had to fail. Where these two were met, the bourgeois state was taken over by fascism or something very much like it in the course of the twenties and thirties—in most of continental Europe west of the Soviet border and in much of Latin America, with considerable fascist elements recognizable in the politics of the United States as well. Fascism, in many ways less revolutionary than Leninism, was nevertheless in one theoretical aspect entirely radical: it indeed offered a true alternative—for with regard to growth, that crucial ingredient of modern society, fascism tended to say no. Growth was materialist and destructive of the mythic values about which fascism loved to effuse so stridently. The renunciation of materialism, however, was just as ambivalent as the rest of the fascist program, and when it came both to courting the people and preparing for war, the reservations were put aside so quickly that we tend to forget that they ever existed. Yet the attacks on modern society and its consumer-oriented growth were sincere.[42]

Also radical was the fascist solution to the problem of alienation. Fascism would attempt to reverse the process of disenchantment spawned by modernism, Max Weber's *Entzauberung,* that progressive erosion of all spiritual and prerational traditions by the steady onslaught of cold reason. Fascism, then, sought to re-create myth. The degree to and manner in which it succeeded will remain for a long time one of the great scandals of Western history. The easy triumphs of its admonishments to zealotry and hatred obviously revealed a great insufficiency in the modern bourgeois state.[43] There was a void there that fascism moved to fill. Not only were the masses enthusiastic but also many of the West's intellectuals, including Gerhart Hauptmann, Carl Jung, Martin Heidegger, Ezra Pound, T.S. Eliot, and even for a moment Benedetto Croce.

In the end fascism revealed itself to have even fewer answers than Leninism. The more Hitler's National Socialism became the dominant fascist power, the more fascism came under the spell of his murderous plans. There was in fascism from the beginning a vicious, neurotic aspect, and under the direction of the Nazis it became primary. The result was the Holocaust, which understandably has then come to overwhelm our memory of the entire era.[44]

But neither Leninism nor fascism did much to change for long the condition of the West's modern politics, except, to be sure, within the area of Soviet occupation. The patterns established by the Modern Age have proved remarkably durable and that even in their vitiated present condition. They have now successfully endured five centuries of buffeting, managing to withstand the attempts of various enemies and ideologies to reshape them. Nor have the occasional efforts on the part of superpowers to subvert the national system in favor of hegemonial spheres met with much success. Perhaps most remarkable, the nation-states have even managed to survive their own overseas empires, the strain of which well might have done them in had they not been so well-established.

Nothing has been said in this brief comment on this last subject, the expansion of the West, and here we shall touch on it only to note its near irrelevance to modern politics. That expansion—carried out in a series of waves that, beginning with the Crusades in the late eleventh century and continuing through the nineteenth-century age of imperialism, exactly corresponded to the periods of internal centralization—had to be sure a tremendous effect on the rest of the world. The world, in short, was Westernized. But the old West remained essentially what it had been: that is true with regard to all of the major lines of development, but here the significant point is that the expansion did not produce a new politics. Once the national state system was in place, imperial experiments came and went without shaking it or even altering it in any fundamental way. In the long run, the Spanish empire did very little for or to Spain. When Spain declined as a power, it lost the empire, and not the other way around. The same can be said of England and its empire. France's overseas venture was even more peripheral to its European interests. The German colonies, an afterthought, were also almost without influence on Germany itself. Italian efforts to acquire an empire only mirrored Italy's domestic difficulties. The American experience has been at best ambiguous and usually also peripheral.[45] The present Soviet empire endures, but has done little to alter the facts of nationalism. Russia remains Russian, Hungary Hungarian, and so on.

The modern political constellation, then, is with us yet. It is a survivor. And if it has its troubles, is it not surely possible, one might suggest, that they can be overcome? The national states continue to maintain order. They even assist in providing a measure of prosperity. Also, it is clear that since the Second World War they are aware enough of the new weaponry so to be no longer eager to fight big wars. Further, even if it is true that the era of bourgeois leadership has been ended without being followed by anything comparable from another source, thus leaving modern politics without any purpose other than presiding over legions of unordered consumers, then certainly that circumstance can be improved upon, with some sort of a solution acceptable to the modern tradition yet to emerge.

Yet is such optimism really justified? We return to the contemporary threats to the present political order: first, the growth economy would appear to be grinding to a halt. That means that the modern political system, which has come into being in good part as the political counterpart of that growth, will be put under pressures the likes of which it has never experienced. Second, and it can hardly be repeated too often, the military balance that supported the national state from its inception has, with the coming of the bomb, been drastically altered. The nation-state can no longer defend itself or even, except in special cases, assert its military power. It is entirely vulnerable to the threat of nuclear terrorism; and its traditional and really only means of resolving ultimate conflicts, warfare among nations, has been lost. If the nation-state is not rushing to war, that is because it cannot, and that fact only underscores its new helplessness. Under these circumstances, the loss of direction takes on new meaning. Modern politics indeed would seem to be a system waiting for a catastrophe. We shall take up the matter of just how we might reshape our political future to reduce some of the risks in the final chapter. But before speculating about the future, there is one more historical segment that requires our attention, and that is that which is to summarize the emergence, maturation, and, finally, onset of the decline of the modern economy.

ECONOMICS

The modern economy has evolved from its medieval predecessor in the course of a thousand-year history. Like its cultural and political counterparts, this progression has been marked by alternating periods of expansion and contraction, and these with much the same chronology. Here too are to be found the three great eras of growth—the first extending from the eleventh century through the thirteenth and in some areas even into the fourteenth, the second from the late fifteenth through the seventeenth, and the third from the early eighteenth to the present—and also the two great eras of regression, those of the fourteenth and seventeenth centuries. One sees as well the many signs of profound, indeed, revolutionary change toward the very end of the millennium, beginning in the late nineteenth century and developing alongside the continuing growth of the twentieth, with the innovations clearly challenging the modern economy and threatening to induce or perhaps force it to move in a very different direction.

Thus a brief overview of the West's economic passage from its medieval to its modern condition looks something like this: from 1000 to 1350, there occurred a long period of growth, as the West began to move beyond the manorial economy; then from 1350 to 1450, a shorter period of regression; then another period of growth, running parallel to the cultural and political developments of the Renaissance, extending from 1450 to 1550–1600; next the second period of regression, lasting until 1720; then yet another long period of growth, from 1720 until the 1870s; and finally, from the 1870s to the present, a time of troubles, during which growth has indeed continued, in many areas even increasing in intensity, but with the basic system, the structure of capitalism itself, manifesting obvious signs of its decay and approaching end.

If one views more closely each of these periods in turn, it is apparent that they are characterized by considerably more than just the presence or absence of growth. In the first place, they are clearly parts of a coherent process, one that might best be described as the rise and fall of the open market, with the last segments of the history yet to be completed. For it would seem to be the open-market system, with its natural encouragement to specialization, commerce, rationalization, large-scale enterprise, and, finally, growth itself, that has been the fundamental economic ingredient in this lengthy evolution; and it is the collapse of that system that we are now experiencing.

Yet if we take the open market as the centerpiece of this history, it would be naive to push it forward as a cause in itself. Growth, scale, trade, specialization, fluid currencies, easy credit, and the various inventions and institutions that lent themselves in their turn to the process—all along with the open market are both cause and effect, the economic protrusions of something deeper, the civilization in all its complexities. In our discussion of the West's economic transformation from primitivism to classical maturity, specialization was taken as the leitmotiv. It might have been used here as well; but in choosing the open market, I have wanted to call attention to a subtle difference, although one with considerable implications, between the two eras: in the ancient world, the market developed to accommodate specialization, while in the modern, specialization has had a tendency to be subordinated to the requirements of the market itself. During the West's first great expansion, the market served the economy; during the second, the economy served the market. The market and its profits have become more and more ends in their own right, steadily more oblivious to the society they once served.

The second fact about the several periods of this economic transition that can be noted here is that each has had a remarkable internal coherence. These periods are not distinctive, not, that is, periods merely with regard to a certain characteristic, but rather to a host of characteristics. Each made, for example, its own distinct innovations in production and distribution. Each had as well (the fourteenth century excepted) its own dominant class or classes. Each (again the fourteenth century excepted) was justified by its own unique theoretical structure. And, finally, each had its own geography, as the primary focus of economic activity shifted from place to place. Thus each period, while representing a stage within the process of building—and more recently dismantling—the open-market economy, has also formed a relatively independent unit, with its own ideals and operational consistency. These characteristics—production-distribution, class, theory, and geography—are sufficiently prominent to provide an easy order for reviewing the periods. We shall use them, then, for facilitating the following summary of the West's economic history during the last millennium.

The starting point for the modern economy was necessarily its predecessor, the manorial economy of the early Middle Ages.[46] The manorial economy had rescued Europe from the progressive disintegration that had followed upon the death of the classical economy. The solution that the manorial system provided to the problems posed by the disappearance of the classical, which had left in its wake an initial economic chaos, was to return to the closed system of the preclassical economies. Imposing itself upon the confusion, a rigid but viable structure built upon the individual manor came to determine the West's productive efforts. This was the essential innovation of the eighth, ninth, and tenth centuries: manorialism

came to provide a self-sufficient, closed economy based on the independent estate as a substitute for the departed open economy of the empire.
Local and almost entirely agrarian, it managed nicely without currencies
and commerce. With a new product—the agrarian output of the unspecialized farm—and a new principle of distribution—grow it at home and eat
it at home—the manorial economy may not have produced abundance, but
it functioned.

The dominant class of this manorial era was provided by the lords of the
manor, linked together to form a political whole by the feudal chain of
mutual obligation. This was a functional aristocracy. It did its own farming,
managing the manor, except, of course, when occupied with the not so
insignificant requirements of feudal warfare. After the many post medieval
centuries during which the aristocracy only pretended to have a function,
it is easy, as already remarked, to fall into the error of assuming that things
were always that way. But, like most dominant classes at the time of their
origin, this agrarian aristocracy fulfilled its economic responsibilities.

As for theory, the workings of the economy during the manorial era
were firmly endorsed by the Church, then committed to the Augustinian
view, with its promises of divine punishment for those who did not
observe the prescriptions of morality and justice. All closed systems are
highly vulnerable to the disturbing effects of those who succeed in violat-
ing their rules. But in this sincerely religious age, the theological restrictions on what little open-market activity managed to survive were
remarkably effective in keeping it from expanding. As is usually the case,
economic theory reflected the general circumstances of the times. The
West's condition was modest, even precarious. Those who wished to
innovate, to enter upon business ventures for the sake of profit, were
pointedly discouraged from doing so. And the Church added that they
should not even want to, for the true business of a Christian was getting on
with the work of saving one's soul.[47]

Regarding the geography of this period, we can observe that the manorial system had its beginnings and earliest successes in that belt of good
soil, plentiful rainfall, and relatively mild climate that extends from the
Loire north and east to the Rhine. Here was the heartland of medieval
Europe. Far enough from the Mediterranean to be free of its economic
heritage and protected from the full consequences of a northern position
by the North Atlantic current, this land of meandering rivers and low-lying
wooded hills was ideally suited to the new effort at self-sufficient agriculture. Game and fish were abundant. So was firewood. And even an
untutored agriculture could hardly go wrong, given a limited and stable
population.

The manorial economy, then, was a distinct entity, with its own way of
production and distribution, its own dominant class, its own theory, and its

own succinct geography. Far from being the mere absence of growth, it formed a coherent system. Therefore when the West around the year 1000 began to grow again and to edge away from the manorial system, when it began, that is, its movement toward the modern economy, it could be expected to innovate across the board. It would most likely make its changes not in isolated fashion, but with regard to each of its several characteristics: with regard, that is, to production-distribution, class, theory, and geographic locus. And that is what it did.

During the first period of growth, that which extended from 1000 to 1350, there were thus significant shifts in all of these areas. To begin with production and distribution, the period can be divided nicely with regard to its centuries. The eleventh century, continuing to build on the foundations laid in the period immediately preceding, saw something of an agricultural boom. The inventions and new practices that had been introduced from the sixth to the ninth century were now producing an accumulated effect. The horse equipped with the new horse-collar was indeed superior to the ox, and the shod hoof to the unshod. The three-field system also made its contribution. It may have put only another sixth of the total land available into production, but such narrow gains are the stuff of economic success. The result was a new prosperity.[48]

The next century, the twelfth, then saw remarkable commercial advances. For the first time since the fall of Rome there were significant surpluses to trade. Europe, it is true, had never been without some commerce, even when things were at their most bleak. Venice and Bari had maintained ties with Constantinople, and the Baltic also had seen considerable trading in the post-Carolingian centuries. But now the West was conceding to commerce a crucial if still distinctly subordinate role within the new economy. The Baltic and Mediterranean networks were joined, fairs provided regular markets, and money and credit came to be progressively more available. The manorial economy was, to be sure, still in place. Without it Europe could not yet survive. However, a new mode of operation was developing above and beyond the manor. Concentrating as this new economy did on luxury goods, its services were hardly crucial; yet their regular provision was resulting in the creation of an economic system ultimately destructive to its manorial host. The manor had been the product of a world without commerce. The return of commerce was certain to put an end to it.[49]

The fall of the manorial system would of course take a long time. But the next century, the thirteenth, saw an even more ominous development, as the West followed the commercial revival with the reestablishment of rudimentary industrial activity. By this time, the development of a bellows operated by water power was revolutionizing the working of iron, which could now be heated until it had become fluid and then cast. The results were typical for the long process of industrialization that was here just beginning: new products, new ways of producing old products, and increased concentration, that is, the growing specialization by geographic area in the production of certain goods. In place of the undifferentiated, homogeneous manorial society with its self-sufficient units, there was appearing gradually but surely an interdependent economy based on specialized production and linked by commerce. With the coming of this initial industrialization, directed as it was to supplying not luxuries but instead the basic work of agriculture and warfare, Europe began to depend on what it received from the non-manorial segments. Even the making of clothing and textiles was leaving the manor, as the Flemish woolen industry rose to prominence.

By the early fourteenth century, the Western economy had, then, experienced a distinct change. It was no longer purely manorial. These successive waves of agricultural, commercial, and industrial innovation—which, it should be understood, overlapped and continued to affect each other reciprocally—had created a mixed economy, still for the most part agrarian and manorial, but now also significantly urban and commercial. For the five centuries preceding 1000, the West had been a civilization almost entirely without trade and towns. From this point on, new urban centers of commerce dotted the landscape.

This circumstance soon came to affect the West's class structure. For within these towns a new class, the bourgeoisie, was in the making. We noted in the discussion of the politics of the Renaissance that even the bourgeoisie of that period was not yet ready to make a bid for direct power. The bourgeoisie of the High Middle Ages could merely hope that the still dominant class, the manorial aristocracy, could be reduced in power. To effect that, to say it again, it sided with the monarchy in the monarchy's struggle to lessen aristocratic influence, withdrawing that support only when the balance seemed to be tipping too far in the royal direction. But whether with the monarchy or against it, the bourgeoisie was able to assert itself and to achieve a certain representation in the places of power. In short, the result of the opening up of the old manorial society in the three and a half centuries that stretched from ca. 1000 to ca. 1350 was not to displace the manorial aristocracy as the dominant class, but to reduce its authority and to force it to share power, especially within the towns themselves, with the new bourgeoisie. Instead of a single dominant class, there were now two, the older, it should be acknowledged, still distinctly superior to the younger.

Theory also responded during this period of innovation with some appropriate changes. This was the time of the Scholastic Synthesis, the reconciliation of faith to reason, and the attitude toward economic activity was also undergoing revision. The Scholastic Synthesis was not a rejection of Augustinian Christianity, but only an attempt to update it, to bring it into line with the first stirrings of things modern. In economic theory the corresponding innovations were just as modest. The insistence on Christian justice based on the conception of a hierarchical society was retained. Regardless of the turn of the economic wheel, each individual was still to receive a proper share based on need and appropriate to his or her station and function within the God-ordained structure. And the cautions against business for its own sake remained. But there was now a greater willingness on the part of the Church—and surely it represented the mood of the times—to tolerate deviations.

For example, Aquinas in commenting on the crucial matter of charging interest for loans argued that yes, under certain circumstances interest was acceptable. If an opportunity for the lender to make a certain profit had occurred after the loan had been made, and because the funds were no longer available to him he had not been able to do so, then certainly it would be just to ask the person to whom the loan had been made partially to offset the loss by paying back something more than the loan itself. And so on. A great deal of water can pass through a small whole. Businessmen were now being told that there were ways in which they could have reasonable profits from entrepreneurial ventures (small profits for the direct provision of goods and services had never been at issue) and still save their souls. The Church before had been against any business that threatened the stability of the manorial economy. Now it was merely against any business that insisted on not making use of the proper conventions. It was helping to open the doors to a very different future.[50]

But so far no one either within the Church or without could have conceived of that future, and had it been possible to, there would have been a chorus of objections. The guilds and leagues of cities kept the new segment of the economy under control. Quality and service to the community came first and profits second. Put differently, profits were expected to be earned at modest rates over a long period of time in a society that could be depended on to be tomorrow much as it was yesterday. And to the medieval mind, that was as it should be.

The geographic story with regard to the West's economy in the years from 1000 to 1350 is of course one that relates consistent expansion, with both internal and external aspects. Europe's population was growing, perhaps not very rapidly by the standards of our century, but nevertheless significantly. It has been estimated that from 700 to 1300 it almost tripled.[51] Whether this demographic increase was the cause of the fermenting economy or its result, certainly there was pressure being put on Europe's land and resources. So the West turned inward and outward at the same time: inward to farm tracts formerly neglected—often with good reason—and outward to push on to new frontiers.

Of these external attempts at expansion, one can count five, some successful, some failures. The first, an effort to reclaim the north-central Mediterranean from the Arabs, can be listed among the successes; the second, the Crusades to the Holy Land, was a most spectacular failure. But the Spanish *Reconquista,* the third, and the German trans-Elbian campaign against the Slavs, the fourth, did manage to add considerable areas to the West. The fifth was the move out into the Atlantic, which began in the late thirteenth century and resulted by the middle of the fourteenth in the discovery of the Canaries, Madeiras, and Azores. In themselves, these explorations were not of much importance, but they served, of course, as a harbinger of remarkable things to come. However, the next wave would have to wait, for at this point the first great growth era in the West's movement from the manorial to the modern economy was rapidly coming to an end. Both the expansion of these first centuries of economic revival and the prosperity upon which it was based were in the process of being interrupted by a period of confusion and general retro-gression.

If one focuses on the most dramatic calamity of the general crisis of the fourteenth century, the Great Plague, that Black Death that ravaged the West beginning in 1347, then the impression is inevitable that the roots of the century-long economic collapse lie in the traumatic dislocations caused by the Plague itself. However, that is wrong. Not, of course, that the Plague did not have direct economic consequences. It could hardly have been otherwise, with Europe's population reduced by one-third in the first four years alone. In some areas, the countryside was all but deserted, and the cities were devastated as well. But the catastrophe did not fall upon a healthy Europe. The good times seem to have come to an end with the turn of the century. From about 1300 on, the West showed every sign of faltering in its advance. And one notes that the collapse of the great banking houses of the Bardi and Peruzzi occurred in 1343, distinctly before the Plague's arrival. We must keep in mind the larger context in trying to estimate the effects of the Black Death.

But just what was this larger context, that is, the larger relevant context? Is it of any significance for the economic history of the fourteenth century that the Scholastic Synthesis was breaking down, that the papacy was disintegrating, that the vigor of High Gothic was being lost, or that the efforts of the monarchs to consolidate their feudal realms were failing? It is always hard to say, but surely the civilization in its entirety was experi-encing some sort of shock. And neither purely economic factors nor the Black Death can be singled out and made responsible for the rest.

Probably the best explanation that can be applied to all areas is that the West had developed too fast and too far. It was overextended. Certainly that was the case with regard to the economy. The crop failures that had led to the sweeping famines of the early decades of the fourteenth century, which in turn undoubtedly prepared the way for the spread of the bubonic and pneumonic pandemics that together made up the Black Death, were an example of this. Had marginally arable acreage not been brought under cultivation, indeed, had the population not expanded to the point where it was necessary to farm more difficult lands, then a few bad harvests would not have had the devastating effect that they did.

Yet however the causes are portrayed, the fact is that for a century and more the West's economic progress was brought to a halt. Production at all levels decreased markedly, and the networks of distribution were badly disrupted. The fairs in and around Champagne declined rapidly—again, they were not so much victims of the Plague as of things that preceded it, in this case, oddly enough, not the later decrease but rather the earlier increase in trade, which necessitated fixed rather than periodic markets. Either way, old economic patterns were being destroyed and replaced by new ones. And the tendency to open up was being generally replaced by a tendency to close down. The West had been moving since 1000 away from the exclusively local economy. Now for a while it would revert to its earlier patterns. Even the towns, formerly the agents of expansion, hurried to protect themselves, and one speaks rightly (the phrase is Shepard Clough's) of a new town particularism.[52]

While the fourteenth-century crisis produced neither a new dominant class nor a new economic theory, it did much to undermine both the old class and the old theory. The manorial aristocrats died along with the rest of Europe, but that was not so much of a problem, for usually for every dead lord there was a live heir. The real difficulty was the changing economy itself, the Plague only adding to the directions and rate of development. The original pressure on the aristocracy was produced by the era of growth, as an urban world of money and commerce made life on the manor less easy. The lord was forced to buy what he needed at increasingly inflated prices while trying to live from fixed services and fees. And the list of what he needed, or thought he needed, was also growing. The less functional within the economy the lord became, the more pretentious he acted, occasioning new expenditures. Moreover, the requirements of warfare alone were enough to strain the budget. Later medieval armor was heavier. So were, necessarily, warhorses. And for-tifications grew apace, as did all of the costs of aristocratic governance.

Then, when the Plague hit, the lord's position was given a second jolt. Now there were many fewer serfs. Labor was acutely scarce, and therefore its value on the open market shot upward, further increasing the tempta-tion of the serf to flee the manor or, short of flight, to make demands that the lord could not easily meet. The Plague shook to its foundations every institution, but it was especially hard on manorialism and its lords, for they were already in trouble.

The changes in theory witnessed by the fourteenth century were subtle, but important. Scholasticism did not disappear, it merely got more contentious. Its intellectual world was collapsing, under attack from science on the one hand and mysticism on the other. To defend itself, it theorized with even greater intensity. Reason had been its forte, and it would preserve itself by even greater exercises of logic. In its efforts in the economic realm, a puzzling thing happened: as the arguments became longer, the late Scholastics on occasion actually began to describe the workings of the emerging economy. Groping toward some sort of compromise between just-price and supply-and-demand economics—put another way, between the workings of a static and a mobile society—they began to explore the problems of what was to become modern economic theory. And that theory would finally be determined not by the dictates of a moral life lived in preparation for an eternal life, but rather by the possibilities for the acquisition of wealth here and now. Moving in this direction, fourteenth-century economic thought—especially considering the despair and frenzy of the times—was at moments remarkably clear-headed in its attempts to deal with the long-range transition from the medieval to the modern economy.[53]

As for the geography of the fourteenth-century crisis, one can see the results on all fronts. Europe went nowhere. There was no successor to Marco Polo, who died in 1324. The German *Drang nach Osten* ground to a halt, as did the Spanish *Reconquista*. The push into the Atlantic, as noted, also came to an end at mid-century and would have to wait for the generation of Henry of Portugal to get it moving again. And internally the new lands that had been cultivated reverted to swamp and forest. The West had expanded for more than three centuries. Now it would lie still for a while.

Toward the middle of the fifteenth century, however, the West's period of economic contraction came to an end, and, seemingly quite suddenly, the early modern economy made its appearance. The impression of rapid change was mostly due to the fact that the fourteenth century had been what it was. The new modern economy seemed to burst forth with explosive force out of the confusion of the immediate past. But a look at the history of economic development since 1000 reminds us that this second period of growth was only a continuation after a relatively brief interruption of the first, different only inasmuch as the features of the modern economy, long obscured by the prevalence of the medieval, now became clearly visible. The age of capitalism, of the dominant open market, had begun. Certainly it would be wrong not to recognize the fact that many aspects of the manorial economy were still present in the late fifteenth century, and not only then, but also later. Some have even persisted on into the twentieth. The same point was made with regard to the politics of feudalism. Yet the balance as we approach 1500 was swinging to the new economy.

This meant that with regard to production and distribution the West's economy was no longer primarily oriented toward the system of local production and consumption. It was gradually being turned around and faced in a new direction, one that pointed it to production for the market, whether the items were manufactured goods, raw materials, or agricultural produce. As for the last, it should be said that the enclosure movement that had had its origins in the thirteenth century was now, in the fifteenth and sixteenth centuries, at its peak. Increasingly the vital center of economic activity was shifting from the unspecialized and self-sufficient to the specialized and commercial sector. Of course the management of the economy was also shifting, from the countryside, where it had been since at least the sixth century, to the towns. It was from the latter that the commercial revolution that is often taken as the most distinctive feature of this Renaissance economy was being directed. And it was from within them that the bourgeoisie was continuing its rise.

The bourgeoisie at present was still not ready to become the dominant economic class of the early modern period, just as it was not yet ready to become the dominant political class. It would renew, however, its claim to share economic leadership with the aristocracy, and this time with still more reason than in the twelfth and thirteenth centuries. In fact, there were now three groups competing: the greater aristocracy, with its huge estates; the lesser aristocracy on the Continent and the corresponding gentry in England, the latter seen by some as a sort of agrarian bourgeoisie; and the bourgeoisie itself. If these three were in opposition, divided by tradition and specific interests, they were also increasingly being joined together in the spirit of capitalism. For they were all now concentrating on the profits. And there were profits to be had because of the existence of the new commerce. Trade encouraged specialization and production for the market. These in turn encouraged trade. The localism of the manorial economy was disappearing rapidly and being replaced by the large-scale activity of capitalism. As that happened, the old aristocracy was forced into crucial compromises: not only was it compelled to tolerate the presence of the bourgeoisie, but also, and more important for the economy of this first modern period, it had to move out into the marketplace. The West was entering a new era, and it was no longer possible to remain aloof.

The economic theory of the Renaissance was mercantilism. On that everyone seems to agree. Just what is meant by the term it is more difficult to say, for there were a variety of mercantilisms, some discouraging trade, some encouraging it, some eschewing industry, some trying to develop it. Yet they all had a number of things in common. One was the conviction that, whatever one might think was the best way to acquire it, success in the economic game was to be measured in bullion. It was the accumulation of gold and silver that was important. Another was the belief that the basic unit of economics was the state, and that would be in most cases now the newly formed national state. Yet another was the insistence that that state intervene consistently to control agriculture, industry, and commerce to its advantage. And, finally, it was assumed that advantage for one state meant disadvantage for another: wealth in mercantilistic thinking was conceived as being entirely static, and therefore gains here must be matched by losses there.

How much of an innovation was this new theory? In some respects, mercantilism represented a sharp break with the past; yet in others it was remarkably traditional. With regard to the four characteristics just mentioned, we might say that the first two looked ahead, to the fully modern economy, while the second two looked backward, to the past—another confirmation of the observation of that now-immortalized student who once wrote that the Renaissance in general stood with one foot in the Middle Ages and the other saluting the rising sun! Bullionism, to take it first, was, for all its rather old-fashioned commitment to a single measure for wealth, also very novel. Money had had a low priority within the initial medieval economy, which operated mostly without it, and as long as the West remained medieval, its economy was never thoroughly monetized. The Middle Ages refused to give or could not give, depending on how one looks at it, to money the top billing. Now indeed the West was saying that money was the economic essence. The root of all evil had become the route to all good for the nascent modern economy.

The elevation of the state to the position of crucial economic unit was also new and modern. Mercantilism here perfectly reflected the political accomplishments of its times. The new monarchs had defeated feudalism; likewise, mercantilist theory replaced manorialism's Thomist theory. One can add that, unlike all medieval economic thought, mercantilism was exclusively secular, infused with a worldly, competitive ethos. Perhaps in some cases, almost certainly with regard to the Spanish economy, the application of mercantilist principles actually made things worse. Still, it was in its emphasis on the welfare of the national community certainly appropriate to the period.

But both the idea of close regulation and the conception of a fixed, unchanging society were medieval. The manorial economy had been entirely regulated and so had its immediate successor, the mixed manorial and urban economy of lords and guild masters. The only novelty in this regard inherent in mercantilism was the application of regulation on a larger scale and at a higher level. The consequences for bureaucracy were not insignificant, but there was nothing here in the theory of regulation itself that was different from the medieval approach to economics. And that is equally true for early modern insights into growth: there were none. Medieval economic thought had, as already said, assumed a stable world. The mercantilists were of the same opinion. The economy had been growing, the fourteenth century excepted, for half a millennium. It occurred to no one, however, that such behavior might be accounted for theoretically. In fact, growth would not be thoroughly recognized by theory until the middle of the twentieth century, by which time it was nearly at an end. Thus in this respect the mercantilists were hardly odd. In any case, mercantilism, to sum it up, was a cross, partly modern, one can even say mostly modern, but occupying, to quote Robert Heilbroner, "a position of unstable rest, not fully emancipated from the past, not fully entrant upon the future."[54]

The geographic expansion of the West's economy during the fifteenth and sixteenth centuries was of course spectacular—so spectacular that economic historians have occasionally been mesmerized by it, resulting in its being made responsible for the boom itself. Certainly two of the three great discoveries had immediate economic effects. Columbus had revealed an accessible new hemisphere and da Gama a water route to the riches of the Far East. Only Magellan's demonstration of the Pacific connection was for the moment of little practical value. But two out of three was not bad. The West undoubtedly received a considerable economic stimulation, as it moved to explore, conquer, and where possible settle the new lands. Europe was forced to manage ventures on a scale hitherto impossible to imagine. The result was not only to put even more pressure on the weakening manorial structure, but also to favor those institutions that were designed to handle entrepreneurial economics, as ventures sought huge profits over long distances and extended time periods.

But the greatest immediate influence regarding economics produced by the discoveries was no doubt made by the influx of precious metals. It has been estimated that the European supply of gold and silver tripled between 1500 and 1650, with the peak with regard to gold imports reached just after 1550 and with regard to silver just before 1600. By 1700 credit and bullion acting together had increased the West's money supply by perhaps a factor of six. The result was instant inflation, easy money, and happy borrowers. The traditional and stable parts of the economy were put at a disadvantage, while the new and mobile were given every inducement to become yet more dynamic.[55]

Yet had there been no discoveries, no new overseas trade, and no influx of bullion, can we conceive of a Renaissance Europe without a considerable economic explosion? The medieval West had already had one long period of growth. And well before the discoveries, noticeable by 1450 and obvious by 1475, the recovery from the period of reaction had been well established. The rise of prices had also started. One can add that when the economic manifestations of the discoveries began to make themselves known, it was the West's determination to employ them to aid the new economy that was the crucial ingredient. The basic prerequisites for the Renaissance economy came from within Europe, not from without. By 1492, every cultural and every political index pointed to economic growth: with a new culture and a new politics, it was unlikely that the West would not turn out a new economy.[56] Had the late-fifteenth-century economic preparation itself not been as thorough as it was, then the effort at expansion would have proved more destructive than stimulating. The discoveries were a factor, but only one among many, as the Western economy, developing within the context of its civilization, made the transition from its medieval to its modern condition.

Much the same can be said of other single possibilities when the talk is of the causes of economic expansion in the late fifteenth and sixteenth centuries. There were important inventions in the later medieval centuries—the use of water power spread from the twelfth century on, the common wheelbarrow and an efficient rudder appeared in the thirteenth, the utilization of canal locks and a workable mechanical clock in the fourteenth, and printing in the fifteenth. But none of these alone nor indeed all of them together would seem to have been capable of doing more than contributing to a trend already set. The demographic increases are, on the other hand, more impressive. Europe's population recovered quickly from the losses caused by the Plague. The data are not entirely reliable, but assuming that the nadir was reached around 1400, by which time there were only half as many Europeans as before the Plague, the population then more than doubled by 1650. This meant that in spite of the Plague there were significantly more people living in Europe by 1650 than had been living there in 1300. It is not unreasonable to suppose that the increased numbers both necessitated and facilitated growth. Yet the old problem remains: did the demographic upswing cause the economic, or the economic the demographic? Again, the suggestion here is that it is impossible to choose, with both better taken as logical pieces in a general civilizational movement.

Even less persuasive as a single cause of the Renaissance economy is the argument that links it to religion, specifically to Calvinist Protestantism. Certainly Puritans made good capitalists, and for just the reasons that Max Weber enumerated: they were frugal, they saved, they invested in capital goods, and they were convinced that prosperity was a sign of election to salvation.[57] But as others have pointed out, other minorities have also made good capitalists. Besides, the chronology is all wrong: capitalism was too far along in its development both in northern Italy and in northwestern Europe before Calvin was born (1509). It was even beginning to do rather well before Luther was born (1483). Double-entry bookkeeping, so often taken as a milestone in the development of early capitalism, was in use by the time Martin was eleven. Luther and Calvin were to live out their lives in a period of economic growth to which they were mostly not pertinent. What specific economic influence they were to have was negative, disapproving, and brought to bear chiefly upon the period that followed, which was one of decline.

By the time of their deaths, or, more precisely, at some point in between them (Luther died in 1546, Calvin in 1564), the West was entering another era of reaction. Not everywhere: the century beginning in 1550 was one of protoindustrial advance for northern England and Scotland, and Holland also did well. As with Eastern Europe during the fourteenth-century crisis, to be out-of-step and a little late was to be fortunate. But most of Europe suffered an economic setback that lasted from the middle of the sixteenth century well into the seventeenth and in certain regards, notably with respect to prices, even into the early decades of the eighteenth. The West would once more appear to have been suffering the consequences of being overextended. And now warfare, religious turmoil, a decline in bullion imports, and perhaps a few degrees drop in average temperatures combined with what might be called the natural cyclic effect—the times were ripe—to put an end to growth; and in some areas, notably Spain and Germany, to cause a severe reversal.

Again there were notable shifts with regard to the dominant classes. This was the period of the great aristocratic reaction. And although it can be explained by reference to politics alone, it is probably true that the aristocracy's relative economic position and thus its will to resurgence was strengthened—even while it was in particular instances also an economic victim—by the long economic depression. For the collapse of the Renaissance expansion meant a weakening of the financial base of that coalition of town and crown that had attempted to bring the aristocracy under control. Now the aristocracy sought to reassume its traditional role, as the early modern economy faltered and began to revert to medieval patterns.[58]

As for theory, the attitude toward economics again changed with the changing intellectual climate. The late sixteenth and early seventeenth centuries were times of intense religious feeling, as the West found itself in the midst of a revolt against Renaissance secularism, with Protestants and Catholics fighting each other to claim the heritage of reaction. And neither side at the outset of this period of reform had anything flattering to say about capitalism. Luther, consistent with his return to Augustinian views, had sharply condemned its practices. His protest against indulgences, although chiefly religious in inspiration, had also managed to decry the drain of money from the agrarian and exploited north to the urban and evil south. The austere Counter-Reformation manifested the same fundamental attitude, if without the specific regional biases.

Within this context, Puritanism to be sure offered something of a refuge, as Hugh Trevor-Roper has pointed out, for the toleration of worldly pursuits that had been formerly sustained by the Erasmian wing of Catholicism.[59] Yet Puritanism was not otherwise noted for its broadmindedness. In this century of cultural reaction and economic depression, it certainly contributed to the general condemnation of the humanist attitudes that lay behind Renaissance capitalism. Puritanism's conversion to capitalism would seem to have been something of an accident: having won over some of the originally more backward areas of the West, notably northern England and Scotland, it just so happened that it soon found itself in the midst of an economy prospering in defiance of the general economic collapse. Puritanism could either find a way to approve of participation in the new growth or be pushed aside by a more compatible faith. And find a way it did: God loved capitalists after all. But the world of Calvin and the world of capitalism only overlapped in places, and largely by chance. The secular and material interests of money-grubbing entrepreneurs and avid consumers were not easily reconciled to Puritanism, which was as typical in this respect as in others of seventeenth-century zealotry. If there was an essential contemporary attitude to expansive economics, it was one of antagonism. For the West as a whole, the economy was suffering; and the response, not unnaturally, was to point again to a better life after death.

The seventeenth century also saw a physical contraction. After such a rapid expansion, it was probably unavoidable. The demographic growth that had characterized the Renaissance came to a halt, although only a few areas, again notably Spain and Germany, experienced big losses. But within the old boundaries of the West, there was much shifting. Many villages stood empty, and wolves reappeared where they had not been seen for centuries. In the new colonies, this period also saw significant interruption. The sixteenth had been the century of discovery and expansion. The seventeenth century, it would seem, served as a time of rest.

Then in the first half of the eighteenth century the West's economy once again put itself back on the path to growth and prosperity. The slow, but long descent of prices that had been continuous since 1640 came to an end in the 1720s, and the inflationary pattern that has usually accompanied growth reemerged. And in the 1740s began the Industrial Revolution. From this point until the latter part of the nineteenth century, for about a century and a half, the West's economy continued to develop effortlessly, advancing toward the dream of the fully specialized, fully commercialized open-market system. In the course of this progression, the landscape of Europe was thoroughly changed and the Westernization of the world begun. The West and the world that it had captured would be re-created as a single economy, with the market deciding who could best produce what and how much was needed. For a long time it seemed to work.

The Industrial Revolution can be divided into major segments with regard to just what was being industrialized, but whether we speak of one or several separate revolutions is not very important, as long as we recognize that from the beginning the same process has been at work, essentially one that has seen the progressive substitution of machinery for manual labor. Of course the use of machinery itself was not new. Both the medieval and the early modern periods of growth had seen a certain amount of it. But the eighteenth, nineteenth, and twentieth centuries brought a tremendous acceleration in the rate of increased application. Now the very business of industry was industrialized, that is to say that systematic work was increasingly brought together from its place of origin in the home, small shop, and farm into central manufacturing enterprises.

The first wave of this modern industrialization came in the late eighteenth and early nineteenth centuries. It brought the start of the initial great mass-production venture that transformed the textile industry, also the perfection of the coal-fired steam-engine. And this latter device produced for the first time vast amounts of that which Watt's collaborator Matthew Boulton rightly described as "what all the world desires to have—Power."[60] The second mid-nineteenth-century wave brought steel, and with it both railroads and steamships, the means of a tremendously expanded commerce; and also the machines of the new agriculture that would provide a good part of the commodities to be traded on the world market. The third wave, arriving in the late nineteenth and early twentieth centuries, brought electric power and the highly mobile gasoline engine, the two combining to bring mechanization to those vast reaches of the economy missed by the original industrialization. Finally (I am using here Heilbroner's schematization[61]), there was a fourth wave, in the middle and late twentieth century, bringing further automation, electronics, and the rest of what has come to be called high tech; yet another round in the mechanization and resultant depopulation of agriculture; and the swelling of the service sector. The last has led to the description of a phase beyond industrialism, often referred to as postindustrialism, but the British sociologist Krishan Kumar has argued convincingly that it is only more of the same.[62] In this regard, the present economy is surely but an extension of its industrial past, although there are other reasons, as we shall see in a moment, to treat it as a distinct period.

The dominant class once the Industrial Revolution had had time to make itself felt came to be the haute bourgeoisie, the upper-middle class, typified by the factory owner—for the moment ownership and management were united, in the classical pattern of industrial capitalism that Marx correctly described. Yet "dominant" here should not be pushed too far. Economics did not alone determine society's direction; and the bourgeoisie could not have enjoyed its position at the top without having captured the imagination of those below. Also it was, after all, an open class. Few would rise to join it, but many thought they could.

But here the important point is that the long contest with the agrarian aristocracy had been won. Agriculture was now commercialized, and thereby the landowners had been reduced to being capitalists among capitalists, and indeed of the lesser breed, for the easier profits were to be had in industry. Furthermore, it was industry, not agriculture, that provided the base for military power. Just as an agrarian age had made it necessary to have a thriving agriculture to support knight and charger, now the new industrial age made it necessary to have a thriving industry to support the industrialized army. Military conventions necessarily both derive from and do their best to reinforce the structure of society.[63]

Economic theory in this era that we might refer to as the high industrial focused on the principle of laissez faire. By the middle of the eighteenth century, mercantilism was being criticized from several sides. Then in 1776 came Adam Smith's *Wealth of Nations*—not a complete break, as the title indicates, but nevertheless a manifesto proclaiming the economic wisdom of the open market.[64] Leave things alone, it said, and the natural laws of supply and demand would ultimately benefit all. Smith's ideas did not find immediate acceptance; toward the middle of the nineteenth century they began to win out, however, first in Great Britain, then on the Continent and throughout the West. By 1860, laissez faire had become an article of faith, although even then it was seldom applied *sans peur et sans reproche*. Where there were certain natural advantages, the doctrine operated well enough for those employing it. But where there were none, where local production was put in competition with cheaper goods, free trade bestowed fewer benefits. Nevertheless, the British said it would work. And Britain was rich. That fact alone persuaded many, even when common sense pointed to regulation and protection.

The geographic dimension of the eighteenth and nineteenth centuries was determined by the return, following the seventeenth-century contraction, of expansion. This was a process whose origins, as noted, can be traced back to the High Middle Ages. Now, with its resumption, whole continents were suddenly being opened up and then filled by the flood of European emigration, which of course brought with it the new economy. The West was now in the last phase of its expansion into the world. Yet if one seeks the center and source of all this activity, it could be found still pretty much where it had always been, even if what had been a small, homogeneous core in northwestern Europe had become somewhat larger, as it spread to new areas, among them central Germany and northern England. Toward the end of the period, to be sure, from about 1850 on, new core areas began to appear overseas, notably in the northern and central United States. But for all the dislocations implied by these shifts, so far nothing in the Old West had been made to suffer for the benefit of the new. Spain and Portugal had fallen by the wayside, but until the early modern period they had been peripheral. Now they were merely peripheral once again. In fact, nothing seemed to be able to hurt the old West and this new, ecumenical version of its economy. Apparently headed toward the creation of a single worldwide economic network that would operate according to the natural rules of the open market, the West was filled with the confidence that things could only get better. Busy enjoying the fruits of its industrial production, it was prosperous. And on top.

Whenever anyone or anything is on top, there is talk of impending decline. And rightly so. We understand from our experience of human affairs at every level that the circumstances that favor our efforts in a particular enterprise sooner or later change. The path of the West's modern economy from the late nineteenth century, by which time it had done all it was ever going to do to create a self-regulating open-market system, would seem necessarily to lead downward. The circumstances would indeed change. Then, in the course of coping with the new economic facts of life, the modern economy would begin the transition to new forms. True, the living standard for the West—that is, the old West, that which had been Westernized by the end of the early modern period—would continue to rise, although there are so many factors that go into that measurement that such observations have little validity. Westerners came to own more things. Whether or not their lives were better is debatable. With regard to the new West, those areas where the West's economy met and destroyed other less aggressive economies, one can only say that some of those regions have since prospered, while others have fallen into a state of near ruin. But with affluence or without it, the essential point is that in the late nineteenth century the economic life of the West ceased to work on its own, without constant monitoring and adjustment. After almost a thousand years of progression toward the open market, the Western economy had begun to close that market and to seek out ways in which it might protect itself from its own more destructive features.

The fact that this reversal of directions was taking place, and it is first evident in the 1870s and continues to the present, has been overshadowed by the much more vivd impressions left by this most recent period's dramatic growth. In the past century, the West and the world with it have been redone as an immense consumer society. But at the same time, a quiet change, fundamental in nature, was occurring. It was unplanned, uncoordinated, and unexplained. It seemed simply to happen. Even when we search today, after having for more than a century watched the gradual breakdown of the modern economy, that is, of the open-market capitalism that culminated in the nineteenth century, it is still very difficult to provide an explanation.

We can, however, point to the events themselves. But first a word of caution: even if all of the economic facts could be known, we would still probably not find our answer. Economics, to say it again, does not exist apart from the other aspects of civilization. And just in this century, that which stretches from the late nineteenth to the present, the West was experiencing the several crises already reviewed: the various cultural crises that invariably put an end to the modern themes in their respective domains; and the developing political crisis that would seem to be putting an end to the modern theme in politics, that national-state system that has been the work of the Modern Age. The implication is clear enough: modernism is failing. If its economic theme appears likewise to be failing, then the suggestion is that there is more here than meets the purely economic eye. The economy would seem to be reacting not only to its own inherent history, but also to a larger history of which it is only a part.

Or could we be deceived here? Could these separate stories, that of thought and art, politics and economics, all of which either have already or seem about to cast off the modern (meaning, again, old modern and not necessarily contemporary modern) forms, not after all be related aspects of the same basic phenomenon? Possible, but not likely. History, like Einstein's God, is not in the habit of playing tricks on us. The appearance of the waning of the Modern Age is surely not the result of a series of remarkable coincidences. The Modern Age is indeed waning, just as the Classical Age and the Middle Ages did before it, and now, as then, that has relevance for each and every area of endeavor within our civilization.

But what are the more purely economic events that since the 1870s have come to mark the decline of the modern economy? Granting, that is, that economic activity never takes place in a vacuum, what nevertheless are the signs of decline that come from within that area traditionally thought of as economic? Here a comment upon them can best be organized by continuing to employ the four divisions that we have been using to describe the rise of the modern economy—that is, production-distribution, class, theory, and geography. In each of these categories, we shall see at work the unfolding of the same underlying process, the devolution of the West's great experiment with open-market capitalism.

The most significant developments with regard to the West's economic production and distribution during the last century have been these two: first, the rapidly increasing intervention in the economy of regional and, much more important, national governments, at first marginal, but later crucial; and, second, the progressive displacement of people by machines, as automation has been turned free to realize its awesome and problematical potential. The beginnings of both are clearly visible from the late nineteenth century onward.

With regard to intervention, one should remember that there had always been some, even in nations like Great Britain, where laissez-faire doctrine was the strongest. Europe was still burdened, as the modern mind saw it, with a considerable remnant of the medieval past. But that remnant had been disintegrating as the modern economy got stronger, and this remained true through the middle of the nineteenth century. Then, however, the flow started to move in the other direction. Domestically, governments, often with the cooperation of big business, moved to suppress the excesses of open-market competition. Established corporations joined consumers in trying to prevent what Karl Polanyi once called "the demolition of society" that one could expect from the uninhibited operation of the market mechanism.[65] The fact that protection for the masses also meant protection of profits for the corporations themselves seems to have assisted the latter somewhat in their altruism. Whatever the motivation, and certainly the hard times brought by the general depression that lasted from 1873 to 1896 also had something to do with it, the West launched its first assault on the mature modern economy. Interference with rates, regulation of food and drug quality, establishment of safety standards in the workplace, and finally, beginning in Bismarck's Germany, the various social insurance programs—these were the work of the 1870s and 1880s. And they were accompanied by the imposition of significant tariffs, as each state moved to restrict the plethora of manufactured goods and farm produce that the new advances in transportation made available on the world market. The enthusiasm for the natural operation of the unfettered market system had obviously been lost.[66]

A second wave of regulation hit the West shortly before World War I and continued through into the postwar period. This time the goal was the redistribution of income. The attempts at realization began in Britain with Lloyd George's "People's Budget" of 1909.[67] The intention was to make the rich shoulder the burden of maintaining the poor, now to be cared for by the growing attentions of the welfare state. But these early measures were modest, more important for the precedent they set than for their actual impact at the time. The greatest influence of these years was exerted by the war itself, as each nation rushed to impose its military priorities, always at the expense of the open market. The war also brought the Russian Revolution. And although Russia was at this point hardly in the mainstream of Western development, we should not pass over Lenin's achievement without a comment on its general relevance: the great European revolution of the eighteenth century, that is, the French, had after a considerable struggle opted for capitalism; the great European revolution of the twentieth century after a comparable struggle did not.

With the peace, most of the West then tried to revert to a more genuine capitalism; but just ten years after the signing of the Versailles Treaty there occurred another catastrophe, as the collapse of the stock market triggered the Great Depression. Accompanying the Depression came the third great wave of intervention, this time so far-reaching in its impact that one can hardly speak of the continued existence of the laissez-faire system. Then World War II arrived hard on the heels of the Depression and of course eliminated any possibility that the tendency to regulation would be soon reversed. The chief result of this decade and a half (1930–45) of growing state power was that the nation took over responsibility for ensuring economic prosperity, specifically, for guaranteeing full-employment. The last step was all but inescapable. The modern economy was by now almost fully monetized. Earlier, one could perhaps get along without a job. But no longer. There was now, short of welfare, no refuge from the ravages of the business cycle. Under the circumstances, with automation paring down the requirements for labor in existing industry, the only solution was for governments to devise ways of encouraging—indeed, forcing where necessary—continual growth.

One should stress here the effects of mechanization. It has been named along with the increase in regulation as one of the two basic developments with regard to the West's pattern of production and distribution over the last century. We shall make no further attempt to trace its history. Yet it should be noted that in this one field, the technological, where we have seen the growing employment of machines and concomitant disemployment of people, a strict laissez-faire attitude on the part of government has been maintained. There is something more than a little odd in that circumstance. Only a society in which the dream of an eventual resolution of capitalism's increasing problems was still alive would have permitted such a failure of regulation in the midst of so much other regulation. Given, however, the commitment to automate and automate again, the only way for capitalism to keep itself from going under, weighed down as it was by the growing mass of the jobless, was to opt for prosperity without end. The alternative in a democracy was welfare-socialism. If the government refused to provide jobs, then it must provide welfare. And jobs were less controversial. Thus capitalism agreed to full-employment despite the implications of automation. Under these conditions, growth provided the only real alternative. For only if the economy continued to grow could it provide new jobs to make up for those lost by the advent of the latest round of mechanization.

Continuing to grow presented no real problem in the post-1945 period. Much to the surprise of those who expected a decline, the West's economy experienced a two-decade boom, from the 1950s through the early 1970s. Prosperity obviated additional increases in government intervention. Faith in capitalism returned. The constant bustle and easy profits even encouraged us to forget to what extent the good times were the product of fortuitous and not-repeatable circumstances, among which were the opportunity to fill the vacuum in consumer-goods production created by the war; the easy availability of cheap resources; and the decision by the United States, in this period the West's economic leader as never before and probably never again, to go on with deficit financing when both a strict Keynesian interpretation and fundamental logic would have insisted on taking money out of the economy rather than putting it in.

But these advantages and stimulants could not last. The shortages created by the war were made up. That perhaps was not so damaging, for it is the business of a consumer society to consume. And ours has shown a consistent ability to rise to the occasion when the price is right. In the early 1970s, however, something of great importance happened. From the eleventh century until 1973, raw materials had been getting cheaper. Now they started to become more expensive. This turnaround was superficially the result of world politics, but at a more profound level it was caused by the fact of developing shortages. The West had based its growth on the use of nonrenewable resources. For a long time it did not matter. Now it did matter. As if the West's aging modern economy had not enough to worry about, the resource problem, made acute as we noted earlier in this essay by the dual phenomena of rapid world population growth and simultaneous expansion of the Western economy into the Third World, all but assured for capitalism and what remains of its open-market system an even more restrictive future.

At the moment, the West is trying to extend deficit financing to the world while also continuing to use it at home in an effort to prolong growth. Again, the United States is the centerpiece. Domestically, the method is the unbalanced budget. And overseas, more important than ever before because it is there that the new markets are located, it is bank loans to nations that cannot afford to repay them. These are inevitably followed by refinancing schedules and further loans that cannot be repaid. The banks are then covered by assistance from the International Monetary Fund, which in turn is supported by U.S. money, which in turn is supported by the government's ability to borrow and, as a last resort, to create new money—to fall back, as it were, on the printing press. If we do not have the money, we, unrepentantly, can simply print up a new batch. One is reminded that the runaway Weimar inflation came to an end when the printers went out on strike. The Modern Age began with the printing press. That Gutenberg's invention should do it in would be all too appropriate. In any case, we are witnessing another great wave of government intervention in the open market, with the scale and stakes going higher and higher. Thus the West's productive and distributive mechanisms have been slowly shifted away from the open market—all for the purpose, oddly enough, of rescuing that venerable institution. Capitalism has called in government to put an end to capitalism. We have had a quiet revolution and now are trying to learn to operate a system that is so new that it as yet has no name.

We have said nothing so far about class, theory, and geography. This commentary on economics is already too long relative to what has gone before, and therefore surely it is best that these be treated only briefly. With regard to changes in the dominant class over the last century, the most significant one is the fall from power of the old class of owners. It is a truism of contemporary economics that those who operate and control today's industry, commerce, and banking are no longer those who own the corporations, and that ownership has been fragmented and reduced to a peripheral consideration in the inner struggles for power. It is more difficult to specify with what the class of owners has been replaced. One can point to the managers, but beyond the label who are they? Do they represent a class, new or old? Probably not. They are bourgeois, to be sure, but in a world where everyone is or is about to become bourgeois that fact is of little significance. And therein lies a predicament, one that was touched on earlier: the twentieth century has seen a fragmentation and diffusion of the old middle class, and so far there is no successor.

Possibly the best thing that can be said at the moment with regard to the new dominant class is, then, that class as a significant demarcation, whether with regard to social, political, or economic alignments, is very rapidly losing its meaning. The Middle Ages did not have a class structure in the sense that we have come to know it, even if we at times speak of a medieval dominant class, for medieval society was divided primarily along vertical lines that ran through the horizontal delineations associated with class. The Modern Age then saw society redivided, as the estates and corporations of the vertical structure were pushed aside to make way for a new organization of society into classes. Now, in the late Modern Age, we would seem to be experiencing the passing of the class structure.

In the changes with regard to theory during the last century one sees more of the same: the shift from the classical capitalist position to a new ground that is, although designed to save capitalism, only dubiously capitalist. In short, the intervention in the open-market system that in fact has taken place has been endorsed by theory. There have been four stages: first, there was the turn to conservatism in the 1870s, which led to the downfall of so many European liberal parties and marked a general turn away from laissez faire, even as an ideal. Then, in the pre–World War I decades, there emerged a new socialism, popular and moderate, stressing reform rather than revolution. These revisionist and Fabian socialists were seldom directly effective until after the war, but their existence certainly edged the theoretical middle point away from laissez-faire economics. Next, with the coming of the Depression, came Keynesianism, which had been developing before Keynes, but was articulated by him and is still generally associated with his name. It called for deficits to prime the pump. But, an important point, one that has already been made but bears repeating, it did not call for permanent measures to stimulate the economy. In times of prosperity, the government was actually to move in the other direction, thus taking steps not only to mitigate the lows of the business cycle, but also to suppress the highs. Yet whether directly attributable to Keynes or not and regardless of just how it was used, used it was. It was an idea for which the West was obviously ready.

The fourth stage in this story of the devolution of the theory of laissez faire has arrived in just the last several decades. It has been marked by the appearance of a theory of growth. In itself there is nothing in such a development that challenges capitalism. The West's economy has been growing, the fourteenth and seventeenth centuries excepted, for almost a millennium. And capitalism and growth have become all but synonymous. But, as already noted, there has never been a clear theory of growth. Neither Adam Smith, nor Marx, nor even Keynes had thought in terms of permanent and consistent expansion. Now, however, in the course of the post–World War II era, both the theory and a commitment to its implementation have come into being.[68] Walter Heller, at one time chairman of the President's Council of Economic Advisers, has written that in the early 1960s "policy emphasis had to be redirected from a *corrective* orientation geared to the dynamics of the cycle, to a *propulsive* orientation geared to the dynamics and promise of growth."[69] In short, government would intervene not only in bad times, but always. Stability was no longer the goal, but rather expansion—and that without interruption.

This new addition to the theory of capitalism in fact signaled, then, the end of capitalism. If the market mechanism is to work, it cannot be committed to any single outcome. If the market is to be open, then it cannot be closed to certain possibilities. There is, of course, always a little of the closed in the most open of markets, and the reverse. But when the West accepted growth as the overriding priority, when it decided that it must have only growth and could tolerate none of the backsliding that an open-market economy would inevitably include, then it opted against capitalism.

It is easy to see villains at work here, in the Western world's obsession with growth. While, however, there are undoubtedly a few, the real cause would seem to be the very success of the open-market system. For it did so well in its competition with the older, traditional economy of the

Middle Ages that it gradually drove the latter out of business. The whole of society became wholly involved with and dependent upon the market. While the new system was still establishing itself, its ups and downs were important to society, but not all-important. There was a more or less stable base economy, local, agrarian, and largely self-sufficient, upon which the West could fall back in times of recession. But once the open-market system had become the only system—and in the West's Modern Age this was the first time in the history of any civilization that this had happened—it could not, as said, be permitted to fail, even for a moment. The Great Depression gave a quick demonstration of capitalism's vulnerability in this regard: of its inability, once society had been entirely monetized, to cope with even a temporary interruption of the flow of money. Therefore the West chose to command perpetual prosperity. If automation had made prosperity dependent on growth, then the West must also choose to grow, even if that meant hastening the flight from the capitalism that had been the original source of prosperity.

Still, the modern economy might have been more successful in its attempt to create a controlled growth had it not been for the fact that it now began to suffer increasingly from the sorts of difficulties that invariably afflict all things that go on growing. If they do not find their natural limits at one point, then they find them at another. Change, especially expansive change, requires the toleration of its surroundings; and eventually that toleration is refused, as it is now being refused to the West's growth economy in the late twentieth century. The specifics of the refusal at the moment have to do with population, resources, and pollution. If it were not these, however, the dynamics of growth would soon bring us to confront another set. But the subject here is theory, and the significant point in that regard, and it contains a woeful irony, is that it is only when at last further growth has become both difficult and dangerous that we have come consciously to opt for it.

Finally, it is time to say something about the geographic shifts in the West's economy since the late nineteenth century. Here the changes that took place are so remarkable that only our familiarity with them keeps our astonishment within bounds. In 1870 most of Africa and Asia and large portions of both North and South American were untouched by the West's open-market system. Despite the grandiose scale of previous intrusions, the vast majority of the world's people still lived as they had for centuries, in some cases for millennia. Then during the next hundred years the Western economy penetrated almost everywhere. Some of the countryside, although less all the time, has remained beyond the pale. But where today is there a city anywhere that is not a Western city? Whatever the flag and no matter the ideology, the world's cities are linked together in a single international economic network. And the goal of all of the newly

Western economies is to become more Western, to advance, that is, to full industrialization.

There is nothing in this particular pattern of geographic expansion that would seem to contribute to the aura of decline found in the other aspects of the West's economic history over the last century. Yet there are three derivatives that do indeed reinforce our impressions of an economy that is failing. First, there is the implication for the population-resources-pollution dilemma, referred to initially in chapter 1 and again just a moment ago. As the West has pressed into the Third World it has acquired for its economy the responsibility for assimilating and providing for those very poor areas where population is the most rapidly increasing. And this final task of industrialization may be more than even a very vital West could have handled.

Second, geography is doing to the West on one level what the bourgeoisie is doing on another: the bourgeoisie by becoming the only class, by eliminating its rivals, has eliminated its raison d'etre—"there cannot be a bourgeoisie without a proletariat," George Lichtheim once noted, "and if the one is fading out, so is the other;"[70] and it is the same with the West and the world. As long as the West was one civilization among several, there was a reason for it to be Western, to be distinctive and to take pride in defending its uniqueness. But the West and the world have become one as the other civilizations have succumbed, whether conquered or attracted to the flame is not in this regard so important. As that has occurred, there has been a weakening of purpose and a decrease in the tensions that bind. The West's modern experiment is perhaps not so much dying as diffusing, with its energies dissipated and not even any longer appropriate. If it has been the work of the Modern Age to make the world Western, then that has been achieved, and the Modern Age and its economy have thereby become superfluous.

And, third, there is the matter of what expansion has done to the center. For a long time, the West expanded and the core seemed to profit—at least, it remained prosperous. Through the nineteenth century that continued to be the case. But since the turn of the century, a few of the newer areas have tended to grow rich at the expense of the older ones. Both France and Great Britain declined rather rapidly relative to Germany and the United States in the period before World War I. Then by the end of World War II, Britain, the first to industrialize, began to show clear signs that it was becoming expansion's first victim. It had led the world in innovation. But now, victimized apparently by its own success, it could no longer compete. British living standards were high. The cost of labor was high. So were prices, and British goods lost their appeal on the world market. The British economy had been displaced. Meanwhile, one has been able to observe another significant displacement at work, as the locus of economic vitality has continued its westward journey across the United States, leaving first New England and then the Great Lakes region seriously weakened.

Next, the cutting edge of this process has passed on across the Pacific, ever in search not only of lower production costs for old industries, but also of suitable homes for those new industries that the highly technological nature of this late modern economy permits to be so effortlessly spawned.[71] It would appear that something of considerable importance is happening here: when the West and its Modern Age were younger, expansion to new areas was harmless at worst and perhaps even at times helpful in raising the general level of the West's economy. But more recently, and unfortunately just as the rate of expansion has quickened, control over the process has been lost, and the old West, including the relatively young United States, is suffering from it. The march outward continues, but now for every new vital area on the frontier that is added to the Western economy, a blighted one appears somewhere in the rear.

With this comment on the implications of our geographic development during the last century, this section, which has attempted to trace the long transition from the medieval to the modern economy, is now complete. It has, to repeat, divided the transition into six periods: an initial one of growth, ca. 1000–1350; a second of reaction, ca. 1350–1450; a third of growth, ca. 1450–1600; a fourth of reaction, ca. 1600–1720; a fifth of growth, ca. 1720–1870; and a sixth of growth and dissolution together, ca. 1870 to the present. The conclusion, which is frankly an interpretation and not proven, for there is no proof in such matters, is a very simple one and hardly original here: it is that the modern economy, based on the open-market system with its attendant phenomena—specialization, rationalization, commercialization, monetization, and both internal and external expansion—has peaked and is now declining.

Also, the discussion of this transition from the medieval to the modern economy brings to a close our review of the West's civilization as it moved from the Middle Ages to the Modern Age. We have looked at the course of the cultural evolution, taking up first style and then thought; and we have also looked at the course of the societal evolution, taking up first politics and then economics. To summarize this history, one can make two points: first, the transition of each of the components—that is, of style, thought, politics, and economics—has in its development evidenced the same pattern, approximately that just described with regard to economics. Therefore one concludes that we are dealing not with four separate histories, but rather with a coherent civilizational progression, what we might call the unfolding of the modern theme.

Second, it would seem clear that that modern theme has now been exhausted. Again, that is not to say that the Modern Age has come to an end. But its period of upward movement is over. Now, in the twentieth century, the West would appear to be passing through a great crisis of adjustment, as it sets out on its journey toward new goals. And it is unlikely that these will involve an attempt to revive the modern ones. This crisis would seem to be not of the sort that we referred to earlier as "intra-eval." Its appearance, rather, is of the sort that leads to the changing of an age, to, that is, the substitution for an old and tired way of life of a new one. If we did not know that from the implicit statement made by the last century's societal history, then we should know it from the very explicit one made by its cultural history, where both the style and content of the modern forms have been destroyed. Thus future goals will be very different from those of the Modern Age.

Our most recent history is, then, necessarily one of decline; and that decline, involving the disintegration of all things modern, will continue. It is also, however one may look upon it, a history of renewed growth— certainly not in the sense, especially with regard to economics, that we have come to understand it, but rather growth with regard to the fundamentals of the culture and society of a future age.

For that is the implication of the West's longer history, its existence as a civilization: the passing of one age is followed by the emergence of another, and passing and emergence are so thoroughly intertwined that they can only be seen as separate in retrospect. There is undoubtedly something very comforting in that thought. By the time the Modern Age is in fact thoroughly dead, we should be, barring catastrophe, safely in the embrace of the institutions and systems of a postmodern age. Ages come and ages go. There is nothing calamitous in that fact; rather, there is contained within it a hopeful promise, the promise of continued life, for in this perpetual cycle of epochal death and rebirth is to be found the means of civilizational regeneration. For a civilization, particularly one as dynamic as our own, to continue to advance in a certain direction, any direction, for very long is to invite, indeed to insure, total destruction. Living things are conditioned by their origins. And this conditioning imposes limits. Therefore civilizations shed ages as acts of self-preservation. Ages, with their finally worn-out forms, are periodically sacrificed in order to maintain the health of the civilization itself. The West dropped classicism because classicism finally threatened, with its passion for expansion, to destroy everything that the West stood for. Then the West sought a corrective solution, medievalism, but in turn dropped it too when, with the achievement of a new stability, it had served its purpose; and when, also, to have continued along the path to a more extreme otherworldliness and particularism would have meant risking what had been so recently won. Thus the antidote for too much medievalism was modernism, a new age of expansion. And now that modernism finally and

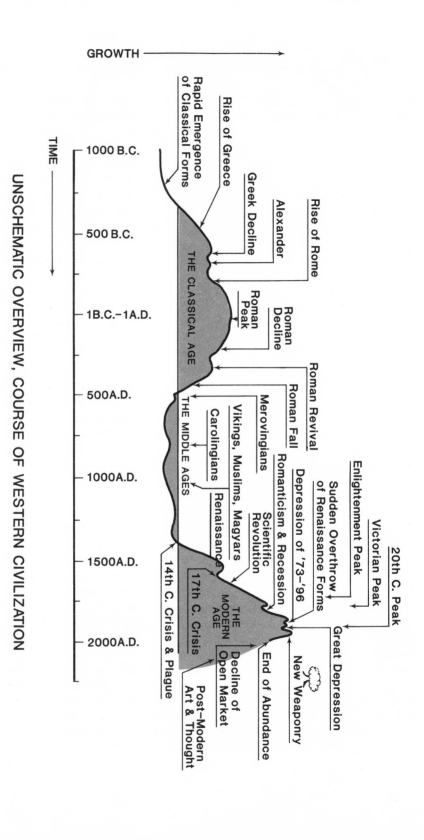

UNSCHEMATIC OVERVIEW, COURSE OF WESTERN CIVILIZATION

GROWTH →

TIME →

1000 B.C.

500 B.C.

1B.C.–1A.D.

500A.D.

1000A.D.

1500A.D.

2000A.D.

Rapid Emergence
of Classical Forms

Rise of Greece

Greek Decline

Alexander

Rise of Rome

THE CLASSICAL AGE

Roman
Peak

Roman
Decline

Roman Revival

Roman Fall

THE MIDDLE AGES

Merovingians

Vikings, Muslims, Magyars

Carolingians

Renaissance

Romanticism & Recession

Depression of '73–'96

Sudden Overthrow
of Renaissance Forms

Enlightenment Peak

Victorian Peak

20th C. Peak

Scientific
Revolution

THE
MODERN
AGE

Great Depression

New Weaponry

End of Abundance

Decline of
Open Market

Post-Modern
Art & Thought

17th C. Crisis

14th C. Crisis & Plague

inevitably has also become more of a danger than a help, the West is moving on to something else—in all likelihood to an age of renewed stability, an age of quiet in which we shall be given the opportunity to seek to undo the damage that the modern furies have unleashed upon us.

But, as said, such a smooth transition is possible *barring catastrophe.* And yet is not catastrophe, a genuine tragedy that the West could not survive, now the more likely outcome? No, it is not. There will certainly be an abundance of lesser misfortunes, but the course of civilization is not usually affected by these. Even an event of the proportions of the Black Death would not seem to have had a lasting impact on the West's evolution as it underwent the transition from its late medieval to its modern condition; for while one can name many results, the chief influence was to make what was happening happen more rapidly. Surely it is true that the catastrophes that the late Modern Age is capable of producing have a far greater destructive capacity than anything seen before. One can answer, however, that, being man-made, they are also necessarily more preventable. Only if our civilization insists on continuing to expose itself to the well-known risks over a considerable period of time would catastrophe appear to be the more likely outcome. And yes, given enough time, where there is a potential for anything, it will occur. But a healthy, still vital civilization will move, respectful of its past and its tradition, to remove such potentials. We can hope that that is the ultimate meaning of the crisis of the twentieth century.

In chapter 2 two highly stylized graphs of the course of Western civilization were offered. Now that we have completed our historical review, it is possible to present a somewhat more realistic portrayal, one that might be useful in providing a context for the remarks on the future that are now to follow (see figure). Again, graphs clarify, but they also trivialize. The course of Western civilization is obviously neither as trivial nor as clear as it is made here to appear. As for a peak with regard to the Modern Age, John Lukacs has put it in his *The Passing of the Modern Age* "between 1750 and 1850, earlier for some nations, later for others," and I would agree, although one could also make a case for extending the latter limit to 1950, especially if the measurement put quantity first.[72]

5

Beyond the Crisis: From the Modern to the Postmodern Age

Most views of the future—all sane views—are based on a view of the past. The question is, which past? But not only which past. We must also ask which future we have in mind. In this chapter, the chosen task is to speculate on the intermediate future on the basis of assumptions that proceed from a consideration of the West's long history, its entire past. Those two phrases, "intermediate future" and "entire past," require elaboration:

By the intermediate future, I mean the period between the immediate future, the next few years, possibly decades, during which we can rightly expect—always barring catastrophe, which now belongs at the end of every sentence—things to be very much like they have been in the immediate past; and the long-range future, centuries distant, when the tendencies that we are observing in their early forms will have resulted in a distinctly different West, perhaps a fully postmodern age, mature and in its own turn already becoming decadent.

Why, then, the intermediate future? Because of the three it is, as it happens, the one most accessible to inspection. The immediate future, while subject to the same influences that are shaping later futures, conceals too nicely its novel aspects in those familiar. The differences from the present will be with regard to nuances, and it is impossible to say just where and how these will make themselves felt. The distant future, on the other hand, remains a relatively closed book. Even if we are correct in estimating the forces that will eventually give it its substance, there will be too many unforeseeable major events, too many chance turnings, to permit an intelligent comment. It is, then, about the intermediate future that we can speculate with the greatest confidence: it is distant enough from the present so that a projection upon it of the sorts of long-range tendencies that we have been discussing in this essay is appropriate; and yet it is not so distant that we should expect our projections to go far astray.

No one, of course, would pretend that even the intermediate future will reveal itself clearly. We peer ahead at it, through a fog that will not lift. No doubt there is a certain protection in our ignorance. If we could really know the future, that would mean that the knowledge would be available to be misused. Still, we remain curious, especially since what we are to become tells us a great deal about what we are. We read the future in the present. But, it is true, we also try to read the present in the future.

Either way, the only adequate guide remains the past, in this case the West's "entire" past. There can never be a scheme, however, that uses the entire past in a literal sense. Unfiltered and unarranged, the past is so much garbage. History is bunk, as Henry Ford once proclaimed, but only to those who do not have the sense to forget most of it. Here we have tried to forget everything except that which would encourage us to concentrate on the mainstream. And from a survey of that mainstream, we come away with the following assumptions relevant to speculating on the future:

1. That the West has behaved throughout its entire life as a civilization, never permitting its major components to deviate much or for long from its course, from which fact we can infer that in the future it will continue to behave as a civilization: style and thought, economics and politics, all will move along together, giving, as they have in the past, an appearance of remarkable coordination that can seldom be explained without reference to the civilization itself.

2. That the history of the West is divided into long periods, usually referred to as ages, during which the civilization remains in its various aspects distinctly different from its constitution in other ages; that these ages have their origins in the age preceding; and that they so far—we should now make the point expressly, although it has no doubt already become apparent—have alternated between growth and stability. This last point is taken to mean that the next age, the postmodern, following as it should upon an age of violent growth, will be one of renewed stability; and that it will one way or another seek to reverse the directions of the Modern Age.

3. And, finally, that the course of events since the latter part of the nineteenth century makes us believe that the West has now begun to execute this reversal and is indeed already on its way to that postmodern age, moving toward, however unstable the passage, an era of recuperation.

But how rapidly? What insights can be provided, assuming that the general scheme of things as here presented proves to be correct, into the rate at which of all this will happen? When we speak of the intermediate future, what specific time period do we have in mind? For those interested in thinking about the future, the rate of change remains one of the more problematical subjects. One would like to avoid it altogether and simply refer to what is to come, leaving the chronology to take care of itself. Yet a view of the future without a chronology is not very satisfying. And we do have some means to help order our reflections concerning rates. Unfortunately, the information gives conflicting testimony. We know two things, and what we learn from the one seems to be negated by what we learn from the other. First, we can see more than a little resemblance between our present situation and the Roman experience during the centuries of decline. If one were to equate our contemporary point of evolution with, say, Rome during the middle of the second century A.D.—when there was still a workable empire, but one in which troubles were rapidly accumulating, with classical culture already giving distinct signs of becoming something else—then the suggestion is that the Modern Age might see its demise stretched out over two or three centuries. However, and this is the second and conflicting piece of information, everything that we know about modern times tells us that today's rate of change far exceeds any that we have known in the past. Change with regard to demography, technological innovation, production, speeds at which we travel, time required for communication, and so on—everything in the Modern Age is faster. Perhaps rates in general are now slowing down a bit, but still the modern condition has been one of rapid movement. Should that not also apply to our fall? Will the Modern Age not continue to hustle along this path, too, the one that leads to its destruction?

Both of these observations are no doubt reasonable: on the one hand, the decline and fall of Rome went very slowly, but, on the other, our impressions are valid, it is true that the civilizational pace has quickened considerably during recent centuries. With these considerations in mind, then, what is the likely chronology of the intermediate future? When are we to expect it? Certainly, there is no formula. One can only offer what amounts to an intuitive judgment, and that is that the changes anticipated here are conceived of as occurring in the course of the next century. By that time, and probably even during the early decades, the West will have entered far enough upon its transition to a postmodern age so that the emerging new solutions will be clearly visible. This chapter, therefore, is devoted to the twenty-first century. It is not intended, it should be understood, as a set of predictions. The purpose, rather, is to speculate, proceeding from the certainty that the future will be in good part a product of its past, and also from the hope that it will attempt to put some of the things right that the Modern Age has gotten wrong. We are aiming, then, at a conjectural description of Western civilization as it passes from its Modern Age.

The organization of these remarks on the future will follow for the most part the same structure that has been used in the historical treatment. We shall first reflect on the nature of the coming culture, taking up initially the matter of possible styles and following that with speculation on the evolution of thought. And then we shall turn to the future of society, first discussing what the West may expect in the way of political change, next doing the same with regard to economic change. Finally, we shall touch upon social change, change in those areas that are infrapolitical and even infraeconomic, change, that is, at the personal and private levels. This essay has not tried to include social history in the survey of the past because the record from which an outline must proceed is inadequate—the public past is fairly well-known, while its more intimate counterpart remains for obvious reasons more of a mystery. Still, we are free as well to speculate on the private aspects of the future, and it is of course a subject, so much of our lives being spent outside the channels of public development, that is necessarily of interest.

STYLE

As for the West's future style—its aesthetic mode of expression—there is every reason to think that it will not change significantly for a long, long, time, possibly not for centuries. That is because the fundamental revolution, as we noted in commenting on the stylistic history of the twentieth century, has now been more or less completed. In this one instance, the future has, so to speak, already arrived. The modern style, to repeat it again, has been driven from the field. And a postmodern style—whatever we wish to call it, even if that is "modern"—that is nearly as different from the style of the Modern Age as black is from white is already dominant. If we try to describe it by saying what it is not, then the basic point to make is that it is not neoclassical, with all that that implies: it is not naturalistic, it is not three-dimensional, it is not imitative of the art of Greece, Rome, and the Renaissance, and, above all, it is not an art of humanism, at least not in the sense that modern style was, with its concern for the portrayal in painting and sculpture of the human face and form. If we try to describe it by saying what it is, then here the essential point is that it is abstract: where the modern style found its ultimate reality in the world as it seems—to the eye or to the unreflecting mind, finally, to the camera—the postmodern style seeks it in the world as it *is*, as it *really* is, as it is taken to be, that is, after considerable distillation and refinement. The first was a style for the here and now; the second points beyond the here and now. The first was secular; the second is religious.

Yet the West is, as remarked earlier, not at the moment a religious civilization. It is still by and large a secular civilization. But it has become a secular civilization with doubts. Whereas the doubts used to be confined during the centuries of modern growth to the still-lingering medieval heritage of religion, now they are directed at secularism itself—and, of course, its fellows, that is, humanism, individualism, rationalism, and the notion of worldly progress. We shall reserve further comment on the West's future thought and the possibilities for the coming world view to the next section. Here we are only concerned with the fact that Western civilization has produced a firm and succinct new style without having moved beyond the various skepticisms to a new intellectual system. The style of the twentieth century is therefore a style looking for a meaning. And it will no doubt find one. We can note in this regard that the modern style's development, if we should date it, say, from Giotto (thus the early fourteenth century), was quite far along before it discovered in a full-blown humanism its obvious—or obvious only in retrospect?—significance. Style, it would seem, always arrives before meaning, or at least perceived meaning.

But if we have, then, already experienced the coming of a postmodern style, is it not likely that it is only the first of several? Probably not. The changes have been very clear and precise, and we know from our experience of the past that such reversals occur only rarely—again, in the West's history altogether just four times: at the very beginning, when the style (or styles) of the West's primitive prehistory gave way to that of classicism; next, when the style of classicism gave way to that of the Middle Ages; yet again, when the style of the Middle Ages gave way to that of the Modern Ages; and finally, this last time, when the style of the Modern Age was overthrown. These are not fashions, which can be taken up in an instant and dropped as quickly. The styles of ages endure with their ages; and once they have been renounced in favor of a new style, that new style is as durable as was the old.

Just because the basic postmodern style is set does not mean that there will not be a variety of schools and periods. The postmodern will have its early, high, and late, its baroque and its rococo. We are already seeing a departure in architecture from what is usually now called the "modern" (here postmodern, again, to distinguish it from the true modern, the style of the Modern Age) to the "postmodern" (not, then, our first postmodern). The initial era of creation, the "Age of the Masters," as Ada Louise Huxtable has called it, is now over. We should not expect to see again the likes of Frank Lloyd Wright, Mies van der Rohe, and Le Corbusier. It is time for variations on the original. But whatever the pattern of innovation, the essential style of what is now emerging will continue to be postmodern. "It will have as its heart," according to Huxtable, and I could not agree more, "the twentieth-century revolution that we call modern (here postmodern) architecture."[1] The basic direction has been set, and we shall proceed along that line. The outlines of the Bauhaus—that is, of the International Style—are here to stay. The same can be said, *mutatis mutandis,* for the other branches of the arts.

Still this is yet the Modern Age, and a number of modern revivals are to be expected. Here or there, for this length of time or that, the old modern will resurface, in architecture, art, music, or whatever. Also, one should assume that there will always be a subversive commitment to modern style. Radicals will flaunt it in the face of the Establishment, defiantly singing Bach or Mozart at official functions, or insisting on restoring the classical canons in drama and shouting down postmodern performances. Presumably little Monticellos will be secretly built in dark glades, where acolytes will gather to praise Newton and read rhymed poetry. Throughout the Modern Age, we should remember, the style of the Middle Ages—in fact all things medieval—continued to hold a certain attraction. Perhaps for every dominant modernist, there has been a Miniver Cheevey. And Miniver, we are told, eyed the modern business suit with loathing, while preferring "the medieval grace of iron clothing."[2] Now the commonplace with regard to style will be the postmodern. It will be the modern, then, that will serve as the source of protest and the object of fond nostalgia. Ultimately, we shall no doubt miss the modern grace of bourgeois clothing.

It should be understood, too, that the casual enjoyment of the works of the long period of modern creativity will not come to an end. Medieval cathedrals, after all, continued in use and continued to be admired, and not just by dissenters but by the vast bulk of the population. Now the old neoclassical buildings will be—are already being—preserved and rightly revered as a part of a valuable heritage. City symphonies will continue to repeat the best of the old modern tradition. And the art of naturalism will always be looked upon with a certain awe. But as the postmodern style grows older, it will become progressively less possible to reproduce those attitudes, always somewhat mysterious, that will permit new work to be done in the mode of the Modern Age.

That fact is already visible in our recent experience with what has come to be called the New American Realism. Not for a long time, perhaps never, has there been such attention to detail and such a finely calculated three-dimensional rendering of nature and the human face. Yet the old naturalism and the old humanism are not recaptured. Theodore Wolff has put his finger on the vital difference in commenting on the painting of one of the most skillful of the New Realists, that of Chuck Close: "If a Rembrandt painting of a man is a window into that man's 'soul,' then a Chuck Close painting of a man is a drawn window-shade upon which a photographically precise copy of that man's physical appearance has been painstakingly and unfeelingly rendered." If a man to Rembrandt is Everyman, to Close he is "nothing but an accident of flesh, skin, hair, pores, and wrinkles." Again, while discussing another neo-Realist, Lucian Freud, Wolff notes that "we are cut off from human contact with the people he depicts—and that's odd, since he goes to such trouble to reveal the humanity in each of them for us."[3]

But that is not really odd at all. It has been the achievement, I think, of this postmodernist realism to reenter—apparently with conscious intent, although conscious or not it amounts to the same thing—the old forms, the forms of naturalism and humanism, to prove that the new art could do so without being tempted to indulge in a true naturalism or a true humanism. In effect, the New Realists have said, "See, we are so completely beyond all that that we can go back and wander the old paths without remorse." And there would seem to be another message as well: "You said we cannot draw. But, as you can see, we can draw very well. You wanted a garden: so, there is a garden. You wanted a human: so, there is a human. Now perhaps you will understand just how meaningless those things are." To be sure, as the postmodernists have rendered man and nature, they are indeed meaningless. The modern mind looks at the results with inevitable disappointment. The postmodern mind, of course, is busy looking elsewhere.

Before, however, we go on to speculate about that postmodern mind, there are several more things that can be said about future stylistic developments. The possibilities might seem to be without number. If we confine ourselves to the parameters set by the past, however, then they greatly reduce themselves. In addition to remarking that the revolution with regard to style has already been made and that it signifies the end of classicism and its replacement by a style of abstraction and geometry, there are perhaps not more than a half-dozen observations that can be reasonably ventured. Here in any case are just that many, six supplementary conjectures on the future evolution of Western aesthetics.

First, we should see as modern influences become increasingly moribund the progressive fusion of art and function. The joining—or rather rejoining, for they had been closely linked in the Middle Ages—of art and function was one of the points that often appeared in the programs of the art rebels when the recent revolution was new. But if the new style was successful, the attempt to bring art and function merely closer, to say nothing of merging the one in the other, was not. Functionalism had some influence upon architecture, but ultimately there was little that was accomplished. The desire to make buildings look like pieces of sleek machinery was no more conducive to making them also functional than had been the effort at making them look like Greek and Roman temples. And painting and music remained about as functional as they had been in previous centuries, that is, hardly at all, made for exhibition only, with little thought to their integration into other sorts of social activity.

Increasingly, however, a number of things should conspire to bring art and function together. For one, the strengthening of the crafts will help, for they have been a traditional bastion of the conception of work as art. By the middle of the twentieth century, the crafts had suffered tremendously from mass production, which had been able to take full advantage of cheap energy. The result was that finally the crafts were almost extinct. But the end of cheap energy should make, and apparently already is making, for a craft renaissance, as human input relative to machine input becomes steadily less costly. It was difficult to fuse art and function when there was a dearth of functioners, that is, craftsmen. That obstacle should gradually disappear, as they now increase in numbers and begin to restore the effortless union that characterized production before machinery came to dominate.

Also influencing the fusion of art and function will be the fact that formal style in several areas has exhausted its potential for creativity. When symphonic music arrives at banging on radiators (as with John Cage) and sculpture evolves to the point where a urinal is accepted as a worthy piece of art (as with Marcel Duchamp), then the only recourse is to build a better radiator and a better urinal. If art has become, that is to say, indistinguishable from its background—music indistinguishable from noise, sculpture from the everyday artifact, and painting from any paint on any surface—then art has disappeared as an independent entity. And if it is to survive at all, it must do so within that general world of function, that is, the world of work, play, and (for some) worship. After the initial demonstration and exhibition of the artifact as art, there is no purpose to further exhibition. Already superfluous are the second banged-upon radiator and the second displayed urinal. One is sufficient. The point has been made. Thereby art as a separate, exhibitable phenomenon is no longer viable.

There is yet another reason to expect art and function to coalesce. The Modern Age's period of ascent was one of affluence. Art was affordable, and its purchase was undoubtedly encouraged by the status requirements of successive generations of rising burghers. But the late Modern Age and its postmodern successor will be austere. Conspicuous consumption will become more and more difficult and perhaps also less tolerated, as pressure increases to take the less expensive, more efficient course and to confine art to the useful. For these several reasons, then, we should expect art and function to draw closer. They will never become one and the same. There are inherent distinctions. As the modern impulse, however, tended to push them further apart, the postmodern impulse will tend to rejoin them.

The second of these conjectures about the future of style is that the gap between style and society, that disparity and even hostility that has existed in this century between art and the general populace, will slowly disappear. Art has been in the awkward position of making a revolution in something of a vacuum. Whatever was happening beneath the surface in the late nineteenth and early twentieth centuries to Western civilization, and there was a great deal, the fabric of society seemed sound and the prospects for the continuation of modern directions good. The appearance of such precipitate discontinuity in the history of Western style was therefore especially shocking. The whole affair was looked on from the outside, from beyond the pale of creative art, as needless and perverse. And that meant, quite naturally, that art attracted more than its share of those who reveled in the role of outsider. There are those in any society who enjoy being found contrary. In this period of sudden change, with culture neatly arrayed on one side and society on the other, it would seem that a great many of these sorts decided to become artists.

But in the future, style and society will probably find less to argue about. Style will become less visible. And society will become more postmodern. It will experience its own dramatic alterations. Art will come to represent and again be more or less compatible with the central forces of its civilization. The bohemian and the philistine will make peace, as art gradually assumes a position within society something like that which it held before recent times, when it was both more accepted and less obtrusive. Postmodern art's adolescence over, it will gradually accustom itself to a more mature station. There will be no more icons left to break. Style will be decreasingly shocking and increasingly supportive.

The third conjecture has to do with the possible development within the postmodern style of certain characteristics that might make it resemble the medieval style. So far, the similarities—other than the fact, very significant in itself, that they are both abstract and nonclassical—are not obvious. While sometimes one can hardly tell a classical, that is, Greco-Roman, from a neoclassical, that is, modern, building, a postmodern building could never be mistaken for a medieval one. Nor could a postmodern painting ever be wrongly identified as a medieval work. Postmodern and medieval styles are distinct. Yet there are other features that would seem to link them together. Medieval art, for example, was vertical, and so is the skyscraper, one of the more significant products of the postmodern style. Medieval art lacked the careful enframement of classical and modern art, and postmodern art has tended also not to enclose its subject. Medieval art looked inward, and so has the postmodern to a certain extent. Medieval art was subtle and implicit, and much of postmodern painting often has been likewise elusive, filled, as it is, with arcane symbols. Medieval art was irregular, and so usually is postmodern art, for it seldom insists on the symmetry of the classical and the modern. Finally, medieval art was almost always anonymous; but here we must admit that thus far modern art has not been that at all. Yet perhaps that is due to the lingering force of humanism. Now to be consistent the artist, having destroyed the naturalistic image of man in his art, should take the next logical step and also destroy his signature. My guess is that that will in fact happen. Engineers, designers, and building contractors are already pretty much anonymous. Perhaps it will not be too long before architects and artists will be as well. That would be, in any case, appropriate to a postindividualist age.

Nevertheless, none of these medieval-like characteristics individually, nor all together, and no matter how intensified, will make postmodern style medieval. Nicholas Berdyaev when discussing the similarities between the Middle Ages and the new age succeeding upon the Modern Age cautioned that there could be no true rebirth.[4] Certainly there will be no repetition of the medieval experience, not with regard to style and also not with regard to any major aspect of the West's future. Still, as we have seen, successive ages tend to run to opposites. Not exact opposites, of course, but they do seem to react, the one against the other. Therefore it is not so surprising that the postmodern age in reacting against the Modern Age would create resemblances to the age against which the Modern once reacted. One looks rightly, then, for medieval similarities in postmodern style and expects them to become even more prominent with the passage of time.

The fourth conjecture on the subject of postmodern style is that style will come to be given new moral purposes. During the modern growth period, aesthetic expression became increasingly secular. And although this secular art was often given a moral message—the sanctity of the family, the virtue of patriotism, or the nobility of labor, for example—more and more the content became merely neutral, a reportorial rendition, satisfied with the presentation of the facts without comment. This trait has carried over into postmodern style, which has so far tended to conform to the custom of being suspicious of all moral statements. Art seems at times to have denounced moral statements as immoral. Thus in painting we look at canvas after canvas, whether abstract or neorealist, where the only message is that there is no message. Surely such an agnostic art will not endure. As the West finds new things to believe in, replacements for the modern values that seem to have been used up, postmodern style will take on the task of reinforcing the commitment to the new order. Is that good or bad? Probably some of both. Artistic production in the service of morality can enrich and ennoble the human condition, as it has in the past; or, as it also has in the past, it can be used to excuse tyranny and suppress the masses. We have seen both and will continue to see both. One should remember that the anticode of amorality has been also both used and abused. However, the prospects for abuse, always present, will not be the issue. Style is given its content by and even in its forms bends to the purposes of the age. In the Modern Age of growth, the canons of style were open and liberal. As we move toward the postmodern age of contraction, they will no doubt be increasingly moral and restraining—some will say closed and illiberal.

The fifth conjecture is that the West's future will see the balance between sacred and profane art—between, that is, intellectual and popular art, the art of the high culture and that of the low—shift in favor of the former. Throughout the Modern Age the balance slowly swung in the direction of the latter, toward popular art. The inherent tendency of modernization to democracy was obviously paralleled by a similar drift with regard to style, until the profane has in certain areas all but eliminated the sacred, "classical" forms. If one wishes to test the thesis with regard to music, there is a simple method: at any moment, scan the radio dial, AM, FM, or both, and perform a simple count—how many popular, how many "classical"? I have just followed my own instructions, and the count is ten to one. And the source of the single classical piece is public radio: classical music subsidized by public agencies because the public, that is, the vast majority of the people, will not listen to it, so that it cannot support itself through advertising.

One might add that the profane style has become rather excessively profane, especially with regard to music. That has happened just in the last several decades. Before, the lyrics and usual mood of profane music were at worst banal (there have always been bawdy songs, of course, but they were reserved for special occasions). Only recently have we converted to a popular style that is consistently and insistently vulgar. (The test here is to repeat the dial survey, this time listening to the lyrics—taking again my own test, I hear something about "give it up, baby . . . want your love," at which point I quit, right where I started.) Can one review the history of the first gradual and then rapid vulgarization of the profane style without coming to believe that a reaction against it is not too far off? If we are edging toward a postmodern world that seeks to return to security and stability, will we continue to permit profane style, for whatever commercial purposes, to carry on a steady propaganda assault on the social order? Almost certainly not. The permit given to profane style to go its own way will surely be revoked and the youth culture that serves as the market and object of its supporting industry severely curtailed. And then perhaps popular style will be returned to the people, who will use it to provide a genuine folk counterpart to the intellectual high culture, both, we can hope, coexisting in keeping with the requirements of the age.

The sixth and last conjecture concerning future style points to a revival of regional distinctions. The Modern Age has been hard on regions. It has encroached upon their domain in every area, and the effects have not been lost on style. Regional styles have generally succumbed to national and cosmopolitan styles. Cities have come to look more alike, cooking has come to taste more alike, and music has come to sound more alike. In a long age devoted to increased centralization, this flattening out of regional differences was inevitable. Now just as inevitable is the reversal of the trend, as various economic and political pressures, shortly to be discussed, encourage a return to the regions as vital centers. The regional styles will remain Western and postmodern, no doubt. They will not have the opportunity to go their own way in total isolation. But it will again come to make a stylistic difference whether one is in this place or that. Maybe even airports will come to be different. If so, that might rank as one of the postmodern style's more appealing achievements.

Before concluding these speculations on postmodern style and going on to a discussion of postmodern thought, there is one more matter deserving of our curiosity: why has the change in style from the modern to the postmodern been so abrupt and so complete? Changes in style in the histories of other civilizations have usually been muted. Even our own preceding stylistic revolutions have been accomplished more slowly, indeed much more slowly, taking a century or two rather than a few decades; and the previous results, at least after the initial jump from primitivism to classicism, have been clearly less overwhelming. One can see more of the Greco-Roman style still alive in the medieval and more of the medieval still alive in the modern than one can see of the modern in the postmodern. The postmodern is so strikingly novel and without firm precedent that some have taken it to be outside the Western tradition. Then, entirely consistently, they have gone on from that observation to wonder about the West's ability to hold itself together as a civilization. Is postmodern art telling us that we are at the end of the road? These are matters open to interpretation, and I can only say that I do not believe that that is what is being said. For all our troubles, we are too obviously vital as a civilization to be dying of old age, and our art reflects that continued vigor. And we will probably not be dying from catastrophe (that is, the bomb) until it very suddenly happens, and then art will not have the chance to brood about it (that will be one of the few consolations). Besides, civilizations do not usually end with dramatic declarations and momentous changes. They die quietly, trying to avoid change.

No, the enormity of the rejection has other explanations. There are two. First, our civilization, as we noted earlier, has been much more dynamic than older civilizations. While others have edged cautiously from a little to one side of the center to a little to the other, ours has veered back and forth from pole to pole. As a later civilization, perhaps it is that we run through notions more adroitly and thus more radically. When we are religious, we are very, very religious. Then when we are secular, we are very, very secular. And as time has gone on we have become even more dynamic. The Modern Age has been the most aggressive and change filled of all, indeed, the most dramatically innovative, and at the same time destructive, era in all of human history. It is therefore fitting that stylistic signals have been equally aggressive and that they have come on early and loud, even before the modern theme would appear to have reached its natural culmination in all other fields of endeavor: thus a loud if somewhat premature wake for a noisy age.

The second explanation has something to do with the first: being dynamic and in search of novelty, the Modern Age became increasingly articulate and self-conscious. And it produced an abundance, perhaps an overabundance, of intellectuals. When the time came to say farewell to the modern style, there occurred a natural competition to see who could say it the most flagrantly, with results that were sometimes brilliant and sometimes foolish, but always extreme. This would be the most thought-about stylistic upheaval ever. Therefore one is unsure just how seriously to take its extremism. If it seems to suggest on occasion that the break with all of the West's past tradition has been nearly total, then we should be skeptical. My own inclination, it should be already clear, is to accept the change of style as an important index with regard to the future direction of the West's progress, an indication that we are moving away from things modern and have instinctively turned our backs on our immediate past. But I do not accept it as a sign of the West's demise, or even as a wish for that demise. The end of modern style would seem to be telling us that the Modern Age is coming to an end—nothing more, nothing less.

THOUGHT

What can be said about the possible directions that will be taken by thought in the transition to its postmodern positions? In the discussion of modern thought in the course of this essay, two assertions especially apposite to our purpose here have been made: first, that modern thought is no longer intellectually vital, its various fundamental beliefs having been attacked and rejected in the course of the last century; and, second, that, unlike the case with style, thought has not yet produced a concise postmodern system. Modern humanism has departed; but so far a successor has not appeared. This circumstance has occasioned that oft-noted peculiarly valueless condition that the West finds itself in at present. Yet there seems to be something of an agreement that this state of affairs will not last and that the West will sooner or later arrive again at a point at which it will be sustained by commonly held convictions.[5]

But there the consensus quickly evaporates. Some believe that humanism can be restored. They see the departure from modern beliefs as
temporary and unnecessary: humankind, responsible for its actions, has
allowed certain contrary sets of values and beliefs to intrude. Among these
opposing and competing systems one can point to behaviorism, revived
religion, totalitarianisms of both the right and left, nihilism, and, perhaps
most dangerous of all to humanism, the general intellectual indifference
and hostility to beliefs of any sort (even to nihilism) that is the hallmark of
this century. The West, according to those who believe humanism still to
be salvable, should return to its commitment to modern values: it should
trust the rational approach, seek to enlarge the scope of freedom for the
individual, and promote at every turn progress toward, to use the language
of the liberal German sociologist (also politician and later director of that
great humanist institution, the London School of Economics) Ralf
Dahrendorf, *"die Vergrösserung menschlicher Lebenschancen"*—the increase of human opportunity.[6]

Aligned against the humanists, although in ranks ill-formed that sprawl
across philosophical and ideological lines, are the antihumanists. They are
not, of course, literally against humans. But they are indeed critical of that
more than trace of arrogance that underlies the humanist argument: the
presumption that mankind can defy both tradition and nature in its hopes
to build a better world. The antihumanist case has perhaps never been put
more succinctly than by Romano Guardini. Our age, Guardini wrote in
The End of the Modern World (1947), has been made painfully aware of the
"reality of the deliberate destructiveness in the human spirit," and precisely because of that is now being given its greatest opportunity: "to
grasp the truth by breaking away from the optimisms of the modern
mind." Modern man, he continued, has for too long denied his potential
for evil and nurtured instead a "revolutionary faith in autonomy." And
thus he has been guilty of believing that he could "simply have power and
rest secure in its exercise." But that has proved impossible, with the result
that we find ourselves in a world in which we are forced to live in constant
danger.[7]

This argument against humanism proceeds, then, not from revealed
religious truths, for which the late modern mind is not yet sufficiently
naive, but rather from the terrible predicaments that modern man by his
refusal to acknowledge human frailties has brought upon himself. But of
course there are other objections to the modern world view that have little
to do with the physical threats created by the misuse of power. These
challenge the worthiness of modern goals even had they succeeded. Yet it
is undoubtedly the realization, brought home to the West only since 1945,
that our new knowledge has an enormous potential for vast destruction
that has given the antimodern pronouncements their wide hearing.

If the antihumanist critique of modern thought does not, as said, dress itself in the robes of revelation—leaving that to the born-again fundamentalists, who would seem to be presiding not so much over a return to the religious spirit as a revival of a system of secular superstition[8]—nevertheless there is an obvious religious orientation to the position. A good part of all religion is the organization of the avowal of mankind's limits into a system of symbols. Therefore the religious cast to the opposition to humanism, which is restating those limits, is to a certain extent inescapable. That being the case, we can posit two basic and antagonistic thought systems: the one hoping for a revival of the West's long modern tradition, the other looking to some sort of religious restoration. And it would seem apparent that this time the latter is destined to prevail, given the drift away from things modern.

For one raised in the habits of and once fully committed to the modern outlook, that realization comes even now as a clear disappointment. Modern methods, after all, clearly produce individual truths. That gives to modern explanations of everything a great appeal. As long as it could be argued that the West was in fact making progress toward its secular goals, all sufficiently noble, it was easy to assume that the methodically acquired individual truths were flowing together to produce truth at a higher level, one at which we would gain the insights needed to make life better, and for all. More goods, better food, improved systems, and correct methodology: these together would bring the future to a new plateau of human fulfillment. But the hopeful plans, although they seemed reasonable extensions of the modern approach to things, remained just what they were, enthusiastic utopias, as much the product of self-delusion as had been the dreams of religion. And as the West first discovered that the paths to its secular goals were blocked, then that not only was progress halted but also mankind's very existence endangered, it became easier to point to the modern fallacy. It was there all along for anyone who might have wanted to see it: there was never a promise inherent within either rationalism or that natural world to which it was to be applied that the little truths, as true as they might be, would someday add up to a relevant big truth, one that could solve the human dilemma.

So the West's intellectual directions as it leaves the Modern Age and approaches its postmodern successor will probably be set toward religious rather than rationalist-secular-humanist systems. Humanism had its chance, and it failed. Religion will also fail, of course, just as it did before. There are no answers to the question that asks after the human purpose and the right way. If there were, we would have agreed on them long ago. But religion with its admonitions to humility and caution will be more appropriate than humanism to the era into which we are moving. Perhaps after a century or two of piety and restraint, when once again our problems are more manageable, then humanism can have another turn. In the meantime, the long process of secularization would appear to be at an end.

If it is assumed that the pendulum is again swinging away from the modern world view, then what can be said to describe the more specific characteristics of a future Western thought? Here perhaps the best procedure is to take a very simple approach and review the several characteristics of modern thought, projecting not a continuation of their development but rather a reversal. When it comes to the big questions, thought has an infinite ability to come up with combinations of ingredients, yet there are still only two choices regarding directions: it can move forward; or it can move backward. In this instance, it would seem, it should move backward for a while. Thought should become, following the general tendency of the West, not more but less modern. To get some sense of what that might mean, let us take the four characteristics of modern thought referred to earlier and ponder what it would indeed entail with regard to each to become less modern.

The first of those characteristics is individualism. Modern thought has been focused upon the individual throughout its history. It has been the individual, not mankind as a whole, who has formed the centerpiece of humanism. It is the individual personality whose development has been one of the great purposes of the age. It is to provide opportunities for the individual that liberty and equality have been championed by its philosophies. And it is to protect that heritage that modern thought has constructed around those rights appropriate theories denying their potential for alienation and building a system of law in which the individual can defend himself—and now, pointedly, herself. But the future of individualism, as argued earlier, looks bleak. Since the late nineteenth century it has suffered greatly, having been deserted by both philosophy and art: no longer considered rational, indeed by the behaviorists not even thought, as said before, to be sufficiently responsible to be irrational, the individual has steadily lost ground.

And in place of theories championing the individual we increasingly find those that exalt the community. One hesitates to use the term *communalist* to describe them, because that word has come to be associated only with the left's communal models. But there are communal models of the right as well. If we understand the term to include both possibilities, then communalism is the obvious choice, and there is no reason not to use it: the theories of individualism of the Modern Age, then, will no doubt continue to be gradually replaced during the future time of transition by theories of communalism. Rather than devoting its energies to encouraging the fulfillment of the personality, the West will increasingly rise to defend once again the sanctity of the community. Instead of liberty and equality, the much-neglected fraternity will assert its own rights.

That is not to say that liberty and equality will be despised by the new thought. But where the modern mind believed with Benjamin Constable, an early-nineteenth-century Frenchman, that "the liberty of the individual is the object of all human association,"[9] the new Western mind will begin to reverse the priorities, that is to say that human association will become the object of the liberty of the individual. The individual should be granted, it will tend to maintain, only what liberty is deemed advisable in order to provide best for the community.

Nor will the new theories be inclined to continue to insist on the legal provisions that preserve the individual from effective prosecution when his or her liberty no longer serves societal ends. Communal rights will grow at the expense of individual rights. And in place of the ideal of equality, which in the context of modern thinking has usually meant equality of opportunity rather than equality of result—the equal chance to succeed rather than equal success—we should see the dual evolution of ideals of hierarchy and social justice. To be sure, it can be pointed out that the Modern Age went to a great deal of trouble to get rid of its medieval hierarchical heritage. And it has always been rightly suspicious of efforts at achieving social justice, that is, equality of result, as inhibiting to growth.

But that is the point: the West will seek to reduce the claims of liberty and opportunity and increase respect for hierarchy and social justice precisely because it is trying to inhibit growth. An open society insures mobility and growth. It did so for the Greeks, and it has for us. A closed society makes growth very difficult. It is inherently stable. Throughout the high modern period we have thought of the open society as being better by almost any measurement. My suspicion is that we shall slowly change our minds. A society motivated by a system of thought based on freedom is destined to be in a condition of constant flux, as its individuals struggle to increase their own advantage relative to that of others. The result is one part creation and an equal part destruction. As long as that is perceived as progress, nothing will be done to limit individual license. When the time comes that society is thought to suffer more from the destruction than it gains from the creation, then the inducements to mobility will be gradually removed. That would seem to be what is happening already, and the process we can expect to continue until a new world view has drawn the necessary boundaries within which a constrained individualism, subordinate to communalism, is permitted to continue.

The second characteristic of modern thought is secularism, that tendency, implicit in the Renaissance and becoming steadily more explicit from the middle of the seventeenth century until the end of the nineteenth, to put this world first and to concentrate on it as the relevant arena of human activity. Sometimes secularism has manifested itself in atheism and sometimes in agnosticism, but more often it has taken the form of a simple shift of attention away from traditional otherworldly beliefs, without the bother of formal renunciation. We should also note that secularism has tended to prefer the nominalist to the realist position, attributing reality to things rather than categories and, when the latter are used, insisting on their limited employment as convenient receptacles and denying to them any independent or transcendental validity. The realist mind upon perceiving several nails had thought, "Ah, there are some earthly and inferior representatives of the eternal nail." But to the modern, nominalist mind each of the nails has been itself taken as the ultimate reality, the very term nail understood to be only a useful way of lumping together individual items with obvious similarities. Of course secularism has also favored materialist theories over their idealist opponents. The world has been taken to be made up of solid matter, not ideas, and run according to the rules of nature's laws.

What, then, will happen to secularism as the West makes its passage from the Modern Age? It will most likely meander in the direction of a postmodern transcendentalism. Modern atheism, which has drawn its followers from the ranks of those who want firm answers, will gravitate toward firm theology. Modern agnosticism has tended to lean in the direction of atheism. Now it will begin to lean toward spiritual assumptions. Instead of saying, "I do not know why we are here, but I find it difficult to believe that it is the work of any sort of god," the new agnostic will argue that it probably is indeed the work of some sort of god. And those who never bothered to renounce their traditional religions will simply shift back to reaffirm and reemphasize those beliefs. The twentieth century has already seen a considerable amount of each of these sorts of ideational relocation. We shall no doubt see still more of them in the future.

Also we can expect the secularist attachment to nominalism and materialism to come to an end. Realism and idealism, both of which have already enjoyed a long revival that began in the early nineteenth century, at the very beginning of the rebellion against the modern world view, should continue to win converts. We mean here, of course, the realism of philosophy, that realism that insists on the reality of categories, not artistic realism, which will remain as neglected as it already is; and we mean likewise the idealism of philosophy, that which insists that the world is more idea than matter, not the popular idealism that clings to its ideals despite practical objections. Both philosophic realism and idealism are of course suggestive of Plato. And, to be sure, if Aristotle was in the long run the ancient philosopher most in accord with the modern mind, Plato should prove to be the ancient philosopher most in accord with the postmodern mind. If modern thought has its roots in Thales, Aristotle, and

Aquinas, postmodern thought will discover its own in Pythagoras, Plato, and Augustine, the spokesmen of the antisecular Western tradition.

The third characteristic of modern thought is rationalism, the faith in reason that has distinguished the Modern Age. Rationalism, as already observed, has assumed a natural world available to investigation by virtue of that world's adherence to laws not subject to exception. And it has then extended that assumption to the social world, thus positing an orderly environment, one with which rational man can live in harmony. In this system only truths that pass the test of reason and experiment have been assumed to be effective, fit contributions to a general knowledge that would when complete assure a contented life on earth. Never before, even during the West's classical age, has the world seen a society so given to following reason and its science wherever it might lead.

Will, then, the course of Western history now carry us beyond our commitment to reason? Not entirely. It is difficult to imagine that where modern thought has proved specific factual relationships the West will ever deny them. There would be no reason to turn our backs on everything that has been learned and perversely to repeat (although, yes, some are doing just that) the ignorance of early times. But where the West will indeed now begin to move beyond reason is, first, with regard to the rational contribution to the prevailing world view, where reason will cease to be the cornerstone and again become simply another piece in the structure; second, with regard to those statements, and there have been many, where the modern claim to insights based on reason and science has been pretense or the obvious result of wishful thinking; and, third, where the application of the work of modern reason and science has proved harmful, and here it will be not so much a moving-beyond but rather a closing-down: the West will move, quickly, one would think, to close down those branches of science that are now encouraged in their efforts to pry open Pandora's box. Only a civilization either entirely out of control or bent on self-destruction would not recognize the dangers inherent in the drift of contemporary science. Certainly it will take a while to get used to the idea of regulating, even suppressing, research, but it will most likely be done, and not just in one nation, but everywhere. We made the Faustian pact. Now we shall renounce it. Appropriately, the first pleas for a return to common sense are coming from within the scientific community itself.

Perhaps in the future Western thought will retrace its way back through something like Scholasticism, in the process reencompassing reason and science within the civilizational whole and insisting upon certain ethical guidelines. As with Scholasticism, there would once again be limits set to what knowledge might independently achieve. One notes a significant difference, however, for this would be a Scholasticism evolving not from Augustinianism to modernism, from, that is, a system in which faith was dominant to a system in which reason was, but rather a Scholasticism evolving backward, devolving, that is, from modernism to something like Augustinianism in the more distant postmodern centuries. But whatever the direction, the result for the intermediate future could well be the rediscovery not to be sure of a literal Scholasticism—that has been too much the captive of Roman Catholicism to enjoy wider allegiance—but of similar syntheses in which reason is allowed to prowl its domain, but with claws removed, an attractive beast, yet no longer capable of violence. Reason would be subordinated to wisdom, if one can still use that word; also truth to morality, knowledge to ethics, the concept of the one path to insight to that of many paths, and scientific method to intuitive judgment.

The fourth characteristic of modern thought is the belief in progress. The older the Modern Age became, the more an explicit view of progress emerged as a conscious part of the West's assumptions about history and man's destiny. This insistence on progress was the logical result of the three other characteristics: because the individual was capable of great things, because this world was the place of primary concern, and because an orderly world was accessible to the rational mind—because of all of those together, the human condition would steadily improve. By the nineteenth century, there was so little doubt that this was the case that every change was assumed to be contributing to progress. And the chief measurement came to be growth itself: growth and progress were all but synonymous. Those who resisted change or even appeared to hinder growth were condemned out of hand. "You cannot stand in the way of progress"—we hear it still.

But probably not for long. As mentioned earlier, the support for progress among intellectuals has been missing for some time now. In the last several decades, the popular mood has also become less receptive. Enthusiasm for progress has become another of this century's casualties, and one can only expect that it will continue to suffer. Certainly to the extent that it has been deduced from the other modern beliefs, all now themselves departing, one could not be optimistic about its chances. Then there are also the sobering facts of the late-modern political and economic circumstances, to which must now be added the possibility of a new pandemic. Thus the assumption of progress, or at least secular progress—and that was really the only kind the Modern Age had in mind—is not apt to return to favor.

The weakening of this concept, once so powerful, is creating a vacuum into which should step an obvious substitute, the ideal of stability. Inexorably, it would seem, we shall come to agree that the lack of progress can also be a wonderful thing. Growth will be feared—as in some quarters it already is—and the burden of proof regarding social utility will be placed on those seeking change, not those opposing it. At the same time, the attitude toward power should undergo basic revision. The modern mind has been fascinated with power and its derivative, speed. Power would remake the world. Speed would dissolve its barriers. But a shift to new attitudes is taking place. Power and speed are coming to be perceived as sources of disruption and danger. And because in their more recent forms that is what they clearly are, the tendency should be strengthened. Instead of the persistence of a world view permeated with the desire for power, speed, and progress, we are more likely to experience the development of one dedicated to labor by hand, repose, and stability. If the actual result is a future with more than its share of inertia and stagnation, then one can only reply that that is to be expected: any new set of ideals will find but imperfect expression, just as the modern set did.

We have designated four characteristics of the postmodern world view toward which Western thought is assumed to be evolving: communalism, the successor to individualism; transcendentalism, the successor to secularism; what we might call reintegrationism, for want of a better way of describing the effort to recapture reason and science for society; and the ideal of stability, the successor to faith in progress. There remain two more questions with regard to the future of thought that we might care to put.

The first of these has to do with the relationship between, on the one hand, a future high culture with its thought and world view and, on the other, a corresponding low culture with its own opinions. We have commented on this relationship in general and more specifically with regard to the disintegration of modern assumptions and need only repeat here the observation that high and low culture usually can be found traveling the same path, but at an interval. To that can then be added the suggestion that during periods of stability the interval narrows: with the avant-garde no longer racing ahead, the popular mind, necessarily committed to filtering and then discarding or digesting the novel ideas and thus always moving slowly, finally reaches a position roughly contiguous to that of the intellectuals. For our future, that should mean that after the experience of the late nineteenth and early twentieth centuries, when an alienated avant-garde managed thoroughly to offend a much less alienated mass culture, the extremes in thought should again be brought closer. A similar observation was made with regard to style. Popular thought will still quite possibly remain more attached to the older modern concepts than will the thought of the high culture. But both should continue to drift away from the modern, eventually coming to share a common allegiance to the newly forming orthodoxy. After high-brow thought has gotten over its blind devotion to the new ways, and the low-brow thought its blind repugnance, they should then come together, proceeding without the early conflict along much the same course.

The second question inquires into the matter of the institutionalization of higher learning during the next century. What sorts of institutions will try to serve it and advance its cause? In the early Middle Ages, it was the monastery that was at the center of things; in the High Middle Ages, the cathedral school; and from the late Middle Ages through the ascendant modern period, the progressively secularized university. The purpose of that modern university was until recently to turn out modern men (later also women) with modern minds. The method was to provide a general, humanist education: literature, history, economics, art, languages, biology, mathematics, and physics. Later more specialized sciences and then the social sciences were added. As noted earlier, it was not professional training that was the central object, but rather training for political participation and the life of the mind, for the citizen in both his public and private aspects. Now, in the late twentieth century, there are obviously basic changes taking place.

And these changes—the shift from the humanist curriculum, the rapid deterioration of ability and standards in what remains of it, the growing attention to professionalism, all again mentioned earlier—are not momentary departures from a tradition that will soon be restored; they are instead milestones on the route to a new ordering of the structures of higher learning. What will be the essential result? Most likely it will be the eventual removal of the university from its position at the center of things. Its old tasks it can no longer perform adequately, for there is no more market, quite literally, for the disciplined studies that it once offered. Thus the drop in standards, as humanities departments struggle to maintain enrollment by pretending to educate without driving away customers. The new tasks, it will sooner or later become clear, can be done better, with greater efficiency and fewer encumbrances, elsewhere—in engineering academies, for example, or in secretarial schools. At the same time, higher education's other present function, that is, research, can also be done better elsewhere. While the bulk of research was general and more or less casual—truly inquisitive and in search of basic knowledge—it belonged in the general, humanist university. Now, however, it has become narrow and funded for specific purposes, serving business and the military. Far from providing a check to the military-industrial complex, the modern university has become a crucial part of the operation. The result will be that either the commissioned research remains and the university thereby ceases to be a true university, or that research will move elsewhere, in which case the university, having come to depend on those funds, will suffer a tremendous financial blow.

However, the difficulties of the university have more profound origins. It was the modern institution *par excellence,* the work of the modern world view, which it propagated—a humanist institution for a humanist age. One can hardly expect it, to take the long view, to survive the fall of its patron philosophy. Yet there will always be universities. They will survive through the late modern transition and on into the postmodern age, just as monasteries have survived to the present. But the universities of the future, the true universities, that is, will deal quite possibly with many fewer students and have much-reduced faculties. With a narrower scope, existing on the peripheries of the cultural world, these schools may indeed have a somewhat easier time carrying out their traditional activities than they are having at present.

What should arise to fill the gap left by the decline of the university? A variety of institutions is the best guess. Higher study and research of the present sort will probably continue to gravitate toward special institutes, existing apart from the university and directly supervised by business and government. In an increasingly religious climate, it would also be reasonable to expect that religious foundations should again become intellectual centers of significance. And the mass university for much of the transition period to a new economy might well serve as a holding place, a work and training center for the unemployable middle classes, with no particular obligation to traditional education. But whatever the institutions, the trend will be away from the general and liberal higher education that sought and found such wide support during the modern growth centuries. The humanism of the Modern Age has been badly weakened. The attempt to mold students in its image, to instill in them the principles of secularism, rationalism, individual fulfillment, and progress, to educate them to participate in a politics based on an informed and reasonably altruistic citizenry—these will no longer be assumed to be the obvious tasks of higher education. That would be a more shocking prospect had it not already happened.

Regardless, however, of the specific fate of modern higher education and its university, the modern world view has undergone in this century and will presumably continue to undergo in the next profound changes. Following in the path already taken by style, Western thought would seem to stand on the threshold of a new era. Indeed, Western civilization's entire cultural foundations appear to be receiving a fundamental reconstruction, as we redo our modern assumptions and prejudices. Modern culture is apparently making a rapid departure, as its postmodern successor enters to replace it. We shall now turn to look at the possibilities for the intermediate future of Western society, beginning with politics, where a similar process is at work.

POLITICS

The nation-state at its peak was the product of nearly a thousand years of history. It could trace its origins to the faint stirrings of new organizational efforts in the extreme fragmentation of the post-Carolingian era. And that long evolution, although beset by many fortuitous turns, was not in itself fortuitous, for it had had its own inner logic. The West, which once before had made its way to a centralized political system only to be forced to dismantle it, had decided to try again. The nation-state was the result. It has been to the Modern Age what the Roman Empire was to the Classical Age, the culmination of the long movement to centralization. Never as centralized in certain respects as its classical counterpart, which after all encompassed the entire West, in others it has been even more so, for the nation-state system came to be applied over a much wider area; had individual units—for example, the Spanish empire of the sixteenth century, the British empire of the eighteenth, and the Soviet empire of the twentieth—that were comparable in size to the Roman state; and also had at its disposal devices for enhancing centralization that were unavailable until modern times. Once developed, the nation-state system flourished because it worked very well. Indeed, the West's division into nation-states in the Modern Age has given its centralization a flexibility and hence vitality that the more rigid classical system never possessed.

But then, just recently, this nation-state system has begun to malfunction. It is still with us, to be sure, but having more and more difficulty providing the essentials, which we can summarize with reference to the benefits described earlier in our discussion of modern politics, that is, security, economic support, and leadership—the last taken to be the ability to order social energies in such a way that the problems confronting the civilization in the course of its development are met and more or less solved. For our purposes here, let us go on assuming that the West will continue to seek to preserve itself by edging away from the old and failing system toward a new one that can at least offer hope. If that is the case, then the future of politics should be determined by efforts to restore the basic political functions: to provide once again a political organization that meets the West's needs for security, that offers a framework of governance in which the economic life of the West can again flourish, and that facilitates a decision-making process with some chance of at least coming to grips with the sorts of problems that lie ahead.

With regard to security, the major problem is and will remain the threat presented by the nuclear bomb and those few other devices that have revolutionized the arts of destruction. In chapter 1 it was argued that the appearance of these new weapons, and particularly the bomb, has fundamentally altered the relationship of politics to warfare. Throughout the modern period, the nation-state's armed force was the greatest source of military power available. No other force, whether from below or above, could prevail against it for long. If a nation was defeated, it was by another nation. And because of the necessity of maintaining a certain balance, even when defeated the nation-state was usually left for the most part intact. But since 1945 the bomb—it absorbs our attention, but other innovations are almost as destructive—has brought such great changes that we are having difficulty in assimilating the implications. Suddenly the potential for the employment of tremendous force has been placed in the hands of small groups. Both terrorist factions and the leadership of small nations now have it in their power to attack and very badly hurt the major nation-states.

We have thought a great deal about the threat to humanity posed by the enormous arsenals of the superpowers. It is indeed a terrifying prospect. However, the superpowers have no interest in destroying themselves. That fact does not eliminate the possibility of these rivalries producing a holocaust but at least reduces it. The same cannot be said of the small groups. There will always be some that are very radical, righteous in the surety that the cause justifies the slaughter, and ready to direct their resentments, sometimes rightly and sometimes wrongly, against the major nation-states. Terrorism is not new, of course. What is new is the nuclear ingredient. When fanatic terrorism escalates to the nuclear level, the demonstration of the vulnerability of the nation-state will be complete.

How will the West react to this remarkable situation? How can it protect itself simultaneously against the great-power rivalry, the threat created by a world of small nations with nuclear armaments, and the realistic prospect of terrorist actions? The dangers are all but permanent. They will be with us as long as the ingredients and the knowledge are available, and that will be for a very long time. No agreement or treaty, no commitment to arms reduction, and no international agency can offer more than a semblance of a solution. And nothing at all will offer a complete solution. The world, quite simply, will never be the same again. There is no refuge from the danger now that it has been created. We can, however, reduce the risks considerably. Once Western civilization has fully absorbed the meaning of its inventions—and because civilizations are complex that takes time—it will move, slowly and falteringly but nevertheless, we can only hope, effectively, to make itself less vulnerable.

If that is to be the case, then the political options for the future are limited. For there are only a few things that the world can do to protect itself. One would be to create a true supranational authority that would try to defuse threatening developments and to guard against terrorism. Another would be to try to remove the source of the problem, the nation-state itself, by redividing it into its regions. And, finally, it might be possible to bring about a change in attitudes toward warfare. We shall look at each of these in turn.

As for a supranational authority, the most likely way in which one might come about is through a gradual fusion of the sovereignty of the major powers. Today that would mean the drawing together of the United States and the Soviet Union. If it is hard to conceive of any course of events prompting such concessions of national sovereignty, then we need to think ahead to the impact of terror. No one reacts very quickly to merely potential problems. But there will be cities lost: terrible, but almost inevitable. Then we should see a rush to cooperation. The cold war will finally come to an end, and so will the Sino-Soviet rivalry, as the true threat to stability, that is, the awesome potential of terrorism—whether from within the developed countries or the suffering areas of the Third World is immaterial—becomes fully manifest.

This coalescing of political power through cooperation, however, would have to produce an effective executive office; and, while one can imagine the task being undertaken, the chances for real success are limited by the vastness of the venture. The world will therefore probably also try to save itself by a seemingly even more drastic strategy: it will seek to remove the target. And that target is the nation-state itself. The nation-state even under the umbrella of a thorough supranational agency would remain what it is today, a victim looking for its assailant. Because we cannot forget how to build the bomb, we shall likely find it necessary to dismantle the only object upon which it might make a coercive impact. Thus there will be an effort to break up the nation-state, for it has become something of a sitting duck, difficult to defend and severely restricted as an offensive instrument.

The suggestion here, then, is that the West will seek to escape the threat of annihilation by moving in two directions at once. It will try to create practical supranational authorities for dealing with terrorism and local warfare, while simultaneously attempting to return to a world of small units. Although we can expect nation-states to remain in existence for some time, they should lose much of their power, identity, and even a good measure of their sovereignty, and that both to networks of organization superior and inferior to themselves. Furthermore, this should happen effortlessly, as they come to see the wisdom of divesting themselves of responsibilities that have become onerous and removing themselves as targets of nuclear terror. Perhaps it will not work entirely. The nuclear bomb, however, like most of modern weaponry, is designed to hit big enemies, remote from the user. It is not effective for small jobs. The West will try to defend itself by offering only small jobs. Although warfare and terrorism will continue with the result that some units will be very likely destroyed, the reasons for seeking to destroy them will be fewer. In any case, the losses will be less likely to affect the civilization as a whole. Yes, perfect, worldwide disarmament would be a better solution. But it will never be achieved.

If the dismantling of the nation-state still seems improbable, then we should remember that we are assuming gradual changes over a considerable time period; that the grand-scale innovations in weaponry have already been introduced and would seem to demand similar grand-scale changes in our political structure; that parts of the framework, both at the supra- and infranational level, are already in place; and, finally, that such complex systems have worked before, and within our political tradition.

Let us consider these last two points at slightly greater length. The framework for the beginnings of a postmodern politics is essentially the same as that for modern politics. The only difference is with regard to the place of emphasis. We can think of the work of governing occurring at five distinct levels: the communal, the local (that is, urban and county), the regional (state in the United States), the national (with its international involvements), and the supranational. All of these are now functioning, to one degree or another. However, during the Modern Age, authority, sovereignty, military power, bureaucratic work—that is, the entire mechanism of politics—everything has gravitated from the extremes to the nation-state. The national level has become vitally important, while the others have been slowly deprived of their functions and prestige. What is envisaged here is a reversal of the process, whereby the communal, local, and regional authorities, on the one hand, and the supranational authorities, on the other, would be strengthened at the expense of the national.

As for our previous experience with such systems, it can be said that for most of the West's history—from the establishment of Rome's imperium until the end of the Middle Ages—the West was ruled by combinations of universal and communal-local-regional governments. During the classical period, the balance clearly favored the universal-imperial constructions, while during the Middle Ages it favored the communal-local-regional set. But in both models, the authority of the institutions at the other end of the scale was maintained. In the imperial period, Roman governance remained somewhat superficial, leaving a considerable amount of discretion to sub-imperial offices. And in the particularist period, that is, the Middle Ages, the Roman papacy remained an institutional force of considerable significance at the universal level. Even though its actual authority always fell far short of pretensions, nevertheless it was able at least during the High Middle Ages to impose its will more than occasionally, especially in regulating warfare. To the objection, then, that a system such as the one here described could not function, one can reply that it did so for the better part of two millennia of Western history. To the objection that such a system could not function in modern times, the response can only be that modern times are coming to an end.

The remaining step that the West could undertake to lessen the peril from its new weaponry is the creation of a new code of morality, specifically concerned with warfare and terrorism, seeking to make the use of nuclear weapons and their ilk immoral—not illegal, for that was the approach of the modern treaty system, but rather fundamentally evil and repugnant, thus weaving around the possibility of their employment a restraining web of taboo. Taboos once established have proved remarkably powerful. But in the Western tradition warfare and violence have been gradually romanticized, and even the contemporary reaction to terrorism has been strangely ambivalent. We shall now see whether or not the world in the future, finally conscious of its new and terrible predicament, can move to reshape its collective attitudes. There would seem to be every reason for it to try.

But certainly the magnitude of the problem makes it very difficult to be genuinely optimistic. In 1945 mankind took a great step backward. Yet possibly this combination of approaches—building up while building down and at the same time working to apply new moral sanctions—could restore to the West and to the world it now dominates the security that it is the first duty of a political system to provide. That is rather implausible, no doubt, but less so than the prospect of long-term survival under the present circumstances.

If to provide security is the first requirement of politics, then the second is to offer support for the economy. Therefore the next question with regard to the West's political future asks how that support, no longer given by the nation-state except in the most immediate and ultimately destructive fashion, might be reestablished. I am not going to elaborate upon the possibilities for the West's economic future just yet, but there is one point that needs to be made here. It has to do with the assumption that we can look forward to a world of shrinking economic dimensions. The Western economy will very likely shift from the path that took it from local to national to world scope and begin to bend back in the direction from which it came. This fact, however it is spelled out, will be of tremendous importance in confirming a tendency already indicated by the considerations with regard to security just reviewed. A progressively decentralized economy should prove just as influential in disuniting the nation-state as the progressively centralized economy of the long modern growth period was in uniting it.

And once that disunification has taken place, the new infranational governments will become as essential to the economy by their contributions to stability as the national governments became through their contributions to expansion. Many of the same devices—for example, tariffs, subsidies, and regulation—will be used that have been already employed to aid growth; but they will next be turned, as they were once before, to the purposes of nongrowth. Again the West's political structures will be brought into harmony with the economy. From the sixteenth century through the nineteenth the nation-state served the growing capitalist economy. Now the reemerging regions should begin to serve a postcapitalist economy of stability. This is not to deny that supranational efforts at regulation will also continue. As long as there is a vestige of a world economy, there will be a need for these. As with the search for security, we should see the nation-state slowly deprived of its economic functions from both sides, losing some authority to world organizations even as most is lost to the increasingly self-sufficient regional economies.

We come to the third requirement of politics, that it facilitate leadership. Politics must provide a structure—appropriate, of course, to the dictates of the current world view, the requirements of the economy, and the construction of society—by means of which decisions can be made, and that with regard both to those everyday conflicts of interest that are endemic to social life and to the long-range well-being of the polity. We have already noted that the ability to make long-range decisions has declined remarkably in this century. Faced with new challenges, the nation-state has been unable to meet them. The result is that at the moment it gives the impression of being a rudderless ship caught in a storm, rolling helplessly in heavy seas. But that has not always been the case. For most of the Modern Age, the nation-state was either given its political inspiration or directly led by the rising bourgeoisie. There is little reason to doubt that, given the venture of creating a modern world, this leadership was effective. The middle class presided over a process that produced what it promised to produce, that is, material growth. And that growth, regardless of unequal distribution, in fact raised the standard of living of all classes. There should be no pretending that everyone was content. Still, the West as a civilization was committed to that pattern of endeavor we associate with modern industrialization and capitalism. The national bourgeois liberal-democracies produced a political climate—and this has been generally conceded by both its capitalist advocates and Marxist critics—in which growth flourished and the world began to fill up with material goods.

Then growth became more difficult. It began to exact a great price. To avoid that price it became increasingly necessary to transfer the payment to the next generations. At the moment, the modern political system is callously passing on to the future—and, unfortunately, the immediate future—the costs of pollution, of the exhaustion of resources, of the heating of the atmosphere (perhaps by several degrees by the middle of the next century), and of the accumulation of huge government debts, all for the sake of a growth that will no longer occur naturally. As if this were not bad enough, the nation-states have managed to lock themselves into an arms race that is as dangerous as it is economically disastrous. It would seem that not only is the political system simply not working as it should, but also that there is no one in charge. Our states function only to confirm a course that, if we insist in continuing on it, can have but one result: the ultimate collapse of Western civilization.

What has happened? As said before, the middle class has expanded its domain to the extent that it encompasses almost the whole of society. And in the course of achieving that victory it would seem to have lost its cohesiveness. Without opponents, it has become nothing. Its political *raison* has disappeared and with that the benefits of its leadership. But that is not the only difficulty. Part of the problem is democracy, or rather democracy as it has come to operate. For democracy as it has been construed permits the people to rule, but only with the provision that their decisions be frequently subject to abrogation. In a democracy of this sort the voice of the people is not merely heard; it is heard and then necessarily must be heard again. At short intervals new dictates must be issued. These may confirm the previous set, or they may not. Under such circumstances, the people can opt only for what is good for them at the moment. They have no way of knowing in what the next mood will result. Both the people as a whole and its individual members are therefore right to see their interest in making as much of the present as possible. If an advantage is deferred to the future, it well may be lost, given the undependable nature of democratic sovereignty—and, again, the fault is not really inherent in democracy, rule by the people, but in the sort of democracy that recently has come to prevail in Western politics, something that we might call democracy-of-the-moment, to distinguish it from systems of popular sovereignty in which decisions once made are not easily reversed.

But the fault that we have here described is not always a fault. If a society is trying to change rapidly, then there is no better way of reshaping the political guidelines than by entrusting them to a system in which the means of constant redirection are incorporated. Rapid change, to say it again, was pretty much the rule during the five centuries of modern growth. And it was no doubt the pressure to find a system that would suit an expansion-bent West that resulted in the development of modern democracy—which of course was modeled closely on the democracy of the expansionist ancient Greek period. At both times, democracy did nothing to inhibit leadership. Under the circumstances, with change as the intended outcome, it in fact facilitated it. Now the implication is obvious: if we are at the end of our growth period, for whatever reasons—because we no longer like the results or because we have actually reached the physical limits, or something of both together—and are now seeking a new political system that will encourage stability, then democracy-of-the-moment will be curtailed. And finally it should be replaced by arrangements that will make it possible to set directions and keep them set, not for a few years, but for decades and then centuries.

What type of government would that be? Here the distinctions between the traditional forms—that is, democracy, aristocracy, and monarchy—are no longer of great importance. Neither are, and not just with regard to the search for stability, such labels as capitalist, socialist, fascist, or communist. All of these meant something in the past, but we are quickly getting beyond the point where their arguments have relevance for the future. If the names continue to be used, and they no doubt will be, then they will invariably come to have different meanings. What will matter is the commitment to regulating social activity in such a way that the populace is well taken care of within a state that is secure and not in the act of destroying itself through growth. And that will, we can speculate, be accomplished by a myriad of innovations, the essentials of which can be reduced to six.

First, the intervals between opportunities for changing directions will be considerably lengthened. Where democracy survives, there will be fewer significant elections, and even when these occur the possibilities for true change will no doubt be constitutionally restricted. Whatever the forms, the principle is apt to be the same, and that will be to insure that decisions once made are not soon altered.

Second, the authority of governments to regulate and restrain will be greatly strengthened. The tendency to government control at all levels witnessed during the last century should continue, with, however, the balance of activity shifting from national to smaller units. More authority for government usually means an increase in executive powers, but because the intention is to discourage innovation rather than promote radical solutions, certainly the executive's freedom of movement will be restricted by various checks. Popular revolutionary demagoguery, whether reactionary or radical, will be rightly perceived as an ever-present threat. And to the extent that constitutional and other safeguards can be constructed to guard against it, they will be. Every effort will be made to enfold the state authority in complex strata of government to ensure that it not be used to innovate.

Third, all pretense of equality will give way to explicit and formal hierarchies. The argument has already been made while discussing the coming changes in ideas: equality, meaning equality of opportunity, the right to aspire to reach a higher level, has clearly been a help to growth. In a society in which growth is anathema, equality of opportunity will be exchanged for a system of assigned position. To the modern mind, such a suggestion is most unwelcome. But we should remember that equality of opportunity has produced its monsters; and systems of place and privilege invariably come with security for the lower stations and duty for the higher. In the correct proportions, it would seem that the moral balance is restored. But even if a hierarchical order should prove to be genuinely oppressive—even as oppressive as the actual results of open systems—

still the restless nature of a society in which initially equal individuals are constantly contending with each other for advantage will not appeal to a future in search of stability.

Fourth, to lessen the chances of provoking the revolutions that unjust societies risk bringing upon themselves, there will be an effort to keep both incomes and benefits within a narrow range. The Modern Age has advocated equality, but produced vast inequalities. Perhaps as we move toward a postmodern age greater de facto equality will be achieved, even as we surrender the ideal. As noted earlier, the Modern Age to facilitate growth opted for equality of opportunity. The postmodern age should choose equality of result, although not perfect equality of result, but that within a spectrum of hierarchical differentiations. That incomes can be kept within close range has been demonstrated by many societies, past and present. Yet the prospect of joining hierarchy to something like equality of result will not be pleasing to many. The left will tend not to like the former and the right the latter. But at present both left and right remain under the spell of the modern dream, which, if worthy in its day, has lost its purpose. We should add that the continuation of the attempt to realize it is taxing the future severely. When the West begins to do what it can to put things back together again, it will have to dream new dreams, and they will be very different.

Fifth, future societies will propagandize the new vision of stability just as sincerely and with as much enthusiasm as modern societies have propagandized the cause of growth. We have been made to believe in growth—not as the result of a conspiracy, although certainly in modern advertising there is considerable cynicism, but rather because the ideal is simply endemic to the age. In the future, the ideal of stability will come to hold a similar position. A society that does not believe in its ideals will not succeed; and a society that does believe will not avoid propagating them as a form of insurance.

Finally, the problems that we have noted with regard to the lack of leadership will most likely solve themselves, as other pieces begin to fall into place. To replace the direction once provided by the growth-oriented bourgeoisie, there will likely appear a new class, or better, estate, since its positioning in society will likely be along vertical rather than horizontal lines—an order designated by status and function rather than by wealth. And this new leadership will be selected with regard to the ability to reconcile to stability. What is in mind here is a lengthy evolution, in which just as once the course of history favored those individuals who were open to expansion, who learned to take advantage of opportunities for growth—and the Modern Age has been the great period of the striving opportunist—now the new course will support those who see their advantage in organizing and maintaining fixed communities. There are always those who like growth, profit from growth, and work for growth, but there are also their counterparts, those who like stability, profit from stability, and work for stability. Between the two it is not a question of moral choice. But for the last five centuries or so, the West has pushed the expansionists to the top. It has blessed them with economic subsidies, political advantages, and ideological assumptions. In the period ahead, growth now having become more problematical than helpful, the civilization will turn against it and gradually induce new leaders to help create what it has come to need, an era of rest and recovery.

To sum up this view of the future of the West's political structure as we move into the twenty-first century, we can suggest the following, that: to cope with the new problem of security posed by the new weaponry, we shall attempt to dissolve the nation-state, that weaponry's easiest target, by building downward while at the same time adding enough of a supra-national authority to try to cope with the problems that remain; next, to improve the troubled relationship between the modern economy that refuses to grow and the modern state that refuses to let it not grow, we shall seek to create a politics that can support economies of stability, these organized at the local and regional rather than national level; and, then, to achieve again direction and leadership, and this in accord with the new purposes, we shall reorder the basic fundamentals of governance, put an end to democracy-of-the-moment, increase the authority of governments to regulate, attempt to decrease the competition generated by equality of opportunity, perform a thorough economic leveling, invent a new propaganda of stability, and permit the rise to influence of an estate distinguished primarily by its compatibility with the new model of society. We should keep in mind that while these are conjectures, they are intended neither as a utopia—I would write it much differently—nor as a nightmare-to-be-avoided, à la Orwell. If the latter were the choice, I would write that differently, too, making it much more horrible, as Orwell indeed did. They are merely reasonable surmises. And I think we all know that the reality will be something else. An unexpected emphasis here, a twist there, an evil or benevolent force intermixed, and things could work out very differently. But once set, the major directions of political movement may prove to be quite durable. Certainly they have been in the past. That should also prove to be the case with regard to the economy, to a consideration of which we now proceed.

ECONOMICS

The modern economy has reached a turning point. Its period of easy growth is over. And the road ahead as it continues to try to force expansion should prove a very trying one. Energy will continue despite fluctuations to become more expensive. The costs of preventing pollution will increase. The numbers of people using and depending upon the new systems will grow larger and larger. The problems associated with the displacement of workers by automation will become more difficult. Expenditures on welfare, ever more necessary because of severe unemployment, will go on rising. National debts and, more significant, the cost of servicing national debts will soar. The rate of default on international debts will discourage new loans, but they will be made regardless, for the Third World must continue to buy. And no one will discover a way out, because there is none. That is the good news. The modern economy is in the process of breaking down. The bad news is that it may take a while.

"What is new to our time," according to Jonathan Schell, "is the realization that, acting quite independently of any good or evil intentions of ours, the human enterprise as a whole has begun to strain and erode the natural terrestrial world on which human and other life depends."[10] And that, of course, is very bad economics. The West is destroying the ecological systems upon which its economic life depends, and eventually upon which all life depends. We are in a difficult position, forced to choose between the short-term interests of an economy that sustains us and the well-being of the natural world that will be needed in the future to sustain us. By now all of us are well aware of what is happening and of both the practical and moral implications of what we are doing. When the chips are down, however, we continue to opt for the present and for the interests of the modern economy. It should be added in our defense that, no matter how harsh later judgments are upon us, it is the only economy we have got. Contemporary society is caught in a dilemma to which it is contributing but over which it has no real control. Therefore we must look forward to the breakdown of our economy to save our future from ourselves.

Possibly, however, that breakdown can occur side by side with a workable transition to a postmodern society, one with an economy that, whatever else may distinguish it, can manage to take care of the future as it takes care of the present. That is presumably not an impossible task, since all other economies but ours have done so, and effortlessly, without even having to think about it. All other economies have of course been relatively simple and could not have done much damage to their natural surroundings even had they wanted to. Now the West, if it is not to force itself into a situation where catastrophe is assured, must return to a more simple economy. In certain regards it would seem that it is already beginning to do that. As it becomes more difficult to operate in the old style, still more alternative efforts should appear, gradually building together to provide the successor to the modern economy. Then, when the breakdown does come, it will be all but meaningless.

To return for the moment to Rome: as noted earlier, Rome, and here the interest is in its economy, took a long time to fall. When it finally was over, Europe was about halfway to another solution. An empire fell, and with it an economic system, and no one noticed. Maybe we shall have the good sense to make our exit from the modern economy in such a way that no one will notice.

Yet that exit will be far from easy. Once things have become as complex as they now are, it is very difficult to reinvent a simple economy. We have developed certain skills while losing others, induced our citizens to concentrate themselves in cities while surrendering the countryside to the machines of single-crop agriculture, and permitted the huge increases in population that put in question the ability of the future to care for the vast numbers, whatever the economic system. Some have suggested that before a true balance can be achieved the world's population must be reduced, one way or another. That would most probably mean great losses from famine or war. Certainly neither of those outcomes is necessary, and it will be the mark of a successful transition if they are avoided. But the longer the worldwide effects of modernization are sustained, the more vulnerable we become. No doubt the key to a viable conversion lies in the rate. If the present pattern of destructive growth continues too long, a genuine human tragedy will be unavoidable. Yet if the modern economy is destroyed quickly, before an alternative system has grown up within it, the results will also be unfortunate. Perhaps, then, it is not really such bad news that the demise will be stretched out a bit.

The most encouraging aspect with regard to this great economic change that we are contemplating is that it has already begun. If we date from the 1870s the beginning of the individual changes that should eventually coalesce to produce an essential conversion to a new economy, then they are already in fact more than a century old. The movements away from free trade and the open market toward regulation and the welfare state were of course begun in order to preserve capitalism, and they were no doubt effective in doing that. They have aimed at furthering growth. But eventually these same mechanisms, that is, the entire apparatus of economic controls, will be put, if we are correct here in assessing the drift, to a new purpose—and that will be to promote stability rather than growth. Controls, of course, can do either. Indeed, they would seem to lend themselves better to assisting the former than the latter. The modern economy, we should remember, had to break loose from the controls of the medieval and early modern periods in order to achieve the easy growth of its vigorous centuries. Only late in the modern period, when growth began to come hard, were controls reimposed. Those who insist that even now growth would be assisted if all government intervention was removed are probably correct. But we are not willing to pay the price. As said earlier, the modern economy has come to embrace all of us too thoroughly. The price of easy growth is periodic failure. Society can no longer tolerate failure, because we have been left with no alternative economy to fall back upon. Therefore we have before us something of an irony: the employment of a system of regulation on behalf of growth that not only can be, but also no doubt will be soon used to halt it. And if we are lucky we shall hardly observe the subtle reversals that turn the West's economy to point in another direction.[11]

What other changes can we expect during this transition? In addition to the employment of regulation to end growth, there should also take place a gradual shift from private to national and then, later, regional and communal ownership. This will be the result of several factors, among them the difficulty in making profits once growth has slowed to a standstill—the running of corporations serving the public will become no longer a privilege, but a public-funded obligation. Also, the end of the ideology of individualism will contribute to the corresponding end of private ownership. The great era of the private economy began with the sunburst of Renaissance individualist humanism and was sustained throughout by its heritage. Now the death of cultural individualism will undoubtedly contribute to the death of economic individualism.

Futher, the profit motive, one of the mainsprings of the private economy, founded as it was upon the encouragement of profits for the individual through private ownership, will be gradually suppressed. Even where there remain profits to be had, the taking of them will be increasingly assumed to be detrimental to the social good. We shall have more statements like that of Robert Heilbroner, who has noted disapprovingly that "no other civilization has permitted the calculus of selfishness so to dominate its lifeways. . . ,"[12] and like that of the historian William Appleman Williams, who argues that "community welfare must replace individual aggrandizement: the moral and social character of the commonwealth must take precedence over the bank account of the individual."[13] Moreover, developing attitudes seem to suggest that if the result is to destroy the consumer society, so much the better: "It laid waste part of our coasts, our mountains, our cities, our way of life, our culture"—here the words are those of Giscard d'Estaing, former president of France—"[and] it caused tremendous havoc. I think that the austere society we are aiming toward is basically better adapted to France."[14] And to the West and the world, the future will quite possibly come to believe.

Just as private ownership should give way to public ownership, we can anticipate that hired labor will give way to a permanent labor of status. In the relatively fixed economy toward which we would seem to be evolving, the open-market system of providing labor, one in which, at least theoretically, labor is contracted for a specific task and paid according to the law of supply and demand, will come to an end. It will be steadily—not steadily at all in the short-run, of course, for there will be many ups and downs—replaced by a closed-market system, in which wages are set, as they were in the Middle Ages and have been in all noncapitalist societies, by a combination of custom, law, and moral pressure; and in which jobs are assigned by tradition, inheritance, and communal and state fiat. The fluidity of labor is as much a threat to stability as is private ownership. The future economy will not restrict the one without a parallel effort to put an end to the other.

Another result of the coming transition will be the end of easy money. From the beginning of the era of growth, governments have favored expansion with the creation of accessible credit and inflated currencies. Businesses were thereby encouraged to expand and consumers to consume. Growth for governments meant popularity at home and power abroad. Inflation was always a problem, but it had its positive side, for it made debt easier to pay off in a long era of accumulating obligations. But as the disadvantages of growth now continue to outweigh the advantages, governments will respond by tightening credit and balancing budgets. Government spending will once again be matched by taxation. Whether expenditures amount to a lot or a little, the government will put back into the economy only what it has taken out, and the effect on stability will be nil. This would not have to be true within every time interval, and a true Keynesian practice, one that insisted in subtracting in good years what had been added in bad ones, would still be possible. There will never be anything to be gained from not seeking recovery during times of depression. It is only the policy of long-term growth that will be increasingly taken to be no longer appropriate.

And, of course, there will also be a transition away from large to small economic units. Growth is promoted by and in turn promotes large units that are highly specialized and interdependent. Stability is promoted by and in turn promotes small units that are not very specialized and largely self-sufficient. "If then self-sufficiency is to be desired," Aristotle wrote in his *Politics,* and certainly it is still true, "the lesser degree of unity is more desirable than the greater."[15] Self-sufficiency will be valued because it will both reduce the pressure on resources and release the small units from their compelled involvement in a world economy that no longer offers economic security. In small units, the needs for energy are necessarily reduced. Tasks are again best accomplished by human labor, and the opportunity is thereby created to dispense with machinery.

Machinery has been an integral part of the modern economy. Like so many things modern, just in this last century there has been a tremendous acceleration in the rate of its employment, even as the end approaches. Shall we in fact now begin to turn our backs on the world of automation that we have called into existence? We shall if the costs of the energy that fuels the machines combined with those of production and maintenance become more expensive than labor. But there is another reason that the future will turn against automation: people need the work, and the machines do not. People need it because, as C. E. M. Joad once put it, "work is the only occupation yet invented which mankind has been able to endure in any but the smallest possible doses."[16] Work—common labor or the work of the mind, and best, as Marx suggested, both together in sensible alternation[17]—has tremendous value as a restorer of the soul. Fortunately, everything is conspiring to return it to people. Once automation has reached the level where it is no longer creating new jobs, and that has now happened, then the welfare costs of the displaced workers need to be added to the costs of the automation itself. Also the fragmentation of the economy will make the renunciation easier. With the disappearance of the vast markets of the present, the potential for the big profits that might seem to justify automation will be diminished. And the autarky achieved by the individual components of the emerging economy will permit societies to put social interest before the requirements of competition. None of this means that a future is being here foreseen that at any point will wish to do without all machinery. But the more sophisticated the particular item, the more designed for the highly specialized economy of today, the less useful it should prove in the economy of tomorrow.

Just as the West will begin to turn away from its radical experiment with automation, it will also no doubt withdraw from space. The smaller political units will not be able to afford the expenses connected with the venture; and also they will have nothing to gain from it. The military uses of space form a tremendous threat, and we can only hope that the breaking up of the nation-state and national economy will prevent space from becoming the next battleground. Again, let us believe that ours is a civilization that will act to preserve itself. Some of the solutions to our problems are very simple, like this one: we only have to say no to a line of development that is inherently suicidal.

If we are fortunate, then the dismantling of the nation-state and national economy will also spell the end of the armaments industry. Without it, the time given us to make the necessary adjustments to a new economy would be considerably increased. Senator Proxmire once called the armaments industry a "pulbic works project." It is that, but one that does not benefit the public. It uses up scarce resources while widening the gap between rich and poor. In any sensible system, the upper and middle income groups would be taxed to aid the lower. In the United States the middle strata are taxed to aid the upper, and the armaments industry serves as the device of distribution. The situation is not essentially different in the U.S.S.R., where the masses are deprived of consumer goods because the momentum of the arms race must be maintained. The problem is the work of neither capitalism nor communism, nor even of the ideological rivalry between them. It is, rather, an entirely natural by-product of the nation-state system. As that system comes apart, both the arms race and the armaments industry ought to be reduced to their proper proportions. Small states do not commit such follies. Or, rather, they commit comparable follies, but the scale and therefore the consequences are proportionately reduced. "In miniature," wrote Leopold Kohr in *The Breakdown of Nations,* "problems lose both their terror and significance, which is all that society can ever hope for."[18] Those words deserve reflecting on.

It was said in the discussion of the West's political future that measures would have to be taken to insure that in a stable society the differences in standards of living not be permitted to be overly great. One can only repeat the thought here: any economic system that seeks stability will reduce the gap between rich and poor to the narrowest possible dimension. Once competition on the open market is no longer the central moving force and various hierarchies have been created to bind society into an immobility designed to last, it will be essential that the economic rewards assigned various functions not be a source of friction. A mobile society can permit wealth and poverty to coexist because the theoretical path from the one to the other is always open. An immobile society, however, cannot afford such disparities. If they continue to exist, then the hopes for reconstructing economic activity in such a way that it benefits the community will surely prove false.

What of the gap between the developed areas of the old West and the developing world, Westernized but not fully? Here there are problems beside which the others necessarily appear diminished. The nations of the older West, meaning not only those of the original Europe, but also of the areas that were Westernized successfully in time to take part in the industrialization of the last two centuries, have gone through the growth era together. They have profited from it and now are beginning to perceive some of the dangers that are gathering on the horizon. The contemplated changes in these long-developed areas could well evolve along more or less natural lines. Already certain types of growth are being curbed. The birthrate has in a few places even declined to the point where one begins to suspect that a crisis is developing from too few rather than too many births. There is, it would seem, a new attitude of restraint that marks the older West in the last decades of this century.

But that is not the case with those nations more recently introduced to the Western economy. They are caught up in their own transition, rapidly moving from the traditional to the open-maket system. And while the innovations have met with disapproval in many corners of these societies, those in control, with the prospect of increased profits for the upper classes, have been generally receptive. The developed nations have also helped, convinced that modernization will eventually solve all the problems created by the dislocations and not unmindful of new profits for themselves, as whole societies are opened up to Western goods. The result has been that those pushing for modernization in the Third World have been given assistance in staying on top. And they are set on completing what they have begun, regardless of both the present effects on local populations and the dim prospects for ultimate success.

And dim they are indeed. If the modern economy as a whole is pushing the limits of growth, then the developing nations are going to find themselves entering upon the scene too late. They will arrive at the take-off point only to crash before fully airborne. Their future would seem to be very dark if they continue along the present course toward modernization. Yet the road back is not an easy one, either. The population explosion makes the chances for an orderly retreat not at all good. Even without the question of what to do with the new millions, the problem is made much more difficult by the fact that now many of the old ways have been lost. The lands that have been converted to new crops cannot be easily restored, and, yet worse, the communal network of custom that supported the traditional economies has broken down beyond repair. Damned if they modernize and damned if they do not, parts of the Third World would seem to be pointed toward economic catastrophe.[19]

What shall the attitude of the older West be to this potential tragedy? Should it take action or withdraw and let the Third World find its own solutions? A problem that affects such a large portion of the globe cannot be one to which any part of the remainder can be indifferent. It is not just a matter of morality, but of survival. The older West will not find much stability in a world in which its more recently Westernized sector is falling apart. Therefore the active course is to be preferred to withdrawal. But what sort of action? For the last century, and especially in the decades since the end of World War II, the older West has contributed only to modernization. Now it should begin to discourage it, not, to be sure, by intervention, but by gradually removing the external stimuli to growth—loans, assistance in acquiring the new techniques that contribute to expansion, Western education, the entire panoply of modern ways. That is the negative part of action.

There will likely be a positive part, too: where the assistance is wanted, the older West may indeed lend its hand in trying to restabilize these societies that have been in fact destabilized by contact with the processes of modernization. One would like to think that there is a point of balance somewhere between the old, traditional societies, to which a return in most places is no longer possible, and a fully modernized growth economy. One would also like to think that the gap between North and South can be brought within reasonable limits, as both rich nations and poor strive toward regional economies, essentially unconnected, of mutual austerity. If there emerges on both sides a clear perception of what the future can be expected to have in store and, here more important, what it cannot be expected to have in store, then despite individual failures it is at least possible to conceive of overall success. And overall success here is crucial. There are three sets of problems that the West cannot fail to solve if it is to make it through its transition to a new society: it cannot fail to solve the problems posed by the threat of nuclear destruction; it cannot fail to solve the problems posed by the internal antagonisms sure to develop as we shift away from growth; and it cannot fail to solve this last set, that posed by the tensions, certain to worsen before they begin to get better, between the developed and developing areas.

Here nothing has been said about two contemporary trends that often feature prominently in discussions of the economic future, and these are the development of the service economy and, more recently, the rapid rise of the computerized information industry. The omission has not been the result of an oversight. If growth does indeed wind down, as assumed here, then both of these innovations will be remarkably reduced in significance in the course of the next century. The service economy is impressive enough at the moment: seven of every ten workers in the United States are now employed in service jobs. The success of the service sector is of course a measurement of the failure of workers to hold their jobs in industry and agriculture: as they have been forced out of the factory and off the farm by mechanization, they have found ingenious ways of positioning themselves along the lines of the cash fallout from the basic money makers. But as human labor once again becomes more economical than machine labor, the service economy will lose much of its work force. There is a core of real service that no society can get along without. Many of the invented services, however, will disappear as quickly and as effortlessly as they have appeared, and few will know that they are gone.

As for the much-heralded computer revolution: its accomplishments are genuine and extremely impressive. Much of what it has produced will endure. However, if the future is indeed permitted to witness the building down of the modern state, economy, and life-style, then the need for computers with their ability to supply information rapidly will consistently decline. Complex systems require complex information to survive. Even though computers do not give better knowledge of these complex systems than the managers of more simple systems have had of their own operations, they do slow the rate of increasing ignorance, and the greater the complexity, the more essential they become. But we shall be moving from complexity to simplicity. Complexity—despite computers and in part, since they permit even greater degrees, because of them—no longer works. And the simple systems will be understood once again by simple people. At least we can hope so.

Finally, what will happen to the modern city as it is caught up in the great transition away from the modern economy? Obviously, in a new economy in which the tasks of industry, banking, and commerce are less important to the system as a whole, the city, which has been the traditional center for those operations, will lose much of its economic significance. But we should also note again—it was mentioned in chapter 1 in connection with the signs of modernism in decline—that the growth of the last half-century has not been at all kind to the old towns and cities. Their outlines have been slowly erased by sprawl, while their cores have fallen on the bad times that only a few of the renewal projects have been able to ameliorate. Quite possibly the slowing down of the growth process will prevent further decay, especially if those who live in the cities decide that they wish to preserve the original areas. Even as the cities are removed from the center of things, perhaps something of their essence can be recaptured. If agriculture is returned to labor-intensive farming, much of the present overcrowding would be eliminated. The West's cities were better places to live before their last growth spurt. They could conceivably again become genuinely attractive.

Now that we are nearing the end of this brief speculation on the West's economic future, we might point to one more implication of the arguments made here, and that is that there can be no winner in the great ideological struggle of the last two centuries between capitalism and socialism. Both were constructed out of thoroughly modern parts and based on legitimately modern assumptions. Capitalism argued that the best way to prosperity and individual freedom was to encourage growth through the open-market mechanism. Socialism replied that, while it agreed with the goals and also credited the open market with having produced a world of abundance, it was now time to make a few major adjustments, especially with regard to the distribution of the rewards and, even more fundamental, to the ownership of the means of production. Both capitalism and socialism thought that growth was good and that it could continue. Socialism thus hoped to build on the success of capitalism. But now capitalism—the open-market system devoted to expansion—is in decline. Therefore, any future socialism will have to build not on its success, but rather on its failure. That fact will make for a profound difference. Socialism can no longer think that it can merely take over a working concern. Rather, it must rethink its premises, wondering what it means to construct a society of justice within the constraints imposed by the end of growth.

In our review of the West's economic progress from its medieval to its modern condition we looked at each stage at the evolving situation with regard to four basic elements: production-distribution, class, theory, and geographic extension. If we try to summarize our foray into the future by extending the commentary on these four, we can say the following:

First, with regard to production-distribution, the economy will move away from the specialization and open-market system of the high modern period and toward diversified production and regulated distribution, all this within smaller, largely self-sufficient units.

Second, with regard to a dominant class, the best guess would seem to be that there will be none, that classes and the entire horizontal structure of society will give way to a vertical structure, and that leadership will emerge from among those who are best able to reconcile their interests to the new requirements of stability.

Third, with regard to a new economic theory, perhaps its most distinctive feature will be that it will not proceed from what we would usually think of as economic considerations, but will be given its parameters by other societal goals. If economics and economic theory have been central to the Modern Age, soon they will no longer be, as all economic activity is more and more scrutinized to make sure that it does nothing to destroy the various balances and compromises that will be necessary to stability.

And, fourth, with regard to the geographic significance of the transition from the modern to the postmodern economy, one can make these observations: that the Westernization of the world is an accomplished fact, for the traditional economies have been forced to give way to it; and yet that this world economy is now going to begin to edge away from its creation and henceforth slowly seek to establish once again units that are more self-sufficient, initially at the national, but later and more lastingly at the regional and local levels. The grand economy of the modern world should be expected, then, to devolve toward less destructive, less automated, and less interdependent forms.

The transformations that have been discussed here are profound. They assume an eventual reorganization of the West's and the world's economy just as thorough as that which took place when the classical economy finally gave way to the medieval and again when the medieval gave way to the modern. But, again, great changes do not come quickly. Even though the process of transition is already a century old, it should, if we are fortunate, continue for another century or so. There is nothing about this conversion that would necessitate violent, precipitate change. Indeed, if the goal is stability, then the more rapid the course, the less the chances for successfully completing the journey. Yet it is also true that there are no inherent guarantees against drastic upheaval. The changes themselves will not be dangerous. They will in fact be designed to avoid danger. The real threats that may appear—and to some degree they are unavoidable—will come not from the process itself, but rather from the way in which it is managed.

And yet little can be said with regard to how it will be managed, or even how it should be managed, except perhaps for one thing. The advice comes from Spengler, who probably deserves to be quoted at least once in a work of this sort. Spengler said that we must "do the inevitable or nothing at all."[20] If that has an application here, it is that it would be very foolish to ignore the signs telling us that the modern growth economy is coming, must come, to an end. However we in fact manage our trek to a future economy, it must be done in such a way that the world's crucial ecological balances are preserved. If we do not do that, then we face the prospect of a very bleak future.

SOCIAL ASPECTS

Although no consistent effort has been made to develop the story of social history in this essay—as said, the record, much of it being of a private nature, is obscure for long stretches—I would nevertheless like to point very briefly to the implications for the future with regard to several social aspects, should the course of events resemble the one that has been outlined in this chapter. We shall take a baker's dozen and say just a few words about each. The subjects are these: where we shall live; the social units in which we shall live; education for the young; the role of youth within society; the future of moral instruction; the fight against crime; the prospects for continuing as a litigious society; the future of racial relationships; the possibilities for resolution of the argument between the sexes; the future of medicine; the likely trends in entertainment; the likely trends in sports; and, last, the outlook for alienation, that great modern disease. As interesting as each is in its own right, the purpose here is not to develop the ramifications at length, but rather only to say enough to position them within the context of this essay.

Where shall we live in the next century, as modern patterns are replaced by new ones? The tendency during the last several centuries has been to concentrate people in urban areas, first mostly in private, individual homes in moderate-sized cities, and then more recently in apartment complexes in gigantic cities, surrounded by suburban layers in which the movement is also away from the single-family unit. Now new influences will be felt, and the result will be to create different patterns. The two basic determinants with regard both to where we live and in what sorts of structures are the cost of building and the place of work. When the costs of building were low, we built large individual units; and when the places of work were concentrated, we clustered the units around those few places.

With the end of cheap energy and abundant resources, the costs of building will continue to climb; and therefore the trend, already established, away from expansive private homes should continue. But will that mean that the movement to apartment housing will also continue? Probably not. If there is a return to small-scale farming, also apparently dictated by more expensive energy and resources, then the cities will start to shrink. Thus the pressure on urban housing should be reduced, putting an end to the trend to apartment living in both the cities and suburbs. And in the countryside, apartments have never been practical for obvious reasons. Therefore, we should see something like this: in the countryside, the return to modest individual units, built out of local materials and with considerable nonprofessional assistance; and in the cities, a stabilization along present lines, with apartments used in the core and individual housing, made up for some time mostly of what has already been built and supplemented by multiple-unit complexes, in the suburbs. Overall, the most dramatic change will be the repopulation of the countryside.

The social unit of the intermediate future will no doubt be the family. Perhaps that would seem to be not much of a speculation, since it merely repeats the present. But here is the reasoning behind it: if we look at our roots in the Middle Ages, there the social unit of prime importance was not the family, but rather the community. As that community slowly broke up under the impact of modern ways—not just of the modern economy, but of modern thought, modern law, and the entire modern nexus—the family, and specifically the bourgeois family, with its significance for the inheritance of private property, became the new social unit. But as the Modern Age wore on, the family was increasingly plagued by certain equally valid modern developments. There was, for example, a distinct reduction of the family's economic significance, as the size of business ventures burgeoned beyond family proportions. Also, the rise of individualism increasingly challenged the demands of family organization. Most damaging was the establishment of the assumed right of the individual to unfettered development, which now was put above the right of the family to endure. The result has been the dramatic increase in divorce in the last half-century.

From this point on, however, we expect individualism to wane. The gigantic corporation of the twentieth century should also begin to break up, allowing to the family, but this time within a restrictive rather than a free-enterprise system, once again a greater economic role. The result should at some point contribute to a revival of the family, although certainly the destructive force of its late-modern enemies is not yet spent. We should note, too, that the family in the more distant future may well begin to lose some of its importance, as a finally achieved economic stability again provides an opportunity for the reemergence of a communal structure. Just as once the West moved from the community to the family to the individual, perhaps it is presently reversing its course and beginning the journey back—that is, from the individual to the family to the community. It would seem that in some respects we are already seeing the earliest manifestations of the transition away from a full individualism and a return to an emphasis on the family. In the course of the next century, the communal network should, our other assumptions proving more or less correct, begin to appear. But it will be a long time before the network is ready to replace the family with regard to its fundamental tasks.

A comment on higher education has already been made in our discussion of trends in thought. Here we shall speculate on the future of school (primary and secondary) education. In evaluating its role as we move from the late Modern Age toward the postmodern, one should remember how important this general education has been to the modern way of life. It has been given the charge of preparing the young for jobs in an industrial society, of schooling them for participation as citizens in a democratic politics, of replacing the mores of traditional society with a modern set, and, finally, of simply providing a care-center, increasingly important with the employment of both parents, for children from the age of five on.

But in the future, as the modern constellation of society continues to lose its coherence, education will be deprived of many of these functions. With the simplification of the economy, there will be less need for the types of skills that schools are best prepared to teach. With the demise of the sort of democracy that compels frequent change and the fall of the growth-oriented ideology that supported it, we should see even less attention given to mass education for these purposes. And with the growing loss of confidence in modern mores and the developing concomitant suspicion that the preachment of freedom for the individual has been much abused, the schools will lose their purpose as defenders of the faith. Education could of course seek to become the defender of the new faiths, and it undoubtedly will do so to a certain extent; but with the reestablishment of other sources of social propaganda, especially the family and the church, there will be less reason for it. And with the increase in the demand for labor and the return of parents to workplaces in or near the home, the need to provide a refuge where children can be retained during working hours will also be diminished.

All of these things should make for a general deemphasis on education. The schools will no longer enjoy the support that they received when they were considered crucial. Compulsory schooling will be in all likelihood discontinued, although not in a moment, but rather gradually, with various categories of exemption being introduced over a long period. The school day will probably be shortened, too, for with the end of mass education those students who remain will be capable of studying on their own. With fewer and better students, standards will rise, and the quality of education for those remaining will be distinctly improved. The matter of discipline, which has come to occupy so much of our attention, will all but disappear, as those who prefer to be elsewhere are permitted to leave. In short, the future should see an end to the modern educational experiment. The quantity of education will decline. Conceivably the quality will rise.

As for the role of youth within society, one would expect that the move away from modernism will undercut the youth culture and restore youth to a subordinate place. The modern attitude toward the concept of youth—although not always to the young themselves—has been consistently adulatory. While the West's medieval culture generally assumed that one got wiser with age, modern culture has tended to take the opposite position: it is the young who are closer to God or, later, closer to the pristine natural state. From the Renaissance to our own times, the West has tended to prefer youth to age. Most recently, we have seen the development, referred to earlier, of a huge youth industry, the obvious result of the achievement of a certain independence of selection on the part of the young. But the end of this modern inclination to identify the desirable with youth would seem already to be approaching. As long as the Modern Age sought to escape the past, it quite naturally venerated youth. As it seeks stability, it will begin, as in so many regards, to turn in the other direction. Once again, we shall come to believe that life is a process by which one gains insight through experience; and wisdom and tranquility through insight. All wrong, no doubt, but no more so than the modern opinion, and more suited to the new needs of society.

In our discussion of the transition to a postmodern thought, we speculated that truth and knowledge would be progressively subordinated to wisdom and ethics. If that is so, then the social application will be the reintroduction of frank moral instruction. The modern mind has shied away from morality, which has been tainted by its association with religious superstition and systems of oppression. In place of morality, modernism has offered the people truth, with the hope that somehow clarifying the facts would eliminate the need for moral judgments. There is no evil, only ignorance. The result has been that, to be sure, morality has declined. But the hoped-for alternative system, with a healthy ego working in an enlightened world, never quite arrived. Now we are ready for morality again. Normative statements will be the rage of the future, as the West seeks to restore to social intercourse the badly needed guidelines of a clearly stated and very unsituational moral code.

Crime has become in the last several decades a major problem, especially in the cities. It is the joint product of several factors. One is clearly unemployment. The breakdown of the family has also contributed. So has racial hostility. Further, city governments, receiving an inadequate share of taxation, are notoriously poor and unable to provide the police armies that are necessary to protect urban populations. Finally, the structure of modern law favors the individual over the community. The already inadequate police forces find it very difficult to put offenders in jail. Nor is the problem confined to the streets. Corrupt but hard-to-prosecute connections between government and business are so frequent that it is becoming increasingly more difficult to find candidates above suspicion to fill the major offices.

No society will ever eliminate crime, but some do a better job of discouraging it than others. And it is a reasonable guess that as we move beyond the modern growth era to a more stable society, crime will be steadily reduced. In a labor-intensive economy that has put capitalism behind it there should be nearly full employment. The reformation of the urban family will provide another check. The stabilization of society should also ease racial tensions, a matter that we shall take up separately in a moment. With the reduction in national government and its high-tech armaments industry, the cities should recapture their rightful portion of tax money. And with the emphasis in all of culture and society swinging away from the individual toward the community, certainly this trend will make itself felt in the area of criminal law. The cumbersome structure that now favors the individual will be rearranged to favor the public interest. Crime, both in low places and high, will be more consistently and probably also more severely punished. The renewed use of the death penalty in some places is undoubtedly an early manifestation of the new directions. Modern society has become increasingly tender-minded with regard to criminals and tough-minded with regard to victims. Now we shall begin to see those positions reversed, as we become more tough-minded with regard to criminals and tender-minded with regard to victims. Neither balance works flawlessly, but we would seem to be ready, as suggested before, to exchange the injustices of the modern system for a new set.

Closely related to the subject of crime is that of law in general. Modern society has been based on law—that is, on secular, man-made law—to an unusual degree. Ours has been among societies uniquely legal, and that has been entirely appropriate to the modern way of seeing things. Each individual has had essentially one and only one right, and that is to equal treatment. Justice is blind. There have been in this age no fundamental privileges, only opportunities. This circumstance has made us very dependent on law, the sole recourse among equals. And as the modern centuries have followed one upon the other, society has become increasingly litigious, to the point where now the lawsuit has become the standard assumed form of social redress. As so often with reasonable ideas, this tendency has produced many unforeseen problems—the rising costs of medicine, for example, as doctors move to insure their practices against the horrendous legal assaults—and a reaction against the process would seem to be developing. Quite possibly there will be an effort made to make access to legal processes more difficult. Not, to be sure, that society will seek to become lawless. On the contrary, as implied in our brief discussion of crime, law and its enforcement will become more important, not less. But we should see as we seek to stabilize fewer inducements to the individual to turn to the courts. Penalties for unsuccessful suits will be increased. Legal expenses will be permitted to escalate. Appellate procedures will become more complex, as the locus of decision making gravitates back toward local and insular authorities. There will be, of course, both good and bad effects, as here too individual rights are sacrificed to social utility. Yet for better or for worse, the decline of the Modern Age will very likely bring with it the decline of the modern legal system.

We come now to the question of race. How will the future handle the problems generated by racial relationships that have plagued the last century? Race is a conception peculiar to the Modern Age. The Middle Ages divided people by religion. The Modern Age has divided them by nationality and by race, conflicting categories, but similar in their both being secular. Where national and racial divisions have been one and the same, racial struggles have been subsumed within the national. But where racial lines have crossed national lines, race has become important as a thing in itself. And just as the Middle Ages was willing to kill in the name of religion, the Modern Age has proved its readiness to kill not only in the name of the nation-state, but also in that of race. Race, in fact, has become one of the great determinants of modern history. The Modern Age has preached the brotherhood of mankind, but true sentiment has rarely managed to extend beyond racial boundaries. Race along with national consciousness would seem to offer that sense of identity earlier found in religion. The commonality of confession has been replaced by one of genes, real or imagined.

But the future should see the matter put within different contexts, with the modern allegiance to race passing along with the rest of modern things. New prejudices—possibly religious—will again take priority. The rise of communal loyalties will also tend to obscure the racial theme. Further, the loss of mobility and the end of constant societal flux will ease the pressures that have been especially acute since ca. 1900, as races formerly apart and distinct have been brought into close contact. The great population migrations that have thrown races suddenly together should come to an end, while areas with established racial combinations ought to find social communication somewhat easier across, where they are still recognizable, the old racial lines. The transition to a postmodern society will create many new problems, but modern racial tensions should be lessened in the long run. But in the short run? If the West presses the modern economy to the point where its potential for sudden collapse is realized, then we can expect to see a revival of a very virulent racism. The more stable the West becomes, the less important race will become; but the more chaotic, then the more important, as the genocides of our recent past should constantly remind us.

We turn next to speculate—and I hope the reader will keep in mind that even when the conditional has been dispensed with, these can be nothing but speculations, given their forms by a set of assumptions—upon the future of the relationship between the sexes. Again, we are dealing with a matter upon which the Modern Age has put its peculiar stamp. Here as in all areas, it has stood for equality—again, equality of opportunity, not of result. As the age has gotten older, the assignment of roles based on sex has been progressively eroded. Competition for position has been on the open market, increasingly without designation as to sex. Just how the benefits have been assigned in this new contest is debated. Women and men have both been exposed to the loss of protective status, while also being granted the theoretical chance to move upward. Certainly the gains and losses have been unevenly distributed, with the more able and aggressive of each sex pushing to the fore, while the less able and aggressive fall behind. Although the general pattern of male dominance in the world of business and public affairs and of female dominance in homemaking, schooling, and child-rearing has not been broken, there has nevertheless been a considerable sharing of opportunities.

Now, as we make our exit from the Modern Age, we can expect the modern goals with regard to sexual equality to be gradually changed. Perhaps because the full thrust of this particular modern experiment has not developed until recently, there may be left in it sufficient vigor so that it will continue for a while. Nevertheless, as with all of the modern drives to create an open society based on competition between individuals equal in all respects but talent, the attempt to eliminate sex as an economically and socially significant attribute will eventually lose its force. Society will choose in this regard as in others to opt for fixed roles, and that in order to discourage the mobility that the removal of those roles was meant to increase. However, one should not suppose that in the future one sex will be held to be generally more capable than the other. As the West begins to return to hierarchies and fixed relationships, we should see a number of vertical orders in which men and women are positioned not at all mindless of sex, but without the assumption of the inherent superiority of either. We could find our way back to something like the premodern system, which insisted on sex distinctions, but was inclined to honor neither men at the expense of women nor women at the expense of men. Both were stereotyped, but with specific tasks in mind, some of which were more honorable and some less. It goes without saying that such thoughts are at best suspect to the modern liberated consciousness.

The Modern Age has been not only a great period for liberation, but also for medicine. For we have aimed, and the effort has been tremendous, at making everyone healthy. And as with the effort at emancipation, the results have been uneven: we live longer, but also are sick longer; and the time spent dying has been greatly extended, with the final denouement still unavoidable. Life, as it has always been, is followed by death. Meanwhile the costs to society are dramatically increasing, and so are the indignities to which the sick are being subjected, even when the endless operations are paid for by someone else. Modern medicine, once a respected and celebrated triumph of the age, has gotten out of hand. It has ceased to put society's needs first. It has become obsessed with what it can do, losing in the process all sense for what it should do—this through no fault of its own, we should add. Modern medicine is merely advancing ineluctably along the course set for it.

Surely that course will now be reset. Society will move to limit the costs of medicine, beginning with fees and proceeding to the charges for drugs and hopsital services. It will also move to limit treatments. Beyond a certain age various operations and devices will simply—and mercifully—be withheld. Unlimited medical aid will no longer be provided when the prospects for restoring an enjoyable life have been already destroyed. No society in its right mind will permit its available places to be occupied by the very sick, the very old, and the very handicapped to the exclusion of life for the new generation. We cannot have it both ways, and the future must decide. Can there be any question that it will opt for the young and the healthy? The difficulty in making the choice is that it must now be made consciously, in defiance of what medicine can do in the individual instance. That will seem merciless. But societies have done more severe things to insure their survival. And if the future is committed to austerity, it will not squander its resources for the purpose of performing medical miracles to no societal purpose. Both the practice and the use of medicine will be increasingly regulated. Yet it need only be the expensive and esoteric ventures that will be cut back. The expansion of inexpensive paramedical services should proceed without hindrance. The net result could easily be more care for more people. Medicine as a spectacle, however, will no longer be enjoyed.

With regard to entertainment, the weakening of the modern impulse can mean but one thing, and that is the decline of entertainment industries and the return of the effort to local amateur and semiprofessional hands. Such a turn of events would indeed make for a loss of quality in certain areas, but both variety and the numbers involved as performers would increase greatly. In the course of modernization, the profits for centralized entertainment corporations grew tremendously, but in the process the local artists were forced out of business. Also, entertainment was increasingly tailored to mass tastes. Only what can appeal to large audiences is now worth performing. Thereby much has been lost. Today we could hardly afford a Shakespeare. The decentralization of the economy should work to break up the modern entertainment business and to return it slowly to the community, where once more we shall come to know our entertainers and learn again to tolerate their inadequacies.

Much the same thing will be likely to happen in the sports world. The modern effect has been to concentrate and centralize athletics. And then through the miracle of television the product is returned to us in our homes. For the spectator nothing could be better. But what will the future bring? Decentralization and austerity will have their impact here as well. Already increased costs are drawing certain limits. And as national firms break up into their regional counterparts, there will be little enthusiasm for national advertising, which, because it has use mostly for national-level sport, has provided one of the two chief inducements to concentration. The other has been the coming of the huge metropolis, capable of supplying the crowds with which to fill the stadiums. As these urban centers are reduced in size, centralized sports will receive another setback. The combined result will be the inauguration of a tendency to return to local and regional competition, with smaller numbers watching more athletes.

Last, a comment on alienation: it too has been peculiarly modern. As the Modern Age created an economy run by machinery in which work was increasingly atomized as a result of specialization, the worker came less and less to identify with the product. Wages went up, but pride, interest, and personal commitment went down. The worker found himself cut off from the flow of creativity, isolated, and condemned to the repetition of dull tasks. A barrier was constructed between the worker and the world. Now that barrier will begin to come down. The force that will bring it down is the rising cost of energy, which will result in less machinery, less specialization, less atomization, and hence less alienation. It will not be a change in the ownership of the means of production that will end the problem—workers in the Soviet Union are just as alienated as they are in the United States—but a change in the means of production itself, as the worker again comes to be permitted to accomplish whole tasks. Perhaps life in the new society will be boring and restricted, even banal; but it should no longer be lived under the curse of alienation.

It is now time to bring this essay to a conclusion. I shall state again its purpose: to think about the future of Western civilization. Everything that has been said has been meant as a contribution to that end. We first reviewed the present crisis, the crisis of the twentieth century, looking at its various aspects as parts within a civilizational whole. We then sought to give that crisis perspective and meaning by an analytical recasting of the West's long history. And, finally, relying upon that context, we have speculated about the future, more specifically, the intermediate future, which has been identified roughly with the next century. One should note, too, that the fate of the West has been taken to hold the key to that of the world itself, since the West in recent centuries has, with whatever result, put its stamp upon the entire globe.

The changes that are here projected upon the future are in most cases— style is the significant exception, where I have argued that the revolution has already occurred—quite radical. They are that because it would seem apparent we have come to another of those great turning points that periodically send the West off in another direction. This time our civilization, having worn out its modern constructions and now very much in danger from their imminent collapse, is trying to flee to new ground. Therefore our problems are radical, ranging from potential demographic and economic disaster to nuclear holocaust; and radical problems necessarily beget radical solutions. But, to repeat with regard to the whole the observation made when discussing our economic future, the course that has been sketched out here is not in another sense at all radical, inasmuch as it envisages gradual change. And here I am assuming that the West will choose to move gradually because it can only choose to move gradually. For it does not quite, despite our helpful remarks, know where it is going and has very little notion of how it would get there even if it did. There may indeed be revolutions, but, like their predecessors, they will work momentarily to confuse things and will have lasting effects only if they confirm what was about to happen in any case. The changes anticipated, then, are expected to take place over a considerable period of time. Also we might remind ourselves that none of them will occur in isolation. And since culture and society will move along together toward the new solutions, the impact of each single innovation will be partly absorbed by the surrounding milieu, also in motion.

But again, we must raise the issue of a possible catastrophe. Shall we be allowed a considerable period of time? Perhaps not. It is not difficult to come up with scenarios that lead to the world's destruction. The likelihood of that happening, however, would not seem to be great *unless,* to repeat, we insist on continuing in our present condition for a long time. Given enough time with the contemporary circumstances and, yes, we shall have our holocaust. Yet we need not. And the assumption here is that, acting slowly and collectively as in the past—acting, that is, as a civilization—we shall move to protect both the present and the future, not only from the nuclear threat, but also from all of the other potential disasters that we have created in the course of constructing the modern utopia.

Civilizations do, of course, die. In the discussion of the fate of the Chaco Indian civilization, presented some time ago in the excellent Public Broadcasting television production "The Chaco Legacy," Richard Loose, an archaeologist, made an interesting comment: he suggested that archaeologists are basically pessimistic people because "time after time, we're dealing with the people who blew it, you know, we're dealing with the losers, the folks that couldn't handle it. I mean, look at the size of that building over there, and there's nobody in it."[21] And the moan of the desert wind breaks the eerie silence. —Will an archaeologist at some point in the future be wondering why we also blew it? At some point, no doubt, but not soon. We are in a dying age, but, again, we do not have the look of a dying civilization. And healthy civilizations do not do themselves in. Sometimes they are conquered from without, and sometimes they grow old and succumb. But they do not commit suicide in mid-life. There is no prospect of the West being conquered from the outside, because there is no more outside, the West having Westernized it. And we are not yet feeble. On the contrary, our problems stem from the possession of too much power, not too little. If we were to put an end to things at this point in our history, it would be a civilizational first, a record that we do not wish to set. So we shall try to escape the foreseeable consequences of our present dilemmas by constructing a very different and more secure future. It too will naturally produce its threats, and someday the West will again want to move on. "In the final analysis," again to quote Dahrendorf, "the only possibility for stability lies in the ability to change."[22] Dahrendorf meant that with regard to contemporary society, but I shall apply it here to the life of the civilization, where it is seemingly even more true.

A last question: what should we in fact *do* about the future? I am sometimes asked that when I have been uncareful enough to reveal that I am venturing beyond my role as a historian to seek to comment on what may lie ahead—and I usually conceal my subject, because I have found that mention of the future, as with all of Balkan history, causes a certain embarrassment. It would seem that we do not really believe in the existence of Bosnia, Montenegro, and Herzegovina and are also instinctively skeptical that there will be, in whatever condition, a twenty-first century. Yet, required to make a sincere response, the only thing that can be said is that we in the present should work to take care of the present, leaving the future to itself. However, and it is a crucial reservation, we must do that in such a way that *the future is left with reasonable options*. That requirement would seem to be obvious. Still, blinded by the imperatives of growth, we are not meeting it at present. We must begin to. If we can return to doing that, the more distant fate of the civilization we need not worry about, for we would not be prejudicing it.

And certainly we can fret too much. Our problems are indeed profound, more so than at any time in the history of mankind. Yet Western civilization has survived until now. Its life has spanned three millennia and three great ages. Given a will to make the necessary adjustments, there is no reason to insist that the West cannot enter a fourth millennium and go on to see the dawning of a fourth great age. The doors to the future are still open.

The New Testament author of *The Revelation of Saint John the Divine* called down retribution—"God shall add unto him the plagues that are written in this book"—upon anyone who might challenge his prophecies. I can sympathize. Those of us who write about the future should be permitted to be a little sensitive. We have wandered out rather far on the proverbial limb. At this point, however, I welcome critics. The appropriate curses can be found later.

Notes

CHAPTER I. THE CRISIS IN REVIEW

1. The topic of the periodization of Western culture, 1650 to the present, especially with regard to national variations, has received a careful treatment in W. Warren Wagar, *World Views: A Study in Comparative History* (Hinsdale, Ill.: The Dryden Press, 1977).

2. See Leonard B. Meyer, *Music, the Arts, and Ideas: Patterns and Predictions in Twentieth-Century Culture* (Chicago: The University of Chicago Press, 1967), 178: "As foreseen here, the future, like the present, will hold both a spectrum of styles and a plurality of audiences in each of the arts. There will be no convergence, no stylistic consensus. Nor will there be a single unified audience." See also p. 217, where Meyer argues that "in our century, the new has not merely been accepted by artists and critics; it has, particularly in recent years, been pursued and cultivated."

3. See, for example, Malcolm Bradbury and James McFarlane, eds., *Modernism, 1890–1930* (Harmondsworth: Penguin Books, 1976).

4. Pico della Mirandola, *Oration on the Dignity of Man,* in Franklin LeVan Baumer, ed., *Main Currents of Western Thought: Readings in Western Intellectual History from the Middle Ages to the Present,* 2d ed., rev. (New York: Alfred A. Knopf, 1964), 126–28. Pico had God address man as follows: "We have set thee at the world's center that thou mayest from thence more easily observe whatever is in the world. We have made thee neither of heaven nor of earth, neither mortal nor immortal, so that with freedom of choice and with honor, as though the maker and molder of thyself, thou mayest fashion thyself in whatever shape thou shalt prefer. Thou shalt have the power to degenerate into the lower forms of life, which are brutish. Thou shalt have the power, out of thy soul's judgment, to be reborn into the higher forms, which are divine" (p. 128). More than two centuries later, Alexander Pope was to say much the same thing, if in a more secular way, when he described man as "Created half to rise and half to fall; / Great lord of all things, yet a prey to all" ("An Essay on Man," in *The Pocket Book of Verse,* ed. with Introduction by M. E. Speare [New York: Washington Square Press, 1960], stanza 1, lines 15–16, p. 63).

5. B. F. Skinner, *Beyond Freedom and Dignity* (New York: Alfred A. Knopf, 1971). "In what we may call the prescientific view (and the word is not necessarily pejorative) a person's behavior is at least to some extent his own achievement. He is free to deliberate, decide, and act, possibly in original ways, and he is to be given credit for his successes and blamed for his failures. In the scientific view (and the word is not necessarily honorific) a person's behavior is determined by a genetic endowment traceable to the evolutionary history of the species and by the environmental circumstances to which an individual has been exposed" (p. 101).

6. See William Barrett's treatment of Heidegger in his *Irrational Man: A Study in Existential Philosophy* (Garden City, N.Y.: Doubleday & Co., 1958), 206–38.

7. For an excellent discussion of Wittgenstein and his milieu, see Allan Janik and Stephen Toulmin, *Wittgenstein's Vienna* (New York: Simon and Schuster, 1973), 167–238.

8. See Eliot's chorus, "The Eagle Soars in the Summit of Heaven," in "The Rock": "Where is the wisdom we have lost in knowledge? / Where is the knowledge we have lost in information?" *One Hundred Modern Poems*, selected with an introduction by Selden Rodman (New York: The New American Library, 1951), stanza 1, lines 15–16, p. 68.

9. Henri Bergson (1859–1941) was a very popular professor at the Collège de France and the Nobel prize winner for literature for 1927. His major work was *L'Evolution créatice* (1907), trans. Arthur Mitchell as *Creative Evolution* (New York: Modern Library, 1944).

10. Robert Nisbet, "Epilogue: Progress and Providence," *History of the Idea Progress* (New York: Basic Books, 1980), 352–57.

11. Regarding limits, see especially the arguments of Gunther S. Stent, *The Coming of the Golden Age: A View of the End of Progress* (Garden City, N.Y.: The Natural History Press, 1969).

12. "A scientific doctrine is not born, however obvious the facts upon which it is based may appear, without a well-defined spiritual orientation. It is necessary to understand the genesis of our thoughts in all their delicate duplicity. No more truths are discovered than those we are already in search of. To the rest, however evident they may be, the spirit is blind." José Ortega y Gasset, "The Theory of Einstein," suppl. to *The Modern Theme*, trans. James Cleugh (1931; reprint, New York: Harper & Row, 1961), 150.

13. See Ludwig Dehio, *The Precarious Balance: Four Centuries of European Power Struggle*, trans. Charles Fullman (New York: Vintage Books, 1962; originally published as *Gleichgewicht oder Hegemonie*, Krefeld: Scherpe-Verlag, 1948), 19–42. Dehio emphasizes the influence of the non-European world in preventing any one power from achieving hegemony over Europe.

14. Arno Mayer has made a persuasive case for the continuation of aristocratic predominance even into the twentieth century in his *The Persistence of the Old Regime: Europe to the Great War* (New York: Pantheon Books, 1982). Certainly the aristocratic presence in politics and the arts is undeniable. But the basic policies, it would seem, were set by those who had aligned themselves with the expansive tendencies of the Modern Age. They then came to form a new entrepreneurial class, one made up of commoner and aristocrat alike.

15. See Wallerstein, *The Modern World-System*, 2 vols. (New York: Academic Press, 1974–80), 1:10.

16. The figures, which of course vary with the years, are from Walter B. Moen, former director of the Federation of Materials Society, quoted in *The Christian Science Monitor*, 11 January 1982. Making much the same point with regard to the reliance of the United States on the Third World, Bradford Morse of the UN Development Committee warns that "Americans, quite apart from the moral dimension, have never adequately understood the practical meaning of their dependence upon the developing countries as the major single market for U.S. exports and as the principal source for many of the raw materials and minerals without which U.S. industry would virtually grind to a halt" ("Where 80 percent of UN resources go," *The Christian Science Monitor*, 19 April 1983).

17. Donella H. Meadows, Dennis L. Meadows, Jorgen Randers, and William W. Behrens, III, *The Limits to Growth* (New York: Universe Books, 1972).

18. The Heilbroner article soon appeared in book form, *An Inquiry into the Human Prospect* (New York: W. W. Norton & Co., 1974); Commoner's arguments

are to be found in his *The Closing Circle: Nature, Man & Technology* (New York: Alfred A. Knopf, 1971); the conclusions of the *Global 2000* report appeared in the work edited by Gerald O. Barney, *Global 2000 Report to the President of the U.S. Entering the 21st Century: The Summary,* vol. 1 (Elmsford, N.Y.: Pergamon Press, 1984); Yergin and Hillenbrand's *Global Insecurity* appeared in 1982, published in Boston by Houghton Mifflin Co. Peccei's analysis is available in *One Hundred Pages for the Future: Reflections of the President of the Club of Rome* (New York: The New American Library, 1982). See also Lester R. Brown, *State of the World 1986: A Worldwatch Institute Report on Progress Toward a Sustainable Society* (New York: W. W. Norton, 1986); and *World Resources 1986: An Assessment of the Resource Base that Supports the Global Economy,* by World Resources Institute and International Institute for Environment and Development (New York: Basic Books, 1986). These last two are to appear annually.

19. According to Population-Environmental Balance, a population study group, the five billionth person was born on 7 July 1986. AP, *Corvallis* (Oreg.) *Gazette-Times,* 7 July 1986.

20. See, for example, Lukacs, *Outgrowing Democracy: A History of the United States in the Twentieth Century* (Garden City, N.Y.: Doubleday & Co., 1984), 161–63.

21. "In fact, youth may best be seen as a separate country, in which young people take out citizenship. That nation has a culture of its own which now reaches every hamlet." Hacker, "Farewell to the Family?" *The New York Review of Books,* 18 March 1982, 42.

22. Arnold Toynbee, *Civilization on Trial* (New York: Oxford University Press, 1948), 9.

CHAPTER 2. HISTORICAL PERSPECTIVES

1. The earliest intra-eval crisis shown on the graph is that labeled "Transition to Hellenism." It is for the most part a theoretical construction, although a good case can be made for its historical existence. It has not, however, been dealt with in the text. See figure on p. 62.

2. Lévi-Strauss, radio conversation with Georges Charbonnier (1959), quoted by John Updike in "A Feast of Reason," a review of recent works by Claude Lévi-Strauss, *The New Yorker,* 30 July 1979, 88.

3. H. W. Janson comments on the use of the human figure in primitivie art in his essay "The Image of Man in Ancient and Medieval Art," *The Western Experience,* ed. Mortimer Chambers, et al., 3d ed. (New York: Alfred A. Knopf, 1983), 1:124b–e.

4. Aristotle, *Poetics* (23), quoted in John Ives Sewall, *A History of Western Art* (New York: Henry Holt and Co., 1953), 65–66.

5. There are different opinions on the question of precisely when it was that the Hellenistic era began and ended, but here it is taken to extend from the fall of Athens, ca. 400 B.C., to the rise of Rome, ca. 200 B.C. The era's name refers to the fact that it was during these centuries that the Near East was being penetrated by Greek influence and therefore was becoming Greek-like, that is, Hellenistic.

6. Sewall, *A History of Western Art,* 154–77, 209–25.

7. Henri Frankfort has warned of the danger when discussing primitive thought of substituting "articulate concepts for unreflected experience." See his *The Birth of Civilization in the Near East* (Garden City, N.Y.: Doubleday & Co., n.d.), 27–28.

8. A highly readable account of the development of Greek ideas and their

adaptation by the Romans can be found in Henry Bamford Parkes, *Gods and Men: The Origins of Western Culture* (New York: Alfred A. Knopf, 1959), 147–370.

9. Becker, *The Heavenly City of the Eighteenth-Century Philosophers* (New Haven: Yale University Press, 1932), 1–31.

10. See E. R. Dodds, *The Greeks and the Irrational* (Berkeley: University of California Press, 1951). A nice summation of the position of Greek irrationalism within the rationalist overview is to be found in H. D. F. Kitto, *The Greeks* (Baltimore: Penguin Books, 1951), 252.

11. One of the best documents of this reaction against Hellenism remains Plato's *Republic*. Available in *The Portable Plato,* edited with an Introduction by Scott Buchanan (New York: The Viking Press, 1948), 281–696.

12. For brief but interesting summaries of the thought of Zeno and Epicurus, see Bertrand Russell, *A History of Western Philosophy: And Its Connection with Political and Social Circumstances from the Earliest Times to the Present Day* (New York: Simon & Schuster, 1945), 240–70. An overview of Hellenistic thought is to be found in Walter R. Agard, *The Greek Mind* (Princeton: D. Van Nostrand Co., 1957), 70–86.

13. Thompson, tape of a public lecture, loaned to me by a mutual student, n.p., n.d.

14. For the history of Greece during the Hellenic centuries, see Robert J. Littman, *The Greek Experiment: Imperialism and Social Conflict, 800–400 B.C.* (New York: Harcourt Brace Jovanovich, 1974).

15. Augustus took great pains to conceal the changes behind a facade of republicanism. See Lily Ross Taylor's excellent chapter "Catonism and Caesarism" in her *Party Politics in the Age of Caesar* (Berkeley: University of California Press, 1949), 162–82.

16. For a survey of ancient Greece, see William I. Davisson and James E. Harper, *European Economic History,* vol. 1, *The Ancient World* (New York: Appleton-Century-Crofts, 1972), 90–142.

17. For the economic history of the ancient world from the Hellenistic era through the Roman period of growth, see ibid., 143–216.

18. See above, introduction to this chapter, figures on pp. 59 and 62.

CHAPTER 3. FROM THE CLASSICAL AGE TO THE MIDDLE AGES

1. The plural usage that has it "Middle Ages" rather than "Middle Age" is too well established to dispense with, although as conceived of here there was but a single age. Oddly enough, the first author to use the term (the seventeenth-century historian Cellarius) used it in the singular, but the plural soon became conventional. See John B. Morrall, *The Medieval Imprint: The Founding of the Western European Tradition* (C. A. Watts, 1967; reprint, Harmondsworth: Penguin Books, 1970), 13–14.

2. There are a number of very good short surveys of the transition from late Rome to the medieval centuries. Two that are outstanding are Peter Brown, *The World of Late Antiquity, A.D. 150–750* (New York: Harcourt Brace Jovanovich, 1971), and Hugh Trevor-Roper, *The Rise of Christian Europe* (New York: Harcourt, Brace & World, 1965).

3. Morey, "The Sources of Mediaeval Style," *The Art Bulletin* 7 (December 1924): 35–50.

4. "Thus over the dying empire the gods were resuming their indomitable sway, and what was dying with the empire was pagan art. . . . For art was now seeking to break away from the human as obstinately as in Greece it had sought to

attain the human." André Malraux, *The Voices of Silence,* quoted in Parkes, *Gods and Men,* 360.

5. A discussion of Romanesque art and architecture can be found in Sewall, *A History of Western Art,* 370–423.

6. Surveys of medieval thought are to be found in Frederick B. Artz, *The Mind of the Middle Ages, A.D. 200–1500: An Historical Survey,* 3d ed. rev. (New York: Alfred A. Knopf, 1967); and David Knowles, *The Evolution of Medieval Thought* (New York: Vintage Books, 1962).

7. See Dagobert D. Runes, editor, *The Dictionary of Philosophy* (New York: Philosophical Library, n.d.), 210.

8. For a discussion of the influence of Neoplatonism, see Brown, *The World of Late Antiquity,* 70–80.

9. Quoted in Parkes, *Gods and Men,* 365.

10. On the influence of Plato and the Neoplatonists, especially Plotinus, on Augustine, see Knowles, *The Evolution of Medieval Thought,* 32–50.

11. Knowles describes John Scotus as a "voice in the wilderness" (ibid., 77).

12. For some aspects of late Greco-Roman thought it is better to speak of an "inner-worldly" rather than an otherworldly orientation. See Brown, *The World of Late Antiquity,* 74.

13. There is a very readable chapter on Augustus that relates the significant yet limited nature of the changes in Michael Grant, *The Twelve Caesars* (New York: Charles Scribner's Sons, 1975), 52–80.

14. For a discussion of the complicated question of the influence of the middle classes during the reign of Augustus, see Davisson and Harper, *European Economic History,* 1 : 196–98. According to Paul MacKendrick, "Augustus' economic policy aimed to advance the bourgeoisie, which would both induce political apathy and increase tax revenues, each, to him, desirable goals." MacKendrick, "The Roman Empire: Augustus to Hadrian," chap. 9 in William L. Langer, ed., *Western Civilization,* vol. 1, *Paleolithic Man to the Emergence of European Powers* (New York: American Heritage Publishing Co. and Harper & Row, 1968), 253.

15. See Parkes, *Gods and Men,* 355.

16. For the effects of Justinian on both the eastern and western halves of the empire, see Brown, *The World of Late Antiquity,* 126–59.

17. A clear description of feudal custom is available in Brian Tierney and Sidney Painter, *Western Europe in the Middle Ages, 300–1475* (New York: Alfred A. Knopf, 1970),121–34. See also Carl Stephenson, *Medieval Feudalism* (Ithaca: Cornell University Press, 1942).

18. On the Roman economy's decline, see Davisson and Harper, *European Economic History,* 1 : 219–34.

19. For a comment on the several possibilities, see Robert-Henri Bautier, *The Economic Development of Medieval Europe,* trans. Heather Karolyi (New York: Harcourt Brace Jovanovich, 1971), 40–49.

CHAPTER 4. FROM THE MIDDLE AGES TO THE MODERN AGE

1. For an example of the first argument, see the seminal work by Charles Homer Haskins, *The Renaissance of the Twelfth Century* (Cambridge: Harvard University Press, 1927); for an example of the second, see Herbert Butterfield, *The Origins of Modern Science, 1300–1800* (London: G. Bell & Sons, 1949), esp. vii–x.

2. For an account of the development of the portrayal of the individual in medieval art, see Colin Morris, *The Discovery of the Individual, 1050–1200* (New York: Harper & Row, 1972), 86–95.

3. The mood of the later medieval period is portrayed in Johan Huizinga's classic, *The Waning of the Middle Ages: A Study of the Forms of Life, Thought and Art in France and the Netherlands in the XIVth and XVth Centuries,* rev. and trans. ed. (1919; London: E. Arnold & Co., 1924).

4. In commenting on the general effects of the Black Death, William H. McNeill has observed that "we cannot assign causal primacy to plague . . . if only because in other parts of the civilized world, where the disaster of the Black Death reached approximately equal proportions, none of the consequences that became manifest in Europe followed." McNeill, "The Plague of Plagues," review of *The Black Death: Natural and Human Disaster in Medieval Europe,* by Robert S. Gottfried, *The New York Review of Books,* 21 July 1983, 28. On the larger context of the Black Death, see McNeill, *Plagues and Peoples* (Garden City, N.Y.: Anchor Books, 1976), 132–75.

5. An example is to be found in George IV's Royal Pavilion at Brighton, designed using Indian and Chinese styles by John Nash and constructed 1815–18. See H. W. Janson, with Dora Jane Janson, *History of Art: A Survey of the Major Visual Arts from the Dawn of History to the Present Day* (Englewood Cliffs, N.J.: Prentice-Hall, n.d.), 461.

6. Huxley, *Tomorrow, Tomorrow, and Tomorrow and Other Essays* (New York: Harper & Bros., 1952), 245.

7. American cities are too recent to have been much shaped by the helter-skelter street construction of premodern nonplanning. They have been laid out instead according to the grid-planning of the eighteenth and nineteenth centuries. Now, in the second half of the twentieth century, we have rejected the grid system, building arterial expressways over it in the inner city and completely disregarding right-angle street construction in the new suburbs. Here again, the twentieth century has shown its disdain for the design of the Modern Age.

8. Stéphane Mallarmé, "Art for All" (1862), in Roland N. Stromberg, ed., *Realism, Naturalism, and Symbolism: Modes of Thought and Expression in Europe, 1848–1914* (New York: Harper & Row, 1968), 200–202.

9. The human figure replete with holes was the consistent theme of the sculptor Henry Moore (1898–1986). For a comment, see William Barrett's *Time of Need: Forms of Imagination in the Twentieth Century* (New York: Harper & Row, Publishers, 1972), 145–83. For an excellent pictorial survey of the course of Western sculpture during the last millennium, see Howard Hibbard, *Masterpieces of Western Sculpture: From Medieval to Modern* (Secaucus, N.J.: Chartwell Books, 1966); a similar survey of Western painting can be found in H. W. Janson and Dora Jane Janson, *The Picture History of Painting: From Cave Painting to Modern Times* (New York: Henry N. Abrams, 1957).

10. See Ortega, "The Dehumanization of Art," in his *The Dehumanization of Art and Other Writings on Art and Culture* (Garden City, N.Y.: Doubleday & Co., 1956), 1–50; and Thomas Ernest Hulme, *Speculations: Essays on Humanism and the Philosophy of Art,* ed. H. Read (London: Routledge, 1936). The latter work was assembled and published posthumously, Hulme having been killed in World War I.

11. The phrase is attributed, perhaps wrongly, to Tertullian. See Runes, *The Dictionary of Philosophy,* 70, and Parkes, *Gods and Men,* 426.

12. On the dangers to faith presented by the Scholastic Synthesis, see Artz, *The Mind of the Middle Ages,* 269b.

13. A good summary account of the fourteenth century and its problems is Robert E. Lerner, *The Age of Adversity: The Fourteenth Century* (Ithaca: Cornell University Press, 1968). For a more leisurely treatment, see Barbara W. Tuchman,

A Distant Mirror: The Calamitous 14th Century (New York: Alfred A. Knopf, 1978).

14. See Tierney and Painter, *Western Europe in the Middle Ages,* 386–94, 436–41, 479–90.

15. "The end then of learning is to repair the ruins of our first parents by regaining to know God aright, and out of that knowledge to love him, to imitate him, to be like him. . . ." John Milton, *Of Education,* in Crane Brinton, ed., *The Portable Age of Reason Reader* (New York: The Viking Press, 1956), 107.

16. An excellent short survey of the Reformation era is to be found in Roland Bainton, *The Reformation of the Sixteenth Century* (Boston: Beacon Press, 1952). See also Richard L. DeMolen, ed., *Leaders of the Reformation* (Selinsgrove, Pa.: Susquehanna University Press, 1984). In choosing 1550–1650 as the dates of the century of religious revolt, I do not, to be sure, want to deny either the earlier origins of the Reformation or, as noted below, the later persistence of something like the original enthusiasm in certain areas.

17. On the witch-craze, see H. R. Trevor-Roper, "The European Witch-craze of the Sixteenth and Seventeenth Centuries," in his *The Crisis of the Seventeenth Century: Religion, the Reformation and Social Change* (New York: Harper & Row, 1968), 90–192.

18. Blaise Pascal (1623–82). For a brief review of his thought, see Roland N. Stromberg, *An Intellectual History of Modern Europe* (New York: Appleton-Century-Crofts, 1966), 51–53.

19. Peter Gay, *The Rise of Modern Paganism,* vol. 1 of *The Enlightenment: An Interpretation* (New York: Random House, 1966), 21.

20. Ibid., 3.

21. For Luther on reason, see Roland L. Bainton, *Here I Stand: A Life of Martin Luther* (Nashville: Abingdon Press, 1950; New York: New American Library of World Literature, 1955), 44, 169, 172.

22. For a review of Hume's philosophy, which is described as "the bankruptcy of eighteenth-century reasonableness," see Russell, *A History of Western Philosophy,* 659–74; also Gay, *The Rise of Modern Paganism,* 401–19.

23. Ibid., 18.

24. "From being *one* of the important ideas in the West it became the dominant idea, even when one takes into account the rising importance of other ideas such as equality, social justice, and popular sovereignty. . . ." Nisbet, *History of the Idea of Progress,* 171.

25. For a succinct commentary on Newton and Voltaire, see J. Bronowski and Bruce Mazlish, *The Western Intellectual Tradition: From Leonardo to Hegel* (New York: Harper & Row, 1960), 189–92, 246–65.

26. A good text on the Romantic period is J. L. Talmon, *Romanticism and Revolt: Europe 1815–1848* (New York: Harcourt, Brace & World, 1967).

27. On Rousseau, Kant, and Hegel, see Bronowski and Mazlish, *The Western Intellectual Tradition,* 280–304, 472–90.

28. Baumer, *Modern European Thought: Continuity and Change in Ideas, 1600–1950* (New York: Macmillan Publishing Co., 1977), 302.

29. There are insightful comments on both Mill and Marx in George L. Mosse, *The Culture of Western Europe: The Nineteenth and Twentieth Centuries, An Introduction* (Chicago: Rand McNally & Co., 1961), 101–2, 173–96.

30. Gay, *Weimar Culture: The Outsider as Insider* (New York: Harper & Row, Publishers, 1968), 2–6.

31. Nisbet, *History of the Idea of Progress,* 318–23.

32. For an account of English medieval political development, see Tierney and Painter, *Western Europe in the Middle Ages,* 255–65, 315–27.

33. See G. Barraclough, *The Origins of Modern Germany* (Oxford: Basil Blackwell, 1952), 24–246.

34. A standard history is to be found in Edouard Perroy, *The Hundred Years War* (New York: Capricorn Books, 1965; originally published as *Le Guerre de Cents Ans,* Paris, 1945).

35. See Eugene F. Rice, Jr., "The Formation of the Early Modern State," chap. 4 of his *The Foundations of Early Modern Europe, 1460–1559* (New York: W. W. Norton & Co., 1970), 92–121.

36. On the crisis of the late sixteenth and early seventeenth centuries, see Trevor-Roper, *The Crisis of the Seventeenth Century,* 46–89; and Theodore K. Rabb, *The Struggle for Stability in Early Modern Europe* (New York: Oxford University Press, 1975).

37. There has been much written since, but one can still profit a great deal from Crane Brinton, *A Decade of Revolution, 1789–1799* (New York: Harper & Row, 1934).

38. See W. E. Lunt, *History of England,* 4th ed. (New York: Harper & Brothers, 1957), 690–92.

39. For a comment on the situation in Germany, see my essay, "Culture and Society in Modern Germany: A Summary View," in *Essays on Culture and Society in Modern Germany,* edited by Gary D. Stark and Bede Karl Lackner, with an Introduction by Leonard Krieger (College Station: Texas A&M University Press, 1982), 36–37.

40. Two journalists commenting on a poll of German youth speak of the coming into existence, and certainly the observation has application throughout the West in these last decades of the twentieth century, of a generation not of citizens but rather of mere burghers. Stephanie Hansen and Hans Joachim Veen, "Auf der Suche nach dem privaten Glück. Jugend heute: Ergebnisse repräsentativer Studien zu den Wertorientierungen und der politischen Kultur Jugendlicher," brochure, no. 37, *Die Zeit. Wochenzeitung für Politik, Wirtschaft, Handel, und Kultur* (Hamburg, 1980), 3.

41. For a survey of the Soviet experience in Eastern Europe since 1945, see H. Stuart Hughes, *Contemporary Europe: A History,* 5th ed. (Englewood Cliffs, N.J.: Prentice-Hall, 1981), 381–98; 469–70; 509–18; 524–33; 553–59; 592–95.

42. For an excellent collection of articles that explores the nature of fascism, see Walter Laqueur, *Fascism: A Reader's Guide* (Berkeley: University of California Press, 1976).

43. For a brilliant analysis of the nature of the relationship between the era's leading fascist and his people, see Sebastian Haffner, *The Meaning of Hitler,* trans. Ewald Osers (New York: Macmillan Publishing Co., 1979); originally published as *Anmerkungen zu Hitler,* Munich: Kindler Verlag, 1978). For a different sort of insight, there is a fascinating study that deserves to be translated into English: Walter Kempowski, *Haben Sie Hitler gesehen? Deutsche Antworten* (Hamburg: Albrecht Knaus Verlag, 1973).

44. A study of the Holocaust that focuses on its treatment at the hands of the historians is Lucy S. Dawidowicz, *The Holocaust and the Historians* (Cambridge: Harvard University Press, 1981).

45. This is not meant to deny American economic involvement overseas (see above, chap. 1), but only to note that that involvement has been recognized neither by the creation of a formal empire nor by significant changes in the domestic political structure.

46. On the formation of the manorial economy, see Georges Duby, *The Early Growth of the European Economy: Warriors and Peasants from the Seventh to the Twelfth Century*, trans. Howard B. Clarke (Ithaca: Cornell University Press, 1974), 3–72.

47. See Artz, *The Mind of the Middle Ages*, 275–76.

48. There is a good review of the medieval agricultural revolution in Jean Gimpel, *The Medieval Machine: The Industrial Revolution of the Middle Ages* (Harmondsworth: Penguin Books, 1977), 29–58.

49. For an account of the impact of the changes on the countryside, see Robert Lopez, "The Response of the Agricultural Society," chap. 6 of his *The Commercial Revolution of the Middle Ages, 950–1350* (Englewood Cliffs, N.J.: Prentice-Hall, 1971), 148–67.

50. Artz, *The Mind of the Middle Ages*, 290–92.

51. Shepard B. Clough, *European Economic History: The Economic Development of Western Civilization*, 2d ed. (New York: McGraw-Hill Book Co., 1968), 90.

52. Ibid., 119.

53. Artz, *The Mind of the Middle Ages*, 292–93.

54. Robert L. Heilbroner, *The Making of Economic Society*, 3d ed. (Englewood Cliffs, N.J.: Prentice-Hall, 1970), 63.

55. Clough, *European Economic History*, 150, 206.

56. With regard to political influence, an interesting connection has been made between the West's growth and the fact that the process of centralization never got beyond the national level: "Where other societies looked upon innovation as socially subversive, . . . Europe, blessed by political fragmentation and multiple sovereignties, was incapable of hobbling novelty and enterprise." See David S. Landes, "To Have and Have Not," review of *How the West Grew Rich: The Economic Transformation of the Industrial World*, by Nathan Rosenberg and L. E. Birdzell, Jr., *The New York Review of Books*, 29 May 1986, 46. This point, however, should no more than other explanations be isolated from the general context.

57. For a discussion of the Weber thesis that compares it as it is generally perceived with what Weber in fact said, see Winthrop S. Hudson, "The Weber Thesis Reexamined," *Church History* 30 (1961): 88–99.

58. The disintegration of centralism did not go far enough to benefit much the lower aristocracy, and it was for the most part the great lords who asserted themselves. This increase in the latter's power was sometimes reinforced by the circumstances of religious conflict, as in France, where the Huguenot aristocracy led the fight against the monarchy. See J. H. Hexter, "Europe's Religious Civil War," chap. 29 in Langer, *Western Civilization*, 1:820–43.

59. See H. R. Trevor-Roper, "Religion, the Reformation and Social Change," *The Crisis of the Seventeenth Century*, 1–45.

60. Quoted in Heilbroner, *The Making of Economic Society*, 74.

61. Ibid., 90. This concentration on the waves of industrialization neglects an early nineteenth-century depression, the economic counterpart of the Romantic reaction.

62. "In what can the novelty of that order consist, if the society continues to be dominated by the persistence of the central and, so to speak, defining process of classic industrialism? . . . When the post-industrial thesis is broken down into specific assertions, examination dissolves it into the more familiar story of *plus ça change, plus c'est la même chose;* or the same, only more so." Krishan Kumar, *Prophecy and Progress: The Sociology of Industrial and Post-Industrial Society* (Harmondsworth: Penguin Books, 1978), 237.

63. For an excellent study of Western military history and its relationship to the workings of society, see William H. McNeill, *The Pursuit of Power: Technology, Armed Force, and Society since A.D. 1000* (Chicago: The University of Chicago Press, 1982); also André Corvisier, *Armies and Societies in Europe, 1494–1789*, trans. Abigail T. Siddall (Bloomington: Indiana University Press, 1979).

64. For a commentary on Smith's arguments, see Robert Nisbet, *The Social Philosophers: Community and Conflict in Western Thought* (New York: Thomas Y. Crowell Co., 1973), 352–54; also Willson H. Coates, Hayden V. White, and J. Salwyn Shapiro, *The Emergence of Liberal Humanism: An Intellectual History of Western Europe*, vol. 1, *From the Italian Renaissance to the French Revolution* (New York: McGraw-Hill, 1966), 311–17.

65. Polanyi, *The Great Transformation* (New York: Farrar & Rinehart, 1944), 73. The remark is quoted with commentary in Douglass C. North, *Structure and Change in Economic History* (New York: W. W. Norton & Co., 1981), 180.

66. For an interesting survey of this imposition of regulation on the open market in the United States, see ibid., 187–98.

67. The "Peoples Budget," the creation of then-chancellor of the exchequer David Lloyd George, not only raised the income tax, but also introduced a progressive element by taxing unearned income at a higher rate. Lloyd George, perhaps not entirely sure of himself with regard to the economics involved, nevertheless understood the political implications clearly enough. He advertised his measures as "a War Budget . . . to wage implacable warfare against poverty and squalidness." It was this bill that led to the crucial veto by the House of Lords, which led in turn to the destruction of the Lords as a political force by the Parliament Act of 1911. For an excellent brief account, see Gordon A. Craig, *Europe since 1815*, 2d ed. (New York: Holt, Rinehart, & Winston, 1966), 328–30. For an interesting comment on Lloyd George, see A. J. P. Taylor, "Lloyd George: Rise and Fall," in his *Essays in English History* (Harmondsworth: Penguin Books, 1976), 254–82.

68. I am following here the exposition of H. V. Hodson. See his *The Diseconomics of Growth* (New York: Ballantine Books, 1972), especially chaps. 2 and 3, 15–50.

69. Quoted in ibid., 32.

70. George Lichtheim, *The New Europe: Today and Tomorrow* (New York: Basic Books, 1963), 194.

71. For more on the threat from the new and highly mobile industries, see Jane Jacobs, "Why TVA Failed," *The New York Review of Books*, 10 May 1984, 41–71.

72. Lukacs, *The Passing of the Modern Age* (New York: Harper & Row, 1970; Harper Torchbook, 1972), 17.

CHAPTER 5. BEYOND THE CRISIS

1. Ada Louise Huxtable, "Is Modern Architecture Dead?" *The New York Review of Books*, 16 July 1981, 17.

2. Edwin Arlington Robinson, "Miniver Cheevy," in *The Pocket Book of Verse*, edited with Introduction by M. E. Speare (New York: Washington Square Press, 1960), stanza 6, lines 2–4, p. 328.

3. Wolff, "Essay on the Many Masks of Modern Art," *The Christian Science Monitor*, 2 February 1982 and 6 October 1983.

4. ". . . There never has been and never will be any return to past times, their restoration is impossible. When we speak of passing from modern history to the middle ages it is a figure of speech; such passage can take place only to a new

middle age, not to the old one." Berdyaev, *The End of Our Time* (London: Sheed & Ward, 1935), 101.

5. See, for example, Nisbet, *History of the Idea of Progress,* 356. For a history and appraisal of humanism, see Alan Bullock, *The Humanist Tradition in the West* (New York: W. W. Norton & Co., 1986).

6. Dahrendorf, *Der Liberalismus und Europa: Fragen von Vincenzo Ferrari* (Munich and Zurich: R. Piper & Co., 1979), 39.

7. Guardini, *The End of the Modern World: A Search for Orientation,* edited with Introduction by Frederick D. Wilhelmsen (London: Sheed & Ward, 1957), 97–108.

8. The reference is to Christian-populist fundamentalism's habit of promising earthly rewards for religious behavior. I remember listening to a college fullback explain that since being born again his yardage-per-carry had increased by several percent.

9. Quoted in Frederick B. Artz, *Reaction and Revolution, 1814–1832* (New York: Harper & Row, 1934), 93.

10. Jonathan Schell, *The Fate of the Earth* (New York: Alfred A. Knopf, 1982), 109–10.

11. With regard to the issue of using controls to obtain a nongrowth economy, the geographer Warren Johnson has argued that, given democratic pressures, controls are more apt to be used to continue forcing growth. His hope is that the pressures of the open-market system will themselves convince us to move toward stability. See his *Muddling toward Frugality* (Boulder, Colo.: Shambala, 1979), 128–35.

12. Robert L. Heilbroner, *Business Civilization in Decline* (New York: W. W. Norton & Co., 1976), 122.

13. William A. Williams, "What Marx Did for Human Freedom," *The Statesman-Journal* (Salem, Oreg.), 29 May 1983. See also the same author's *The Great Evasion: An Essay on the Contemporary Relevance of Karl Marx and on the Wisdom of Admitting the Heretic into the Dialogue about America's Future* (Chicago: Quadrangle Books, 1964).

14. Interview with *Paris-Match,* September 1979, quoted in Peccei, *One Hundred Pages for the Future,* 126. The full passage reads: "It has always been my feeling that the consumer society did not suit either France or the French. It laid waste a part of our coasts, our mountains, our cities, our way of life, our culture; it caused tremendous havoc. I think that the austere society we are aiming towards is basically better adapted to France."

15. Aristotle, *Politics,* quoted in Leopold Kohr, *The Breakdown of Nations* (New York: E. P. Dutton, 1978), 113.

16. Joad, *Diogenes, or the Future of Leisure* (London: Kegan Paul, Trench, Trubner & Co., 1928), 19; quoted with commentary in Dennis Gabor, *Inventing the Future* (New York: Alfred A. Knopf, 1964), 121.

17. See, for example, his comments in *Capital* (orig. *Das Kapital,* 1867), bk. 1, chap. 10, available in Robert C. Tucker, *The Marx-Engels Reader,* 2d ed. (New York: W. W. Norton & Co., 1972), 361–64.

18. Kohr, *The Breakdown of Nations,* 70.

19. Peter H. Raven, director of the Missouri Botanical Garden in St. Louis, points out that the less-developed countries in their present situation are actually discouraged "from putting in place productive agricultural and forestry systems," for they must "produce as much cash as quickly as possible in order to be able to stay a part of the system." Rushworth M. Kidder, "When the Rain Forests Go . . .," *Christian Science Monitor,* 7 August 1986.

20. For those who prefer not to struggle with Spengler's original production, there is an admirable commentary in H. Stuart Hughes, *Oswald Spengler: A Critical Estimate,* rev. ed. (New York: Charles Scribner's Sons, 1962). The quoted phrase is to be found on the final page of Spengler's great work, which then is concluded with "Ducunt Fata volentem, nolentem trahunt," a Latin rendering of the same sentiment. Oswald Spengler, *Decline of the West,* 2 vols., trans. Charles Francis Atkinson (New York: Alfred A. Knopf, 1926–28; originally published as *Der Untergang des Abendlandes,* Munich: C. H. Beck'sche Verlagsbuchhandlung, 1922), 2:507. Thomas Mann made Spengler's dictum the subject of a short and very critical essay, "Über die Lehre Spenglers" (1924), available in Mann, *Sieben Aufsätze,* edited by Frederick L. Pfeiffer and Felix Wittmer (New York: Prentice-Hall, 1930), 67–76.

21. Documentary Educational Resources, *The Chaco Legacy* (film; Watertown, Mass.: Public Broadcasting Associates, Inc., 1980).

22. "Am Ende liegt die einzige Stabilität immer in der Fähigkeit zum Wandel" (Dahrendorf, *Der Liberalismus und Europa,* 7).

Works Cited

Agard, Walter R. *The Greek Mind*. Princeton: D. Van Nostrand, 1957.

Artz, Frederick B. *The Mind of the Middle Ages, A.D. 200–1500: An Historical Survey*. 3d ed., rev. New York: Alfred A. Knopf, 1967.

———. *Reaction and Revolution, 1814–1832*. New York: Harper & Row, 1934.

Bainton, Roland. *Here I Stand: A Life of Martin Luther*. Nashville: Abingdon Press, 1950. New York: New American Library, 1955.

———. *The Reformation of the Sixteenth Century*. Boston: Beacon Press, 1952.

Barney, Gerald O. *Global 2000 Report to the President of the U.S. Entering the 21st Century: The Summary Report*. Vol. 1. Elmsford, N.Y.: Pergamon Press, 1984.

Barraclough, G. *The Origins of Modern Germany*. Oxford: Basil Blackwell, 1952.

Barrett, William. *Irrational Man: A Study in Existential Philosophy*. Garden City, N.Y., and New York: Doubleday & Co., 1958.

———. *Time of Need: Forms of Imagination in the Twentieth Century*. New York: Harper & Row, 1972.

Baumer, Franklin LeVan, ed. *Main Currents of Western Thought: Readings in Western European Intellectual History from the Middle Ages to the Present*. 2d ed., rev. New York: Alfred A. Knopf, 1964.

———. *Modern European Thought: Continuity and Change in Ideas, 1600–1950*. New York: Macmillan Publishing Co., 1977.

Bautier, Robert-Henri. *The Economic Development of Medieval Europe*. Translated from the French by Heather Karolyi. New York: Harcourt Brace Jovanovich, 1971.

Becker, Carl L. *The Heavenly City of the Eighteenth-Century Philosophers*. New Haven: Yale University Press, 1932.

Berdyaev, Nicholas. *The End of Our Time*. Translated by Donald Attwater. London: Sheed & Ward, 1935.

Bergson, Henri. *Creative Evolution*. Translated from the French by Arthur Mitchell. New York: Modern Library, 1944. Originally published as *L'Evolution créatice* (1907).

Bradbury, Malcolm, and James MacFarlane, eds. *Modernism, 1890–1930*. Harmondsworth: Penguin Books, 1976.

Brinton, Crane. *A Decade of Revolution, 1789–1799*. New York: Harper & Row, 1934.

———, ed. *The Portable Age of Reason Reader*. New York: The Viking Press, 1956.

Bronowski, J., and Bruce Mazlish. *The Western Intellectual Tradition: From Leonardo to Hegel*. New York: Harper & Row, 1960.

Brown, Lester R. *State of the World 1986: A Worldwatch Institute Report on Progress toward a Sustainable Society.* New York: W. W. Norton & Co., 1986.

Brown, Peter. *The World of Late Antiquity, A.D. 150–750.* New York: Harcourt Brace Jovanovich, 1971.

Bullock, Alan. *The Humanist Tradition in the West.* New York: W. W. Norton & Co., 1986.

Butterfield, Herbert. *The Origins of Modern Science, 1300–1800.* London: G. Bell & Sons, 1949.

Chambers, Mortimer, et al. *The Western Experience.* 2 vols. 2d ed. New York: Alfred A. Knopf, 1974.

The Christian Science Monitor. 11 January 1982; 19 April 1983.

Clough, Shepard B. *European Economic History: The Economic Development of Western Civilization.* 2d ed. New York: McGraw-Hill Book Co., 1968.

Coates, Willson H., Hayden V. White, and J. Salwyn Shapiro. *The Emergence of Liberal Humanism: An Intellectual History of Western Europe.* Vol. 1, *From the Italian Renaissance to the French Revolution.* New York: McGraw-Hill Book Co., 1966.

Commoner, Barry. *The Closing Circle: Man, Nature and Technology.* New York: Alfred A. Knopf, 1971.

Corvallis (Oregon) *Gazette-Times.* 7 July 1986.

Corvisier, André. *Armies and Societies in Europe, 1494–1789.* Translated from the French by Abigail T. Siddall. Bloomington: Indiana University Press, 1979.

Craig, Gordon A. *Europe since 1815.* 2d ed. New York: Holt, Rinehart, & Winston, 1966.

Dahrendorf, Ralf. *Der Liberalismus und Europa: Fragen von Vincenzo Ferrari.* Munich & Zurich: R. Piper & Co., 1979.

Davisson, William I., and James E. Harper. *European Economic History.* Vol. 1., *The Ancient World.* New York: Appleton-Century-Crofts, 1972.

Dawidowicz, Lucy S. *The Holocaust and the Historians.* Cambridge: Harvard University Press, 1981.

Dehio, Ludwig. *The Precarious Balance: Four Centuries of European Power Struggle.* Translated from the German by Charles Fullman. New York: Vintage Books, 1962. Originally published as *Gleichgewicht oder Hegemonie* (Krefeld: Scherpe-Verlag, 1948).

DeMolen, Richard L., ed. *Leaders of the Reformation.* Selinsgrove, Pa.: Susquehanna University Press, 1984.

Documentary Educational Resources. *The Chaco Legacy.* Watertown, Mass.: Public Broadcasting Associates, Inc., 1980. Film.

Dodds, E. R. *The Greeks and the Irrational.* Berkeley: University of California Press, 1951.

Duby, Georges. *The Early Growth of the European Economy: Warriors and Peasants from the Seventh to the Twelfth Century.* Translated from the French by Howard B. Clarke. Ithaca: Cornell University Press, 1974.

Eliot, T. S. "The Eagle Soars in the Summit of Heaven," chorus from "The Rock," in *One Hundred Modern Poems.* Selected with an Introduction by Selden Rodman. New York: The New American Library, 1951.

Frankfort, Henri. *The Birth of Civilization in the Near East.* Garden City, N.Y.: Doubleday & Co., n.d.

Gabor, Dennis. *Inventing the Future*. New York: Alfred A. Knopf, 1964.

Gay, Peter. *The Rise of Modern Paganism*. Vol. 1 of *The Enlightenment: An Interpretation*. New York: Random House, 1966.

———. *Weimar Culture: The Outsider as Insider*. New York: Harper & Row, 1968.

Gimpel, Jean. *The Medieval Machine: The Industrial Revolution of the Middle Ages*. Harmondsworth: Penguin Books, 1977.

Grant, Michael. *The Twelve Caesars*. New York: Charles Scribner's Sons, 1975.

Guardini, Romano. *The End of the Modern World: A Search for Orientation*. Edited with an Introduction by Frederick D. Wilhelmsen. London: Sheed & Ward, 1957.

Hacker, Andrew. "Farewell to the Family?" *The New York Review of Books,* 18 March 1982.

Haffner, Sebastian. *The Meaning of Hitler*. Translated from the German by Ewald Osers. New York: Macmillan Publishing Co., 1979. Originally published as *Anmerkungen zu Hitler* (Munich: Kindler Verlag, 1978).

Hansen, Stephanie, and Hans-Joachim Veen. "Auf der Suche nach dem privaten Glück. Jugend heute: Ergebnisse repräsentativer Studien zu den Wertorientierungen und der politischen Kultur Jugendlicher." Brochure, no. 37. *Die Zeit. Wochenzeitung für Politik, Wirtschaft, Handel, und Kultur*. Hamburg, 1980.

Haskins, Charles Homer. *The Renaissance of the Twelfth Century*. Cambridge: Harvard University Press, 1927.

Heilbroner, Robert L. *Business Civilization in Decline*. New York: W. W. Norton & Co., 1976.

———. *An Inquiry into the Human Prospect*. New York: W. W. Norton & Co., 1974.

———. *The Making of Economic Society*. 3d ed. Englewood Cliffs, N.J.: Prentice-Hall, 1970.

Hibbard, Howard. *Masterpieces of Western Sculpture: From Medieval to Modern*. Secaucus, N.J.: Chartwell Books, 1966.

Hodson, H. V. *The Diseconomics of Growth*. New York: Ballantine Books, 1972.

Hudson, Winthrop S. "The Weber Thesis Reexamined." *Church History* 30 (1961): 88–99.

Hughes, H. Stuart. *Contemporary Europe: A History*. 5th ed. Englewood Cliffs, N.J.: Prentice-Hall, 1981.

———. *Oswald Spengler: A Critical Estimate*. Rev. ed. New York: Charles Scribner's Sons, 1962.

Huizinga, Johan. *The Waning of the Middle Ages: A Study of the Forms of Life, Thought and Art in France and the Netherlands in the XIVth and XVth Centuries*. Revision and translation of the original Dutch edition of 1919. E. Arnold & Co.: London, 1924.

Hulme, Thomas Ernest. *Speculations: Essays on Humanism and the Philosophy of Art*. Edited by H. Read. London: Routledge, 1936.

Huxley, Aldous. *Tomorrow, Tomorrow, and Tomorrow and Other Essays*. New York: Harper & Bros., 1952.

Huxtable, Ada Louise. "Is Modern Architecture Dead?" *The New York Review of Books,* 16 July 1981.

Jacobs, Jane. "Why TVA Failed." *The New York Review of Books,* 10 May 1984.

Janik, Allan, and Stephen Toulmin. *Wittgenstein's Vienna.* New York: Simon and Schuster, 1973.

Janson, H. W., with Dora Jane Janson. *History of Art: A Survey of the Major Visual Arts from the Dawn of History to the Present Day.* Englewood Cliffs, N.J.: Prentice-Hall, n.d.

———. *The Picture History of Painting: From Cave Painting to Modern Times.* New York: Harry N. Abrams, 1957.

Joad, C. E. M. *Diogenes, or the Future of Leisure.* London: Kegan Paul, Trench, Trubner & Co., 1928.

Johnson, Warren. *Muddling toward Frugality.* Boulder, Colo.: Shambala, 1979.

Kempowski, Walter. *Haben Sie Hitler gesehen? Deutsche Antworten.* Hamburg: Albrecht Knaus Verlag, 1973.

Kidder, Rushworth M. "When the Rain Forests Go. . . ." *Christian Science Monitor,* 7 August 1986.

King, David B. "Culture and Society in Modern Germany: A Summary View." In *Essays on Culture and Society in Modern Germany.* Edited by Gary D. Stark and Bede Karl Lackner, with an Introduction by Leonard Krieger. College Station: Texas A&M University Press, 1982.

Kitto, H. D. F. *The Greeks.* Baltimore: Penguin Books, 1951.

Knowles, David. *The Evolution of Medieval Thought.* New York: Vintage Books, 1962.

Kohr, Leopold. *The Breakdown of Nations.* New York: E. P. Dutton, 1978.

Kumar, Krishan. *Prophecy and Progress: The Sociology of Industrial and Post-Industrial Society.* Harmondsworth: Penguin Books, 1978.

Landes, David S. "To Have and Have Not." Review of *How the West Grew Rich: The Economic Transformation of the Industrial World,* by Nathan Rosenberg and L. E. Birdzell, Jr. *The New York Review of Books,* 29 May 1986.

Langer, William L., ed. With Paul MacKendrick; Deno J. Geanakoplos; J. H. Hexter; and Richard Pipes. *Western Civilization.* Vol. 1, *Paleolithic Man to the Emergence of European Powers.* New York: American Heritage Publishing Co. and Harper & Row, 1968.

Laqueur, Walter, ed. *Fascism: A Reader's Guide.* Berkeley: University of California Press, 1976.

Lerner, Robert E. *The Age of Adversity: The Fourteenth Century.* Ithaca: Cornell University Press, 1968.

Lichtheim, George. *The New Europe: Today and Tomorrow.* New York: Basic Books, 1963.

Littman, Robert J. *The Greek Experiment: Imperialism and Social Conflict, 800–400 B.C.* New York: Harcourt Brace Jovanovich, 1974.

Lopez, Robert S. *The Commercial Revolution of the Middle Ages, 950–1350.* Englewood Cliffs, N.J.: Prentice-Hall, 1971.

Lukacs, John. *Outgrowing Democracy: A History of the United States in the Twentieth Century.* Garden City, N.Y.: Doubleday & Co., 1984.

———. *The Passing of the Modern Age.* New York: Harper & Row, 1970; Harper Torchbook, 1972.

Lunt, W. E. *History of England.* 4th ed. New York: Harper & Brothers, 1957.

McNeill, William H. "The Plague of Plagues." Review of *The Black Death:*

Natural and Human Disaster in Medieval Europe, by Robert S. Gottfried. *The New York Review of Books,* 21 July 1983.

———. *Plagues and Peoples.* Garden City, N.Y.: Anchor Books, 1976.

———. *The Pursuit of Power: Technology, Armed Force, and Society since A.D. 1000.* Chicago: The University of Chicago Press, 1982.

Mallarmé, Stéphane. "Art for All" (1862). In *Realism, Naturalism and Symbolism: Modes of Thought and Expression in Europe, 1848–1914.* Edited by Roland N. Stromberg. New York: Harper & Row, 1968.

Mann, Thomas. "Über die Lehre Spenglers" (1924). In *Sieben Aufsätze.* Edited by Frederick L. Pfeiffer and Felix Wittmer. New York: Prentice-Hall, 1930.

Mayer, Arno. *The Persistence of the Old Regime: Europe to the Great War.* New York: Pantheon Books, 1982.

Meadows, Donella H.; Dennis L. Meadows; Jorgen Randers; and William H. Behrens, III. *The Limits to Growth.* New York: Universe Books, 1972.

Meyer, Leonard B. *Music, the Arts, and Ideas: Patterns and Predictions in Twentieth-Century Culture.* Chicago: The University of Chicago Press, 1967.

Morey, C. R. "The Sources of Mediaeval Style." *The Art Bulletin* 7 (December 1924): 35–50.

Morrall, John B. *The Medieval Imprint: The Founding of the Western European Tradition.* 1967. Reprint. Harmondsworth: Penguin Books, 1970.

Morris, Colin. *The Discovery of the Individual, 1050–1200.* New York: Harper & Row, 1972.

Mosse, George L. *The Culture of Western Europe: The Nineteenth and Twentieth Centuries, an Introduction.* Chicago: Rand McNally & Co., 1961.

Nisbet, Robert. *History of the Idea of Progress.* New York: Basic Books, 1980.

———. *The Social Philosophers: Community and Conflict in Western Thought.* New York: Thomas Y. Crowell, Co., 1973.

North, Douglass C. *Structure and Change in Economic History.* New York: W. W. Norton & Co., 1981.

Ortega y Gasset, José. *The Dehumanization of Art and Other Writings on Art and Culture.* Garden City, N.Y.: Doubleday and Co., 1956.

———. *The Modern Theme.* Translated from the Spanish by James Cleugh. London: C. W. Daniels, 1931. Reprint. New York: Harper & Row, 1961.

Parkes, Henry Bamford. *Gods and Men: The Origins of Western Culture.* New York: Alfred A. Knopf, 1959.

Peccei, Aurelio. *One Hundred Pages for the Future: Reflections of the President of the Club of Rome.* New York: The New American Library, 1982.

Perroy, Edouard. *The Hundred Years War.* New York: Capricorn Books, 1965. Originally published as *Le Guerre de Cent Ans* (Paris, 1945).

Plato, *The Republic.* In *The Portable Plato.* Edited with an Introduction by Scott Buchanan. New York: The Viking Press, 1948.

Polanyi, Karl. *The Great Transformation.* New York: Farrar & Rinehart, 1944.

Pope, Alexander, "An Essay on Man." In *The Pocket Book of Verse.* Edited with Introduction by M. E. Speare. New York: Washington Square Press, 1960.

Rabb, Theodore K. *The Struggle for Stability in Early Modern Europe.* New York: Oxford University Press, 1975.

Rice, Eugene F., Jr. *The Foundations of Early Modern Europe, 1460–1559.* New York: W. W. Norton & Co., 1970.

Robinson, Edwin Arlington. "Miniver Cheevy." In *The Pocket Book of Verse.* Edited with an Introduction by M. E. Speare. New York: Washington Square Press, 1960.

Runes, Dagobert. *The Dictionary of Philosophy.* New York: Philosophical Library, n.d.

Russell, Bertrand. *A History of Western Philosophy: And Its Connection with Political and Social Circumstances from the Earliest Times to the Present Day.* New York: Simon & Schuster, 1945.

Schell, Jonathan. *The Fate of the Earth.* New York: Alfred A. Knopf, 1982.

Sewall, John Ives. *A History of Western Art.* New York: Henry Holt & Co., 1953.

Skinner, B. F. *Beyond Freedom and Dignity.* New York: Alfred A. Knopf, 1971.

Spengler, Oswald. *The Decline of the West.* 2 vols. Translated from the German by Charles Francis Atkinson. New York: Alfred A. Knopf, 1926–28. Originally published as *Der Untergang des Abendlandes* (Munich: C. H. Beck'sche Verlagsbuchhandlung, 1922).

Stent, Gunther S. *The Coming of the Golden Age: A View of the End of Progress.* Garden City, N.Y.: The National History Press, 1969.

Stephenson, Carl. *Medieval Feudalism.* Ithaca: Cornell University Press, 1942.

Stromberg, Roland N. *An Intellectual History of Modern Europe.* New York: Appleton-Century-Crofts, 1966.

Talmon, J. L. *Romanticism and Revolt: Europe 1815–1848.* New York: Harcourt, Brace & World, 1967.

Taylor, A. J. P. *Essays in English History.* Harmondsworth: Penguin Books, 1976.

Taylor, Lily Ross. *Party Politics in the Age of Caesar.* Berkeley: University of California Press, 1949.

Tierney, Brian, and Sidney Painter. *Western Europe in the Middle Ages, 300–1475.* New York: Alfred A. Knopf, 1970.

Toynbee, Arnold. *Civilization on Trial.* New York: Oxford University Press, 1948.

Trevor-Roper, H. R. *The Crisis of the Seventeenth Century: Religion, the Reformation, and Social Change.* New York: Harper & Row, 1968.

————. *The Rise of Christian Europe.* New York: Harcourt, Brace & World, 1965.

Tuchman, Barbara. *A Distant Mirror: The Calamitous 14th Century.* New York: Alfred A. Knopf, 1978.

Tucker, Robert C. *The Marx-Engels Reader.* 2d ed. New York: W. W. Norton & Co., 1972.

Updike, John. "A Feast of Reason." Review of recent works by Claude Lévi-Strauss. *The New Yorker,* 30 July 1979.

Wagar, W. Warren. *World Views: A Study in Comparative History.* Hinsdale, Ill.: The Dryden Press, 1977.

Wallerstein, Immanuel. *The Modern World-System.* 2 vols. New York: Academic Press, 1974–80.

Williams, William Appleman. *The Great Evasion: An Essay on the Contemporary Relevance of Karl Marx and on the Wisdom of Admitting the Heretic into the Dialogue about America's Future.* Chicago: Quadrangle Books, 1964.

———. "What Marx Did for Human Freedom." *The Statesman-Journal* (Salem, Oreg.), 29 May 1983.

Wolff, Theodore. "Essay on the Many Masks of Modern Art." *The Christian Science Monitor,* 2 February 1982; 6 October 1983.

World Resources Institute and International Institute for Environment and Development. *World Resources 1986: An Assessment of the Resource Base that Supports the Global Economy.* New York: Basic Books, 1986.

Yergin, Daniel, and Martin Hillenbrand. *Global Insecurity: A Strategy for Energy and Economic Renewal.* Boston: Houghton Mifflin Co., 1982.

Suggested Reading

Ariès, Philippe. *Centuries of Childhood: A Social History of Family Life*. Translated from the French by Robert Baldick. New York: Vintage Books, 1962. Originally published as *L'Enfant et la vie familiale sous l'ancien régime* (Paris: Librairie Plon, 1960). A thorough and insightful history of the West's varying attitudes toward childhood and the family, with an excellent chapter on games.

———. *The Hour of Our Death*. Translated from the French by Helen Weaver. New York: Alfred A. Knopf, 1981. Originally published as *L'Homme devant la mort* (Paris: Éditions du Seuil, 1977). A survey of the conception of death in Western thought since the early medieval period.

Barraclough, Geoffrey. *An Introduction to Contemporary History*. Baltimore: Penguin Books, 1967. An attempt to synthesize the many changes that the West has had to deal with in the twentieth century.

Barzun, Jacques. *Darwin, Marx, and Wagner: Critique of a Heritage*. 2d ed., rev. Garden City, N.Y.: Doubleday Anchor Books, 1958. An interesting analysis that demonstrates the influence of a single idea in three different areas.

Braudel, Fernand. *Civilization and Capitalism*. 3 vols. Translated from the French with revision by Siân Reynolds. New York: Harper & Row, 1981–84. Originally published as *Civilisation matérielle, économie et capitalisme: XVe–XVIIIe siècle* (Paris: Librairie Armand Colin, 1979). A vast store of information, these volumes also make an argument for the open market and against monopoly, be it capitalist or socialist.

Brinton, Crane. *Ideas and Men. The Story of Western Thought*. 2d ed. Englewood Cliffs, N.J.: Prentice-Hall, 1963. Originally published in 1950, it still offers a stimulating account of the West's intellectual experience. Caustic, perceptive, and eminently readable.

Brodie, Bernard, and Fawn Brodie. *From Crossbow to H-Bomb*. Rev. ed. Bloomington: Indiana University Press, 1973. A history of mankind's efforts to cope with the evolution of the technology of destruction.

Burns, Edward McNall; P. L. Ralph; R. E. Lerner; and S. Meacham. *World Civilizations: Their History and Their Culture*. 7th ed. New York and London: W. W. Norton and Co., 1986. There are many very good texts that treat the history of Western civilization. This is one of several to include a sufficient account of other civilizations to permit the reader to attempt to view the West in a world context.

Choron, Jacques. *Death and Western Thought*. New York: Collier Books, 1963. An entertainingly written history of Western views of death and thereby of life as well.

Clough, Shepard B. *The Rise and Fall of Civilization: An Inquiry into the Relationship between Economic Development and Civilization*. New York and

London: Columbia University Press, 1951. An essay on the history of the West from the standpoint of an economic determinist.

Frank, Philipp. *Modern Science and Its Philosophy.* Cambridge: Harvard University Press, 1941. A careful attempt to discuss the implications for thought of twentieth-century physics.

Gay, Peter. *The Science of Freedom.* Vol. 2 of *The Enlightenment: An Interpretation.* New York: W. W. Norton & Co., 1969. A continuation of the author's vast, but very readable survey of Enlightenment thought, the first volume of which is referred to here under "Works Cited."

Gillis, John R. *Youth and History: Tradition and Change in European Age Relations, 1770 to the Present.* New York: Academic Press, 1974. The historical approach to a subject too often viewed in nonhistorical contexts.

Harman, Carter. *A Popular History of Music: From Gregorian Chant to Electronic Music.* Rev. ed. New York: Dell, 1969. A clear survey that assumes no specialized knowledge.

Harrington, Michael. *The Accidental Century.* New York: The Macmillan Co., 1966. The optimistic left's answer to the cultural pessimism of Ortega y Gasset.

Heisenberg, Werner. *Physics and Beyond: Encounters and Conversations.* New York: Harper & Row, 1971. Especially interesting for its illustration of the role of Platonic thought in twentieth-century physics.

Hughes, H. Stuart. *Consciousness and Society: The Reorientation of European Social Thought, 1890–1930.* New York: Vintage Books, 1958. A profound and sympathetic analysis of the initial "revolt against positivism" and its continuation in the early decades of the twentieth century.

Landes, David S. *The Unbound Prometheus: Technological Change and Industrial Development in Western Europe from 1750 to the Present.* Cambridge: Cambridge University Press, 1969. An account that manages to be both thorough and thoughtful.

Leff, Gordon. *The Dissolution of the Medieval Outlook: An Essay on Intellectual and Spiritual Change in the Fourteenth Century.* New York: Harper & Row, 1976. A sophisticated treatment of a key period in the history of Western thought.

McNeill, William H. *The Rise of the West: A History of the Human Community.* Chicago: The University of Chicago Press, 1963. One of the few attempts by a contemporary historian to write an analytical history of the West's civilization.

Masur, Gerhard. *Prophets of Yesterday: Studies in European Culture, 1890–1914.* New York: Harper & Row, 1961. A first-rate history of the great cultural upheaval of the late nineteenth and early twentieth centuries.

Morazé, Charles. *The Triumph of the Middle Classes.* Translated by George Weidenfeld and Nicolson Ltd. New York: World Publishing Co., 1966. Originally published as *Les Bourgeois Conquérants* (Paris: Max Leclerc et Cie, 1957). An interesting presentation, tracing middle-class successes from the late eighteenth century to the eve of the twentieth.

Munsterberg, Hugo. *Twentieth Century Painting.* New York: Philosophical Library, 1951. Short and to the point, with good chapters on Picasso and Matisse.

Myers, Bernard. *Sculpture: Form and Method.* New York and London: Reinhold and Studio Vista, 1965. A rapid but informative survey with illustrations, from ancient Egypt to the present.

Ortega y Gasset, José. *The Revolt of the Masses.* Authorized anonymous translation from the Spanish. New York: W. W. Norton & Co., 1932. An attempt to analyze the negative effects of democratization upon the West and its culture.

Pollard, Sidney. *The Idea of Progress: History and Society.* Harmondsworth: Penguin Books, 1971. Traces the concept, to which the author is frankly devoted, from the eighteenth century to the present.

Schorske, Carl E. *Fin-de-siècle Vienna. Politics and Culture.* New York: Alfred A. Knopf, 1980. A close look at the cultural revolution of the late nineteenth century, focusing on the Viennese experience and viewed primarily through biography.

Schumacher, E. F. *Small Is Beautiful.* New York: Harper & Row, 1973. One of the classic statements of the argument for building down.

Seidenberg, Roderick. *Post-Historic Man: An Inquiry.* Chapel Hill: University of North Carolina Press, 1950. A postwar discussion of Western directions, critical of the tendency to increasing organization and automation.

Shattuck, Roger. *The Banquet Years: The Origins of the Avant-Garde in France, 1885 to World War I.* Rev. ed. New York: Vintage Books, 1968. Approaches the art history of this crucial period of transition through biography.

Sorokin, Pitirim. *Social Philosophies of an Age of Crisis.* Boston: Beacon Press, 1950. An excellent guide to the great modern theorists of civilization: Danilevsky, Spengler, Toynbee, Berdyaev, Kroeber, and others.

Stavrianos, L. S. *The Promise of the Coming Dark Age.* San Francisco: W. H. Freeman & Co., 1976. A search for the more hopeful prospects offered by decline of the old order.

Thompson, William Irwin. *At the Edge of History.* New York: Harper & Row, 1971. An imaginative approach to thinking about the West's future directions, arguing for myth, intuition, and "a new Whiteheadian science."

Timasheff, Nicholas S. *Sociological Theory. Its Nature and Growth.* Garden City, N.Y.: Doubleday & Co., 1955. A digest of the major theorists of civilizational behavior.

Toynbee, Arnold. *A Study of History.* Rev. and abr. by the author and Jane Caplan. New York: Oxford University Press, 1972. A usable condensation of the original.

Wagar, W. Warren. *Good Tidings: The Belief in Progress from Darwin to Marcuse.* Bloomington: Indiana University Press, 1972. An optimistic approach to the subject of optimism.

Index